Law and Community in Three American Towns

Law and Community

in Three American Towns

CAROL J. GREENHOUSE,
BARBARA YNGVESSON,
& DAVID M. ENGEL

Cornell University Press
ITHACA AND LONDON

First published 1994 by Cornell University Press.

Library of Congress Cataloging-in-Publication Data
Greenhouse, Carol J., 1950–
    Law and community in three American towns / Carol J. Greenhouse,
Barbara Yngvesson, and David M. Engel.
        p.   cm.
    Includes bibliographical references and index.
    ISBN 0-8014-2959-5 (cloth : alk. paper). — ISBN 0-8014-8169-4
(paper : alk. paper)
        1. Law — Social aspects — United States.   2. Law and anthropology.
3. Sociological jurisprudence.   I. Yngvesson, Barbara, 1941–   .
II. Engel, David M.   III. Title.
KF371.G74   1994
340′.115 — dc20   93-44353

Printed in the United States of America

⊗ The paper in this book meets the minimum requirements of the American National Standard for Information Sciences — Permanence of Paper for Printed Library Materials, ANSI Z39.48-1984.

For FRED, SIGFRID, DAG, FINN, JARUWAN, ANYA, & MARK

Contents

Acknowledgments

This project had multiple origins. Each of us initiated our research independently, and indeed we did not realize we had common concerns until our separate projects were well under way (and, in one case, thought to have been completed). Although the questions that guided each of us in our fieldwork differed, we were all interested in how ordinary people view the law and in how they handle problems in and out of the courts. In addition, each of us was concerned with connecting the ethnographic study of law to the ethnographic study of the United States.

Our first meeting as incipient collaborators took place at the annual Law and Society meeting in 1985. It was followed by working holidays, with our families in tow, in the Finger Lakes district of New York and by collaborative presentations hosted by the SUNY Buffalo Law School and by the Cornell University Law School. These informal and productive exchanges with interested and insightful audiences helped to advance our joint endeavor and led to more formal presentations at Law and Society and Anthropology meetings in the late 1980s. We acknowledge with gratitude the many helpful comments we received from colleagues at those meetings. Although it is impossible to name all of them, we want to single out two for special thanks: Felice Levine and the late Fred DuBow. We are also grateful to Peter Agree for his interest and encouragement.

We gratefully acknowledge permission to use previously published material in this volume. David Engel's "Oven Bird's Song: Insiders, Outsiders, and Personal Injuries in an American Community," *Law & Society Review* 18 (1984), appears here as Chapter 1; Chapter 2 is Barbara

Yngvesson's "Making Law at the Doorway: The Clerk, the Court, and the Construction of Community in a New England Town," *Law & Society Review* 22 (1988); Chapter 3 is Carol Greenhouse's "Courting Difference: Issues of Interpretation and Comparison in the Study of Legal Ideologies," *Law & Society Review* 22 (1988). These articles are reprinted by permission of the Law and Society Association.

Chapter 4 includes a passage based on an early draft of Carol Greenhouse's "Signs of Quality: Individualism and Hierarchy in American Culture," *American Ethnologist* 19 (May 1992). We are grateful to the American Anthropological Association for permission to use this material. Chapter 5 includes quotations from Carol J. Greenhouse, *Praying for Justice: Faith, Order, and Community in an American Town*, copyright © 1986 by Cornell University, used by permission of the publisher, Cornell University Press. Chapter 5 also includes quotations from Carol J. Greenhouse, "Interpreting American Litigiousness," in *History and Power in the Study of Law*, edited by June Starr and Jane Collier, copyright © 1986 by Cornell University, used by permission of the publisher, Cornell University Press. Chapter 6 includes a section of David Engel's "Law, Time, and Community," from *Law & Society Review* 21 (1987), revised slightly here, reprinted by permission of the Law and Society Association.

For acknowledgments related to our three original studies, please see the notes to Chapters 1, 2, and 3. In addition, David Engel acknowledges funding from the National Science Foundation, Grant Number SES 8511105, and Carol Greenhouse is grateful for a study leave at Cornell University and research support from Indiana University.

For assistance with research and production of the manuscript, we thank Christine Farley, Anne Gaulin, Linda Kelly, and Cynthia Werner.

Our three studies began in conversations with the people of Hopewell, Riverside, and Sander County. We are grateful to them, and we have enjoyed the fact that this project has renewed such conversations, both literally and figuratively.

Our families have, almost from the beginning, been a part of this collaboration in many important ways, and we are happy to dedicate this book to them.

Bloomington, Indiana	C. G.
Amherst, Massachusetts	B. Y.
Amherst, New York	D. M. E.

Law and Community in Three American Towns

Introduction

Ethnographic Issues

This book is about community, law, and change in the United States and the ways these shape people's sense of identity in three different American settings. The places are towns, counties, and suburbs in New England, the Midwest, and the South. In each, certain people identify themselves and their places with what some of them might call mainstream America. The same people also readily label undercurrents and cross currents in the local segment of the mainstream that trouble them: the loss of traditional values and practices, the decline of family life, a rising tide of materialism, and increasing numbers of people — outsiders, troublemakers — whose very presence is a reminder of the threats to a way of life they value. In their eyes, the landscape bears the marks of this altered stream: housing developments or industrial sites where farms once were, old landmarks disappearing. On the street, they meet unfamiliar faces.

In Hopewell, Riverside, and Sander County (these are pseudonyms), people who are concerned about change stress what they perceive to be the new role of law and the courts in the local and national society. Indeed, in the social commentaries spontaneously offered by citizens in conversation, law and law use provide the key terms for broad analyses of community and change. For these citizens, the court is a crucial but ambiguous symbol of community. On the positive side, it is the very emblem of local autonomy and classical republicanism. On the negative side, the court symbolizes the reach of the state into the fabric of local society. Accordingly, in this book, we address the irony that, although courts and law are central to the ways some residents construct their sense of community, these same individuals disparage the courts as having been captured by the "wrong" people for the "wrong" kinds of cases.

One of our main findings is related to this irony, in that law and law use provide ordinary citizens with a potent social discourse that they use in a variety of settings to explain and comment on their everyday experience. By discourse, we mean an interrelated set of cultural meanings — symbols, values, and conventionalized interpretations — that shape and make comprehensible the terms people use to converse in everyday life (see Chatman, 1978). In Riverside, Sander County, and Hopewell, we found a discourse, shared by people who claimed "insider" status, that placed law and law use at the center of "community." In that discourse, harmony and conflict are presented as opposites, corresponding to the oppositional processes of making and unmaking communities in which the law is perceived to play a central defining role. "Harmony" encodes positively valued practices and persons associated with those practices; "conflict" encodes negatively valued practices and persons. One of our ethnographic emphases is on the nature of these ascriptive references and the significance of their local and translocal meanings.

A second major finding is that, in each of our three sites, the harmonious community is a myth that is predicated on — and reproduces — a symbolic distinction between insiders and outsiders. By calling the harmonious community a "myth," we draw attention to its place in the discourse of identity through which "insiders" in each locale construct themselves *as insiders*. People who claim to be "insiders" represent local social identity as involving oppositions (them versus us), in ways that encode specific hierarchies (high versus low, restrained versus uncontrolled, included versus excluded).[1] In each town, these people place law use symbolically at the fulcrum of these distinctions.

In addition to exploring this system of differences in terms of local semiotics, we feel that we have developed some understanding of their importance in structuring major local contests, past and present. Although people claiming to be "insiders" draw an explicit link between litigiousness and outsiders by defining excessive litigation as a characteristic of that "group," we also consider the untestable nature of such ascriptions (and of the concept of "excessive litigation" itself) and the fact that any and every group boundary is constantly in motion, constantly transgressed. The myth of the harmonious community "is elaborated vis-à-vis" (Clifford, 1988:11), in dialogues with specific others and in contests at specific historical moments.

One by-product of the "moving target" quality of the conceptual boundaries around local social classifications is that it became difficult for us, in writing this book, to find a lexicon for social and symbolic dynamics that was not already predefined by "native" (that is, "insiders' ") meanings. Given our concerns with the referents of symbols of identity, we found it impossible not to refer to "insiders" and "outsiders," although we stress as often as is practicable that these are terms that express a particular point of view within the settings we studied. Ethnographically, the narrative structure and organization of the book derive primarily from the point of view of people who define themselves as "insiders," but we make every effort to provide readers with independent vantage points. Certain other native terms, such as "individual," "community," "harmony," and "conflict," were more easily presented almost exclusively in terms of local usage without blurring the boundary between local meanings and our own language of analysis. Such words should be read as if they had quotation marks around them; they refer to "native" speech. Our sense of what these terms mean in the three towns is explained fully in the text. For now, we want to register an important caveat: "Insiders' " symbolic distinctions are not necessarily reciprocated by those with whom they see themselves in contest relationships.

It is important to connect terminological difficulties such as these to the central issues of the study. From the local point of view, learning the discourse of "insiders" and learning to mark social and conceptual boundaries appropriately are valued forms of cultural expertise. There is much at stake in putting things, people, and behaviors "in their place." For example, praise or condemnation of court use has much to do with local insiders' sense of things and people being "out of place" — dirty, degenerate, reprehensible (see Douglas, 1966, and Perin, 1977).

One way of summing up these comments (in highly abstract terms) would be to say that in all three towns, local space has moral meaning. When people talk about order, they invite their interlocutors to visualize their towns' former "way of life" (another key term from local lexicons). Thus, the distinction between people who are where they belong and people who are out of place is highly charged. It evokes the image of rival moral orders sharing the same space, as if the local landscape itself were contested ground. In Part II of the book, we consider at length the subtleties of local concepts of space and probe their multiple moral referents.

Competition and conflict are not only symbolic, of course. The differing concerns of local people are very much grounded in their personal experience. That is what gives the symbols their relevance and force. Individualism charters their prevalent sociological discourse — although individualism is expressed somewhat differently in each setting. In context, individualism is also their prevalent ethical discourse. In ethical terms, the forms of individualism we describe emphasize and valorize self-reliance. In relation to law use, sometimes self-reliance means invoking rights and entitlements; sometimes it means *not* invoking them. This ambiguity is another refrain in the book's ethnographic discussions.

The ethical aspects of individualism are inseparable from the concept's more sociological aspects. This mutual embeddedness of the moral and the social is evident in the way local people talk about economic competition. Competition in the marketplace is for "insiders" a legitimate expression of individualism. Litigation is appropriate in community terms when it is consistent with the norms of the local market, that is, for purposes of contract enforcement, debt collection, or landlord suits to evict or collect back rent. The same people draw a distinction, however, between local economic activity and the anonymous, dollar-driven national and multinational companies that, in a variety of ways, symbolically and materially disrupt local practices and local exchanges and interdependencies. Such disruptions as these merge with others: Insiders also disparage people who seem to them to be seeking to advance their individual interests through certain kinds of litigation, such as personal injury or civil rights actions. These "abuses" are perceived by insiders as greedy and selfish — as anticommunitarian. Like other American towns, our three sites have experienced major economic transformations within the memories of middle-aged adults. We believe that those developments shaped the dynamics and significance of the distinctions that are central to our comparative project.

LEGAL KNOWLEDGE, LOCAL KNOWLEDGE: THE ANTHROPOLOGY OF LAW IN THE UNITED STATES

Our focus on Americans' ideas about legal institutions and their role in the lives of communities places this work at the intersection of two literatures with separate traditions. As we explain in the next section, this project has its genesis in our independent research activities as ethnographers of law. The anthropology of law, both before and after the rise of the "law and society movement" in the United States, offers one context for the present work. The other major literature to which we hope to contribute is the anthropology of the United States — also a collective project of long standing (since the 1920s), though its revival since the 1970s has had a particular character, as we explain below. Since our independent case studies (Chapters 1–3) were developed specifically for sociolegal audiences, this introduction emphasizes the sociolegal aspect of the present work's context; we introduce the U.S. ethnographic context more briefly, and return to additional American themes in the book's conclusion.

One way of introducing both the sociolegal and American dimensions of the book is to observe that the standard terms of analysis in sociolegal studies are themselves embedded in the cultural field under investigation. Europe's secular legalism in the eighteenth century left a contemporary legacy in scholars' concerns with social order, social systems, and the relationship of the individual to the state. Eighteenth-century European concepts of society were highly legalistic; the very notion of the individual was of a free contracting agent, and, more generally, law was assumed to be among the primary signs of cultural difference. The romanticism of the nineteenth century defined a research tradition whose heritage also survives today, particularly in anthropologists' concerns with culture, symbols, worldviews, and ideologies. Modern anthropologists continue to seek evidence of people's understandings of the universe in institutions and practices that claim to ensure order, protect individuals and property, and facilitate exchanges (see introduction of Starr and Collier, 1989). To some extent, this book reflects the legacy of these ideas — a legacy shared by the social sciences and academic law — in the American context. We have already sketched some of the ways in which people in Hopewell, Riverside, and Sander County identify the law with particular expressions of community, and law users with particular forms of social identity. We also attempt to keep constantly in view the reflexive turn that places our informants in conversation with Emile Durkheim, Max Weber, and other classical social science theorists who dwelt on the genesis and social reproduction of normative ideas in ordinary life (for a related experiment, see Peacock and Tyson, 1989).

Legal anthropology emerged in the first decades of the twentieth century, as scholars in Europe, Great Britain, and the United States turned to the customary law of the indigenous societies of Africa, native North America, Southeast Asia, and Melanesia (for examples of early works, see Barton, 1919; van Vollenhoven, 1918; Malinowski, 1989 [1926]). The American tradition, in which we situate this volume, can be linked to simultaneous developments in Great Britain and the United States in the 1930s. In Great Britain, anthropologists of law were primarily concerned with indigenous jural traditions and modern practice in Britain's colonies in Africa. The nature of colonial administration and of the indigenous societies themselves combined to lead to a research emphasis on local jurisdictions, customary law, the role of the chief and counselors in mediation and adjudication, disputes and their outcomes, and the relationship of dispute settlements to the broader fabric of village life. Cast as comparative questions, these themes became the research foci of legal anthropology in general; their genesis, however, was in the African colonial experience.

In early contrast to the African emphasis, Bronislaw Malinowski's writings from the Trobriand Islands off the coast of New Guinea provided another orientation toward law. Malinowski (1989) emphasized law "in the broad sense of the term," as cultural practice, to use today's terminology. His classic work on law is a small monograph that ranges over Trobriand exchange, kinship, science and magic, formal and informal sanctions, and mores. There is no direct discussion of legal institutions, nor does Malinowski record rules or cases of dispute; rather, he emphasizes the dynamic and interconnected structure of social life and develops the links between the society at large and the existential conditions in which individuals function. Although its language is dated, the book is as much about the furnishings of the inner life as it is about the normative apparatus of a small-scale society and its anthropological observers.

Both the Africanist and the Malinowskian influences survive today. The Africanists — perhaps by virtue of the nature of the cultural ideas they studied — represent a research tradition more oriented to legal institutions and their internal conflict-resolution processes.[2] It can be found today among anthropologists who attend especially to courts, disputes, and the negotiation and articulation of implicit and explicit norms and rules. The Malinowskian tradition also survives in anthropological questions of the interrelationship of language, social organization, and personal experience in the construction of social order. Both traditions inform this book, particularly in giving shape to the questions in Part I.

In the United States, legal anthropology had independent origins, although the British traditions were eventually deeply influential. The foundational work in the United States was Llewellyn and Hoebel's *The Cheyenne Way* (1941), which emphasizes the relationship of legal processes to cultural norms and, in particular, the multiple sources of order in society — law, custom, religion, myth, and so forth. This breadth of scope (no doubt in part the Cheyenne contribution to the anthropology of law) remains an important aspect of American research traditions in legal ethnography. *The Cheyenne Way*, with its expansive inquiry into "law jobs" and "trouble cases," tends to obviate distinctions between legal norms and legal practice that might have been discovered in the differing emphases of the Africanist and the Malinowskian traditions. Traces of its influence may be found in our book, in both our emphasis on informants' complex sense of the relationship between normativity and practice in everyday life and our particular attention to the symbolic aspects of modern local myths.

Although it is possible to identify overarching themes and their origins in canonical works, legal anthropology also involves internal debates and unresolved questions. These, too, shape our questions and methods. For example, differences between approaches emphasizing legal norms and those emphasizing legal practice surface periodically and then resubmerge amid expressions of agreement that the two approaches are ultimately inseparable. Investigating the implicit or explicit rules of indigenous social practice, as opposed to uncovering the processes by which legal institutions operate, involves more fundamental differences of perspective. Thus, the debates involving Max Gluckman, Paul Bohannan, and, later, Richard Abel and their aftermath left the discipline with a sense of crisis. In part, this was a political crisis, as the Gluckman-Bohannan debate involved the cultural politics of cross-cultural comparison and the domination of possible vocabularies of comparison by the legal lexicons of the British colonizers.

The response to such issues came in the form of an intensified search for empirical data. Under the direction of Laura Nader, the Berkeley Village Law Project became a massive project of data collection by ethnographers in Africa, Europe, Latin America, Irian Java, and the Middle East. Whereas contemporary theoretical debates focused on the ultimate possibility of ethical and scientifically valid comparison, the Berkeley Project sought new possibilities close to the ground, among the actual disputes and dispute-resolution practices at the grassroots. The empirical emphasis of these and other studies enabled scholars to appreciate the relationship between local "legal" practices (that might or might not have had the status of official law), local social structures, and the dynamics of local political interests.

By the 1970s, the accumulation of ethnographic data from around the world by numerous scholars seemed to reopen the possibility of new comparative models and more synthetic approaches. The search for comparison began in what Collier (1975) termed the "ecology" of law — her phrase for the relationship among legal practice (broadly speaking), social relationships, and cultural norms. Over the course of the decade, anthropologists undertook this search in two principal directions: outward, toward the cultural and political context of law and law users, and inward, to the legal institutions in which norms are negotiated. Thus, one vein of research addressed issues of access to law (see, for example, Nader, 1980), and another focused on the deployment of local and regional political interests in legal arenas (see, for example, Moore, 1977).

At the same time, the theoretical openness and empirical commitment among legal anthropologists facilitated their dialogues across disciplines through the then-new Law & Society Association, a professional association for all social scientists interested in law in the broad sense of the word and for academic lawyers interested in empirical social science approaches. In the social sciences generally, the 1970s were an era of subdisciplinary specialization and interdisciplinary partnerships; among legal anthropologists, a term that began to be used with increasing frequency, the basis of these collegial improvisations was in the idea that legal institutions and "dispute processing" contained within themselves the elements of a general cross-national and cross-cultural theory.

By the 1980s, the aggregate ethnography of law seemed to cast doubt on the proposition that a general theory was possible. The ethnographic literature confirmed a relationship between the construction and reproduction of normative repertoires in local social life and between norms and other institutional practices and interests; however, each case study also contained compelling evidence of its own singular distinctiveness. The necessity of confronting cultural difference and the cultural complexity of law was most fully voiced by Comaroff and Roberts (1981) in their introduction to their book, *Rules and Processes*, which is both a legal ethnography of the Tswana and a critical essay on the conceptual deficits of an anthropology of law conceived as such. Working from very different starting points in symbolic and interpretive anthropology, Geertz (1983) also outlined an anthropological approach to law that questioned the possibility of holding "law" conceptually constant as a basis for comparison and theorizing (significantly, his essay is titled "Local Knowledge.)"

In the late 1970s and early 1980s (the period of our research), as anthropologists became increasingly convinced that the reality of law is profoundly local, the law itself was expanding considerably in the United States. Some said litigation was increasing; all agreed that the number of lawyers was on the rise. The scope of federal regulation increased in the 1970s, although growing antiregulatory movements gained legitimacy under the Reagan administration in the early 1980s. Civil rights law, which had witnessed important benchmarks in the 1950s and 1960s, continued to expand, although its pace began to slacken. Debate over the very concept of rights was beginning, but it seems fair to characterize the late 1970s and early 1980s as a period of rights consciousness, as people continued to press for new protections for women, minorities, consumers, and others.

Anthropologists were not studying these developments per se (neither were we), but they had considerable impact on the shape of ethnographic problems at this time. Our informants found myriad ways of expressing to us their own sense of identification or difference (and sometimes both) with these rights movements and the state's legal innovations. Indeed, their expressions are the ethnographic starting point of this volume. Had we collected our data ten years later, when deregulatory movements were in full swing and civil rights movements were increasingly embattled, our informants might have voiced different concerns; this context plays a definite, yet undefinable, role in our study.

Perhaps as a result of these significant shifts in the role of the state in our society — and the varying reactions of our informants — we found it increasingly difficult to rely on Malinowski's general allusions to law "in the broad sense of the term." Along with other legal ethnographers, we felt compelled to reorient our comparative questions around specific problematic aspects of state norms and institutions in everyday life. At the same time, the Malinowskian commitment to exploring the normative dimensions of social life at the grassroots continued and, indeed, flourished, as ethnographers in anthropology and other disciplines became increasingly sensitive to the complexity and indeterminacy of everyday negotiations of social life (see, for example, Clifford, 1988). The quest for methodology and theory continues, but it now takes greater account of both the law's power and the self-regulatory processes of social life for ordinary people.

In this book, we address the dual question of the power of law and the importance of everyday practice by emphasizing the ways in which law engages systems of local meaning. That is, we came to see use of the court and talk about law as ways local people have of making claims about the legitimacy of a particular way of life. Bourdieu's analysis of law as a form of symbolic power for "creating" the social world (Bourdieu, 1987:234) is central to this approach, which underscores the struggle between different social groups to control powerful symbols. Those struggles often take place in legal arenas, and, even when they do not, "the law" symbolically marks the place of those actual and hypothetical contests. In this volume, we explore the local experience of courts as sites where worlds are not only made but also unmade (although Bourdieu leaves the latter possibility relatively unexplored).

The prevailing sense among our informants that communities can be destroyed by people who assert their claims to entitlement in courts of law is a recurrent theme in our ethnographic chapters. If litigation is at times interpreted by local elites as a sign of a lack of virtue, then we must attend to the dynamic of law in everyday life that can turn ideologies of rights and of virtue into competing interpretive frameworks in this way. It is through such frameworks that local contests for power and recognition are carried out. Merry (1990) pursues related issues in her study of American working-class legal consciousness, which links class and court use. Hers and related works confirmed our sense that Americans communicate a broad range of messages through their uses of the law and through their talk about law use. Those works also confirmed our sense that there is a legitimate ethnographic problem in the many ways in which law comes into play in adjudicating among varied visions of order through which people imagine their own lives in some predictable relation to others.

It is probably apparent already that we view our work in terms of its connection to a long-standing ethnographic concern with cultural definitions of otherness and, indeed, with concepts of culture itself. We are particularly interested in the ways in which such concerns manifest themselves in American settings. We hope that our work can contribute to the understanding of how symbolic distinctions between "insiders" and "outsiders" (and the shared discourse of community they imply) emerge in contests through which people compare themselves with other people and their ways of life. These contests presume antagonists who are, culturally, "others" (that is, "outside" a particular system of meanings), but, as our discussion implies, the cultural boundary between "insiders" and "outsiders" is contestable in at least two ways. First, the category "outsider" is a code for the perceived intrusions of materialism, self-interest, and the state into a local economy mythically shaped by family, collective interest, and love. We refer to this oppositional array of institutions and values as the "myth of community." We investigate this myth, examining the close connections between local and translocal economies. We also acknowledge the different ways in which contemporary "insiders" are positioned vis-à-vis people they term "outsiders," some of whom do not share their vision of community or their interpretation of the meanings of law and the court.

Second, the boundary between "insiders" and "outsiders" is selective, fluid, somewhat arbitrary, and sometimes even nonexistent. That is, the concept of outsider does not necessarily apply to any actual group. "Outsider" status might be a collection of signs, but the coherence of such signs does not necessarily mean that they describe some set of people. Both the fluidity of social boundaries and their hypothetical character were important in our three-way study. For example, although our three locales had separate and distinctive histories, their portraits of "the outsider" had much in common.

In our book, we both follow a particular legacy of cultural analysis found in classic works of American cultural anthropology (Schneider, 1968; Perin, 1977; Varenne, 1977) and depart from this legacy. With David Schneider and others, we view cultural analysis as the study of ideas about society, an approach that builds on Claude Lévi-Strauss's insight that culture can be seen as "a system of differences" and as the models (or symbolic strategies) people use to distinguish their own societies from others. These models are accessible in what Lévi-Strauss (1983) terms "myth" — that is (for our purposes), people's talk, memories, stories, accounts of their past, and their fears and visions of the future. Social interactions might or might not enact these models in some observable way. (We should probably also note what reservations Lévi-Strauss might have about the capacity we see for modern society to generate myth.)

In this spirit, we focus on "the myth of community" when we discuss the great cultural weight borne by images of a harmonious small town, a face-to-face society, in Part II of this book. As we show, people go to considerable lengths, in both their inner lives and in their more public efforts, to "live" this image. Indeed, these images supply American institutions with some of their basic premises and cultural legitimacy. In pursuing their influence, we are assuredly not implying that such images are merely hollow, meaningless, or mystifying fictions. Rather, we reaffirm their importance and explore their subtexts in particular social contexts.

In doing so, we have found specific links to earlier works in cultural theory. For example, in his classic "cultural account" of what he called "American kinship," Schneider (1968) traced a basic mythic distinction between "nature" and "culture." For his informants, the distinction between "blood" and "law" was literally crucial to their sense of who people their universe of relatives. In our work, too, people drew on this distinction, as a means of expressing the difference between people who make trouble and others who exert a laudable self-control. The image of the litigant as polluting recurs in our findings; in Yngvesson's study particularly, the image is vivid, as in the court clerk's reference to certain plaintiffs' problems as "garbage" cases. In other ways, too, our informants seemed to fuse their general sense of law with equally broad propositions about common sense, polite society, and moral community, that is, with their own sense of what "culture" means.

We also depart from the legacy of cultural analysis represented by the work of Schneider and others, however, by examining the openness of cultural models to contestation in the struggles of people who "do not belong" with those who do. Accordingly, we focus on the emergence of myths of community at particular historical and contemporary conjunctures. These myths bespeak a cultural discourse, shared by some but not by others, in which "rights" are juxtaposed to "relationships" and "money" is juxtaposed to "love." These same myths also point to the historical and contemporary struggles of real people, with very different histories, who are symbolically linked in a discourse that locates them "outside" the community. These people speak a language of rights that is trumped by the (unarticulated) right to belong — a right claimed by people whose corollary claim is that they themselves speak for the "community" on the grounds that they are "insiders." In this sense, as Ginsburg (1989: 196) has noted, cultural meanings emerge in dialogue with an adversary, "real and imagined." Culture is not simply a model encoded in myth that can take us beyond the complexity and diversity of American society but also one that emerges *from* this diversity and complexity, silencing parts of it in that the very concept of "a" culture cannot tolerate "sharp contradictions, mutations, or emergencies" (Clifford, 1988:338).

Our project is a comparative study, most explicitly in its exploration of parallels and divergences in our findings from three U.S. settings. Implicitly (and with occasional references), its comparative terms are considerably broader, as the theoretical and methodological frameworks of ethnography are defined by anthropology's long-standing practice of cross-cultural research.

As we have noted, "culture" itself is a comparative concept, both for social scientists and the people they study. Writing on anthropology's comparative discourses, Boon argues that culture and comparison are corollaries. He identifies anthropologists' comparative efforts as an expression of every "culture's" inescapable need to draw distinctions for the sake of maintaining an intelligible self-identity in a constantly changing world:

> Without comparative analytic frameworks, every culture, whatever its "genius," remains impenetrable. . . . A "culture" can materialize only in counterdistinction to another culture. This statement is no hocus-pocus but merely acknowledges that before any culture can be experienced *as a culture* displacement from it must be possible; and contrary to notions of the Enlightenment, there is no place outside it to be except in other cultures or in their fragments and potentialities. (Boon, 1982:ix)

The technologies of such displacement operate in language, symbols, discourses, ideologies, and so forth. All claims to map the world as it "really" is simultaneously assert and deny the power of these technologies to distinguish among peoples and their cultural forms.

Our comparative project began with our general sense that the people we had known in the course of our three separate endeavors in the field might have something to say to all of us as anthropologists. They certainly did. Moreover, we became convinced by and committed to the idea that they also had much to say to one another. As we sought to understand the experiences and concerns encoded in local affirmations and critiques of law and law users, we became increasingly persuaded that these centrally involved the recent impact of national and international developments at the local level—impact of multinational corporations, loss of agriculture, urbanization, shifting demographics, new rights, and so forth. This theme appears throughout the book.

Indeed, we concluded that the significance of the variation in our findings pointed to ways in which these large-scale forces of social change were perceived, acknowledged, welcomed, or resisted in our separate locales. Our comparative approach is justified, we feel, by the fact that these three towns have experienced in common (though differently) the national and global restructurings of economy and society that contemporary scholars call late modernity. To put this another way, our comparative method is a means of recovering some of the ways in which the people about whom we write were already linked as actors on a world stage. That they are actors who generally go unobserved does not alter the significance of their roles or the importance of attempting to understand their experiences, perceptions, and beliefs.

THE UNITED STATES IN ETHNOGRAPHIC AND COMPARATIVE PERSPECTIVE

This book is very much a product of the conceptual trends outlined in the preceding section, because it both deals with American cultural material and is the work of three individuals who were trained in these research traditions. The "Americanness" of the data can be found in several currents that run through the volume. The idea that law is—or somehow ought to be—a popular creation rather than the command of a sovereign (Austin, 1965) reflects a liberal democratic outlook that comes easily to most of our informants and is, not coincidentally, also pervasive in the conceptual apparatus of empirical sociolegal research. Our study is also shaped by this liberal research tradition, although we do emphasize the limits and problems of this idea when it is voiced as a cultural premise by the people whose experiences we are most concerned to understand.

Another American hallmark in the volume is in our informants' premise that the term "American" is meaningful as a name for something distinctive, integral, and affirmative. They identify themselves as Americans in this sense, adding, when invited to do so, that the American nation is as much a creation of shared character as it is the result of anything else. "Belonging" thus carries the connotation of a natural, familistic tie that continually renews the nation's fabric. As we have already suggested, this view of the nation and its component communities is also hedged with serious reservations and anxieties, and these are explored in depth. Although we ourselves do not share our informants' expressed belief in national character, we are concerned with the question of how to juxtapose our independent studies and make sense of them together.

This book originated in a research problem that American sociolegal scholars shared with our informants, that is, in their concern with how disputes were handled in our society. Did Americans lack access to justice? Were they excessively litigious? Did they use, or need, informal mechanisms to "resolve" their conflicts? In this respect, our informants shared the view of vociferous social critics and other public figures, including the then–chief justice of the Supreme Court, Warren Burger, that our society was experiencing a litigation explosion (for discussion and critique of this view, see Galanter, 1983). Although our own aims were broadly ethnographic, each of our original research projects leaned toward questions of how ordinary people were handling problems in and out of the courts.[3]

We independently began our studies thinking of ourselves as ethnographers of law, but we ended them preferring to think of our work as contributing to the ethnography of the United States. Given the particularly legalistic quality of American republicanism, it is indeed a small step from popular conceptions of the law to larger idioms of social life; we are primarily concerned to understand the proximity of these ideas. Yet, in some respects these intellectual currents seemed to challenge the validity of the sort of comparative ethnographic project that we attempt in this volume. Quite apart from the fact that there were few publications on the ethnography of American law when we began our original projects from the early 1970s to the early 1980s (indeed, American ethnography itself was at a standstill in the early 1970s), Americans' individualistic conceptions of society — emphasizing the personal as well as asserting the universality of fundamental interests and motivations — seemed to mitigate against applying standard anthropological concepts (especially the concept of culture) to the United States (for a related argument, see Varenne, 1984). In effect, it was as if there were two entities: law and the individuals it addressed. What difference could culture make?

From that point of view, except to the extent that he or she might track the contours of cultural diversity (in the sense of difference from some alleged mainstream), an anthropologist might seem to have little to do in the United States. Our informants' concerns about the implications of new forms of diversity and pluralism in their own towns and regions illustrates this point. Paradoxically, where the impression of diversity was prevalent, the possibilities of anthropology were said by many social science skeptics to be even more remote, as if culture (like some Americans' notions of equality) were a synonym for sameness (again, see Varenne, 1984).

In the late 1970s, American ethnographic writing began to appear again after a period of relative silence. Lloyd Warner's synoptic volume *American Life: Dream and Reality*, summarizing his entire Yankee City and Jonesville corpus, had been republished in 1962 (1953), and David Schneider's classic *American Kinship: A Cultural Account* was published in 1968. Americans rearranged their ideas of diversity, national identity, and the role of the United States in the world in the 1970s, and anthropologists returned to the United States as a field of study. Among the first results were Varenne's *Americans Together: Structured Diversity in an American Town* (1977) and Constance Perin's *Everything in Its Place* (1977); these and subsequent works shifted the ground of American ethnography from the operations of national character to the ways in which Americans perceive and manage diversity in their daily lives.

Beyond the general ethnographic project that connects this work to others, this book is in close conversation with at least several others. In particular, we recognize some of Varenne's "Appleton" in our respective sites and have also drawn on his subsequent analyses and critiques of the ethnography of the United States (1977, 1984, 1986, 1987). We expect that people in Hopewell, Riverside, and Sander County would find much in common with people from Appleton when talk turns to local identity and the vexed nature of modern times. Beyond any ethnographic parallels, we value the Appleton study for Varenne's deployment of a concept of culture that attends to diversity not only as a subject for research in its own right but also as evidence of other cultural principles and processes that make diversity significant in the public symbols of the United States.

Specific parallels to findings reported in this volume can also be found in the work of Perin (1977, 1988), who argues convincingly for a cultural "reading" of local regulation (her study focuses on urban American zoning categories). Essentially, she finds that categories of land use express cultural categories of land users. In Part II of this volume, we explore the ways in which the concept of community defines both a location and a symbolic site where social classifications are produced and juxtaposed. Her later work on neighboring and belonging is also relevant: for example, the relationship between "belonging" and purity, and, more generally, the inevitability of taking some cultural perspective in writing about urban landscapes and their tenants. In general, Perin's work is oriented toward the ways in which Americans attempt to structure their lives around chosen principles and myths. We pursue these questions in the context of local attitudes toward courts and court use.

In our field sites, these principles include the notion of voluntarism or "choice" as central to the construction of identity and community and an ideology of restraint and self-control as fundamental to civic life. An ethic of autonomy pervades local understandings of what "community" consists in, as well as people's interpretations of the appropriate and inappropriate uses of law. The same themes emerge in other recent ethnographic studies of American life, from the interpretive analysis of a Montana rodeo (Errington, 1987, 1990) to the documentation of the struggles of abortion activists (Ginsburg, 1989). In each of these studies, local practice and translocal knowledge intersect in ways that produce concepts of "diversity" along similar cultural lines.

In the places we studied, as in those examined by Ginsburg, Errington, Varenne, and others, "community" is seen as "a matter of choice on the part of the 'I' " (Varenne, 1977:34). At the same time, only certain people are deemed capable of making this kind of choice. Thus, not surprisingly, quite specific "others" come to be excluded from "community" — "litigious" people, people "with dollar signs in their eyes" (these quotations are from our informants), people whose lack of self-restraint, whose "excess, audacity, and irresponsibility" (Errington, 1990:632) are said to disqualify them for community life. Paradoxically, it is precisely these qualities that make for success in the marketplace and thus are valued as market practice in local epistemologies. One of the themes in this book is the simultaneous condemnation and celebration of forms of individualism that are seen as destructive of community yet are also essential (and admirable) in economic arenas on which an elite "community" depends for its existence.

The relationship between people's sense of community and the cultural meanings and tensions encoded in it also provide a point of departure toward comparative studies beyond the United States. Certainly, it is not only in the United States that people construct local, regional, and national identities around the specific sorts of distinctions that our informants raised for us, between the city and the country, multinational capital and local commerce, national government and local forums, a "standard" national culture and the distinctive character of the local society, state law and the "normal" rhythms of reciprocity, and so on (see, for example, Handler, 1984, on Quebec; Dorst, 1989, on the United States; Greenwood, 1989, on Spain; Eidson, 1990, on Germany; Herzfeld, 1990, on Crete; and Kelly, 1986, on Japan). These works are related to each other (and to this volume) in that they trace the daily negotiations of ordinary life to referents in state bureaucracies, global markets, the creation of new forms of wealth and power, and the reification of "culture" at the very moment when local cultural expression ceases to be a voice of effective power.

BACKGROUND AND HISTORY OF THE PROJECT

Although our collaboration on this book has continued now for nearly eight years, it originated less in careful planning and coordinated study than in happenstance and serendipity. We initiated our research independently; we did not meet until after our respective early years of fieldwork. As our collaboration now reaches printed form, we have asked ourselves how it was that we undertook in relative isolation from one another three studies that were readily integrated into a shared interpretation of law and community in American society. We have also asked ourselves how it was that circumstances brought us together in such a way that a collaborative project suggested itself years after we had independently begun (and, for some of us, imagined that we had concluded) our separate research endeavors.

Each of us initiated research in an American setting after fieldwork in other cultures and, for Engel and Yngvesson, earlier extended experience abroad (see Engel, 1978; Yngvesson, 1978). In different ways for each of us, we returned from our respective "fields" in the 1970s with the sense that the sort of work we had done abroad might well be attempted usefully in our own society, given the nature of the times and their questions for the discipline. The repertoire of the Second City company in the late 1970s included a skit about anthropologists venturing up the Chicago River to explore the bizarre behavior of natives in the outlying suburban villages. Earlier, anthropology had spawned its own parody, in the form of Miner's (1956) essay on "the Nacirema." To attempt to find the exotic in the familiar may appear quixotic or even parodic, yet creative ethnographic research has been undertaken, as we have seen, in so-called mainstream American towns: Warner (1962 [1953]) in Yankee City; the Lynds (1929, 1937) in Middletown; Hollingshead (1949) in Elmtown; and Vidich and Bensman (1958) in Springdale. None of these studies focused particularly on law; yet each of them demonstrated the powerful impact of notions of community on local norms and interpersonal engagements. These works ranged in age from almost twenty to over fifty years when we met for the first time to explore the possibility of a collaborative project; we wondered vaguely if pursuing that possibility might not be viewed (even by ourselves) as a futile effort to recapture a lost era of American ethnographic certainty. We now suspect that, rightly or wrongly, our earlier field experiences elsewhere, where ethnographic traditions are much less inhibited by the doubts of those working "at home" (see Messerschmidt, 1981), predisposed us to believe in the possibility of writing a comprehensive ethnography around our three sites that would conceal neither their respective distinctiveness nor their internal diversity.

In retrospect, it is clear that once we had decided to do legal ethnography in our own society, our prior immersion in other cultures led us to understand "our" three American field sites in distinctive and distinctively similar terms. To the observer living in an unfamiliar culture, even the most mundane and obvious behavior or expressions are exotica demanding interpretation. When the observer returns to her or his own culture, what was once familiar, everyday, or "given" can take on a different cast and raise interpretive questions of a very fundamental kind. As it happened, each of us began to do fieldwork at a time in our lives when few aspects of everyday life in American towns struck us as obvious or self-explanatory. Beyond our personal experiences, our separate returns coincided with the crest of the American engagement in Vietnam, the antiwar movement, as well as a period of heightened national self-consciousness in the domain of civil liberties. In that moment of cultural self-scrutiny, new terms—"middle America," "the silent majority"—named terra incognita that invited study. The law was centrally involved in the definition of cultural identity within this newly unfamiliar society, as the judiciary expanded equal protection from racial classifications to those of gender, ethnicity, legitimacy, and so forth and as Affirmative Action entered the public vocabulary.

As our independent work and analysis progressed, we each became increasingly conscious of the complex interconnections of myth, belief, and perception in the cultural experience of these three towns. This cultural fabric included the legal institutions and behaviors that we sought to understand. Law and beliefs about law in these American settings began to take on some of the culturally constitutive attributes we recognized from our research into the belief systems and behaviors of people in Asia, Europe, and Central America.

Of the three of us, Yngvesson's study is closest to the courtroom itself. Her interest was in the use of the criminal complaint procedure as a way of structuring moral order in a New England town; she focused particularly on the court clerk. Engel worked more on the users' side of the law's doorway, examining patterns of civil court use in Sander County, a formerly agrarian midwestern town. Greenhouse, working in a southern town, was interested in local attitudes toward conflict and disputes and only more or less incidentally in courts and litigation as themes in their own right. The first three chapters summarize major themes from our independent projects.

In turning our ethnographic attention toward "home" (though none of us was raised in the area we studied), we certainly were not alone. Moore's (1973) influential discussion of "semiautonomous social fields" as a unit of analysis in the study of complex societies was a clear invitation to find settings in the United States whose partially regulated and partially autonomous workings could be comparatively analyzed (her essay compares the interlocking social fields of the New York garment industry and those of the Chagga villages of Tanzania). Merry (1990) studied the disputing practices of different ethnic groups in the Boston area. Nader (1980) turned to large-scale questions of access to law in the United States. In sociology, Baumgartner (1988) explored informal practices of social control in a middle-class northeastern suburb. The expansion of ethnologists' efforts in the study of law, social control, and politics made sustained comparative theory building inviting across related disciplines, especially among American legal scholars who read anthropological works: Abel (1973) on the role of dispute institutions in different social contexts, Felstiner (1975) on the social contexts and dynamics of disputing, and Galanter (1975) on "why the haves come out ahead" are leading examples. Today, though cultural inquiry on U.S. law is by no means mainstream in either anthropology or law, it is nevertheless difficult to recapture convincingly the sense of how new these early projects were. Suffice it to say that when we first met at the Law & Society Association's annual meeting, we in no way took for granted the nature of the conversation that would result.

By the time our collaboration began in earnest late in 1985, its context in our respective disciplines had changed somewhat, both in the availability of a new generation of American ethnographers and in new approaches within the sociolegal research community. For example, although earlier sociolegal studies emphasized disputes as a unit of analysis, later works moved in the direction of the systems of knowledge and power that frame disputes and connect them to social relationships (see Collier, 1975; Santos, 1977; Kidder, 1980–81; Comaroff and Roberts, 1981; Cain and Kulcsar, 1981–82; Mather and Yngvesson, 1980–81; Geertz, 1983; and Rosen, 1984). Accordingly, we do not treat "conflict" and "injury" or "equality" and "inequality" for that matter as neutral terms of analysis but as cultural concepts whose meanings are locally constructed. We are also interested in how those meanings are negotiated, articulated, reproduced, and challenged in practice and in what they imply as to these Americans' ultimate visions of justice and social order.

It is probably not a coincidence that our collaboration came about at a time when cultural attention to the United States was proliferating in both anthropology and sociolegal studies. Had we undertaken our original projects as a collaboration, this book would undoubtedly look very different. Following the then-current anthropological tradition, we would have been inclined, perhaps, to assume that each town was a microcosm of some larger cultural and national "whole," and that the important difference among our separate research enterprises was that of region. Indeed, we can recall an early conversation in which we considered region, religion, and ethnicity as separate factors likely to account for the three towns' expressions of distaste for open disputing in and out of the courts. We set these factors aside for various reasons and, more appropriately, settled on the fact that each of these towns was in the midst of a particular kind of social change. That point of departure was productive, we now think, because rather than developing the comparison by juxtaposing the sites in terms of three sets of more or less static attributes, we instead pursued it by thinking about local dynamics of identity and social experience. In effect, we turned from who we thought local people were to who they told us (and, we think, themselves) they were and were not.

This collaboration has been satisfying to us, in no small part because it allowed us to participate in new ways in the broadening scholarship on cultural aspects of law and society in the United States. Closer to home, it was satisfying, too, in that it brought together three separate and complementary data sets and transformed them into a conversation about a common subject. In this, there was much to enjoy, not least the sense that it was our respective disciplines and the work of our colleagues that made the conversation possible and fruitful. The format of this book is our attempt to recreate the process of collaboration and mutual discovery through conversation and reflection, beginning in Part I with three separate studies and progressing in Part II to a more fully integrated perspective.

ORGANIZATION

This volume is organized in two parts, designed to introduce readers to both the independent projects and the collaborative conversations that constitute the present study. Accordingly, Part I presents Riverside, Sander County, and Hopewell in separate chapters; each one was individually authored. The central themes of these chapters are local individualisms, perceptions of law and law use, the symbolic role of litigation in defining community and important social categories, and the various ways in which courts and court personnel participate in the cultural construction of local ideologies. They are reprinted here in their original form. Observant readers will note some changes in our usage from Part I to Part II, especially with respect to terms distinguishing "insiders" and "outsiders." We abandon this terminology in Part II. "Community" also changes from a neutral term of description (or so we thought) in Part I to a culturally laden object of study in Part II.

Part II is the result of the prolonged conversation among us. Although we never lost the sense of experimentation that first led us to try to juxtapose our separate projects and never lost sight of the diversity within or among the towns, we became increasingly convinced that the comparative effort yielded interpretive problems that we would not have entertained on our own. We think that this is the case not only because three heads are better than one, but also because, by collaborating, we gained a vantage point from which to reassess the townspeople's convincing but somewhat misleading claims as to the nature of local social change, as if their communities, once integral and distinctive, were now under siege from the future. Such claims are misleading, in that these towns have always been diverse places, structured by significant conflicts that reverberate in the terms in which people define and analyze local experience. They have always been places connected to the world beyond their jurisdictions. After all, these are places settled by immigrants — whose descen-

[handwritten marginalia: Part 1 / language, insiders, outsiders, & community / Each is problematic, yet essential]

dants' principal (and paradoxical) claim to liberty is based on their own belonging.

It is probably significant that our collaborative study reached its largest conclusions when we attended most closely to the local particularities of our separate sites. Anthropological theory and practice, which are predicated on the concept of culture as a system of differences, encouraged us to think about what three widely separate research projects and research sites might have to say to one another. No doubt, the fact that each of us had originally designed an ethnographic study facilitated our efforts to juxtapose our findings and develop new questions. Ethnography is a research methodology that is close to the ground. Based on the premise that what is essential about human experience is its public aspect, ethnography watches, reads, and listens to the lived, written, and spoken records — past and present — people make as they go about their daily lives. Thus, the raw material for this ethnographic work consists of countless conversations, memories, testimony, prayers, formal and informal interviews, as well as observations at public events, trials, and hearings, as invited guests at private homes, or as a member of the general public.

At the same time, anthropological theory and practice, which tend to reify "community" (as do the town residents whose points of view we discuss), are also available to challenge any comparative enterprise. In particular, the interpretivist stance that each of us takes (in somewhat different ways) is also one that casts a long shadow over any search for similarities and differences across cultural systems, given its priority on "the native's point of view" in defining ethnographic problems. In this context, it is worth emphasizing that the volume's conclusion is not that people in "our" three towns are somehow "the same" but that they share a vocabulary — individualism, law, community, and so on — with which to carry on a conversation that transcends their particular locales.

That vocabulary's key terms are the subject of Part I. Part II examines the language in which that vocabulary has meaning: moral categories, *Part 2* concepts of place, and concepts of history. In part, this is a language of myth. The concept of community does indeed — like myth or as myth — generate a structured diversity (the term is Varenne's, 1977) that claims to be total. If we examine those claims, it is not to dismiss the myth, but to understand how the myth defines the ways in which people link the existential conditions of their lives to the world around them.

PART ONE

Ethnographic Studies

CHAPTER ONE

The Oven Bird's Song

Insiders, Outsiders, and Personal Injuries in an American Community

DAVID M. ENGEL

Although it is generally acknowledged that law is a vital part of culture and of the social order, there are times when the invocation of formal law is viewed as an *anti*social act and as a contravention of established cultural norms.[1] Criticism of what is seen as an overuse of law and legal institutions often reveals less about the quantity of litigation at any given time than about the interests being asserted or protected through litigation and the kinds of individuals or groups involved in cases that the courts are asked to resolve. Periodic concerns over litigation as a "problem" in particular societies or historical eras can thus draw our attention to important underlying conflicts in cultural values and changes or tensions in the structure of social relationships.

In our own society at present, perhaps no category of litigation has produced greater public criticism than personal injuries. The popular culture is full of tales of feigned or exaggerated physical harms, of spurious whiplash suits, ambulance-chasing lawyers, and exorbitant claims for compensation. Scholars, journalists, and legal professionals, voicing

---

The title refers to Robert Frost's poem "The Oven Bird," which describes a response to the perception of disintegration and decay not unlike the response that is the subject of this chapter. The poem portrays a woodland scene in midsummer, long after the bright blossoms and early leaves of spring have given way to less attractive vistas and to age, fallen leaves, and "highway dust." With the approach of fall (the word has a double meaning in the poem), the "loud song" of the oven bird echoes through the woods: "The question that he frames in all but words / Is what to make of a diminished thing."

60 minutes from a piece on this topic in 1994

concern with crowded dockets and rising insurance costs, have often shared the perception that personal injury litigation is a field dominated by overly litigious plaintiffs and by trigger-happy attorneys interested only in their fees (Seymour, 1973:177; Tondel, 1976:547; Perham, 1977; Rosenberg, 1977:154; Taylor, 1981; Gest et al., 1982; Greene, 1983).

To the mind agitated by such concerns, Sander County (a pseudonym) appears to offer a quiet refuge. In this small, predominantly rural county in Illinois, personal injury litigation rates were low in comparison with other major categories of litigation[2] and were apparently somewhat lower than the personal injury rates in other locations as well.[3] Yet Sander County residents displayed a deep concern with and an aversion to this particular form of "litigious behavior" despite its rarity in their community.[4]

Those who sought to enforce personal injury claims in Sander County were characterized by their fellow residents as "very greedy," as "quick to sue," as "people looking for the easy buck," and as those who just "naturally sue and try to get something [for] . . . life's little accidents." One minister describing the local scene told me, "Everybody's going to court. That's the thing to do, because a lot of people see a chance to make money." A social worker, speaking of local perceptions of personal injury litigation, particularly among the older residents of Sander County, observed: "Someone sues every time you turn around. Sue happy, you hear them say. Sue happy." Personal injury plaintiffs were viewed in Sander County as people who made waves and as troublemakers. Even members of the community who occupied positions of prestige or respect could not escape criticism if they brought personal injury cases to court. When a minister filed a personal injury suit in Sander County after having slipped and fallen at a school, there were, in the words of one local observer, "a lot of people who are resentful for it, because . . . he chose to sue. There's been, you know, not hard feelings, just some strange intangible things."

How can one explain these troubled perceptions of personal injury litigation in a community where personal injury actions were in fact so seldom brought? The answer lies partly in culturally conditioned ideas of what constitutes an injury and how conflicts over injuries should be handled. The answer is also found in changes that were occurring in the social structure of Sander County at the time of this study and in challenges to the traditional order that were being raised by newly arrived "outsiders." The local trial court was potentially an important battleground in the clash of cultures, for it could be called on to recognize claims that traditional norms stigmatized in the strongest possible terms.[5]

SOCIAL CHANGES AND THE SENSE OF COMMUNITY

Sander County in the late 1970s was a society strongly rooted in its rural past, yet undergoing economic and social changes of major proportions. It was a small county (between 20,000 and 30,000 population in the 1970s), with more than half its population concentrated in its county seat and the rest in several much smaller towns and rural areas. Agriculture was still central to county life. Sander County had 10 percent more of its land in farms in the mid-1970s than did the state of Illinois as a whole, but the number of farms in Sander County had decreased by more than one-third over the preceding twenty years, while their average size had grown by almost one-half. Rising costs, land values, and taxes had been accompanied by an increase in the mechanization of agriculture in Sander County, and the older, smaller farming operations were being rapidly transformed. At the same time, a few large manufacturing plants had brought blue-collar employees from other areas to work (but not always to live) in Sander County. A local canning plant also had for many years employed seasonal migrant workers, many of whom were Latinos. In recent years, however, a variety of "outsiders" had come to stay permanently in Sander County, and the face of the local society was gradually changing.

To some extent, these changes had been deliberately planned by local leaders, for it was thought that the large manufacturing plants would revitalize the local economy. Yet, from the beginning there had also been a sense of foreboding. In the words of one older farmer:

> A guy that I used to do business with told me when he saw this plant coming in down here that he felt real bad for the community. He said, that's gonna be the end of your community, he said, because you get too many people in that don't have roots in anything. And I didn't think too much about it at the time, but I can understand what he was talking about now. I know that to some extent, at least, this is true. Not that there haven't been some real good people come in, I don't mean that. But I think you get quite a number of a certain element that you've never had before.

Others were more blunt about the "certain element" that had entered Sander County: union members, southerners and southwesterners, African Americans, and Latinos. One long-time rural resident told us, "I think there's too many commies around. I think this country takes too many people in, don't you? . . . That's why this country's going to the dogs." Many Sander County residents referred nostalgically to the days when they could walk down Main Street and see none but familiar faces. Now there were many strangers. An elderly woman from a farming family, who was struggling to preserve her farm in the face of rising taxes and operating costs, spoke in troubled tones of going into the post office and seeing Spanish-speaking workers mailing locally earned money to families outside the country. "This," she said, "I don't like." Another woman, also a long-time resident, spoke of the changing appearance of the town:

[It was] lots different than it is right now. For one thing, I think we knew everybody in town. If you walked uptown you could speak to every single person on the street. It just wasn't at all like it is today. Another thing, the stores were different. We have so many places now that are foreign, Mexican, and health spas, which we're not very happy about, most of us. My mother was going uptown here a year ago and didn't feel very well when she got up to State Street. But she just kept going, and I thought it was terrible because the whole north side of town was the kind of place that you wouldn't want to go into for information or for help. Mostly because we've not grown up with an area where there were any foreign people at all.

There was also in the late 1970s a pervasive sense of a breakdown in the traditional relationships and reciprocities that had characterized life in Sander County. As one elderly farmer told me: "It used to be I could tell you any place in Sander County where it was, but I can't now because I don't know who lives on them. . . . And as I say in the last twenty years people don't change work like they used to—or in the last thirty years. Everybody's got big equipment, they do all their own work so they don't have to change labor. Like years ago . . . why, you had about fifteen or twenty farmers together doing the exchange and all."

Many Sander County residents with farming backgrounds had warm memories of the harvest season, when groups of neighbors got together to share work and food:

When we had the threshing run, the dining room table it stretched a full 17 feet of the dining room, and guys would come in like hungry wolves, you know, at dinner time and supper again the same thing. . . . And they'd fire the engine up and have it ready to start running by 7:00. . . . You know, it was quite a sight to see that old steam engine coming down the road. I don't know, while I never want to be doing it again, I still gotta get kind of a kick out of watching a steam engine operate.

And all could remember socializing with other farming families on Saturday evenings during the summertime. In the words of two long-time farmers:

A: Well, on Saturday night they used to come into town, and the farmers would be lined up along the sidewalk with an ice cream cone or maybe a glass of beer or something. . . .
B: If you met one to three people, you'd get all the news in the neighborhood. . . .
A: If you go downtown now, anytime, I doubt if you'll see half a dozen people that you know. I mean to what you say sit down and really, really know them.
B: You practically knew everybody.
A: That's right, but you don't now.
B: No, no, no. If you go down Saturday night. . . .
A: Everything is dead.

THE STUDY

Perceptions of personal injury claims in Sander County were strongly influenced by these social changes as local residents experienced them and by the sense that traditional relationships and exchanges in the community were gradually disintegrating.[6] I cannot say that the frequent condemnation of personal injury litigation elsewhere in the United States is linked to a similar set of social processes, but investigation in other settings may disclose some parallels. The sense of community can take many forms in American society, and when members of a community feel threatened by change, their response may be broadly similar to the kind of response I describe here.

My discussion is based on fieldwork conducted from 1978 to 1980.

Besides doing background research and immersing myself in the community and in the workings of the Sander County Court, I collected data for the study in three ways: (1) I analyzed a sample of civil case files opened in 1975 and 1976;[7] (2) I contacted and interviewed in broad-ranging, semi-structured conversations plaintiffs and defendants in a subsample of these civil cases;[8] (3) I identified and interviewed at length strategically placed "community observers." These were individuals who had particular insights into different groups, settings, occupations, or activities in the community.[9] Discussions with them touched on various aspects of the community, including the ways in which the relationships, situations, and problems that might give rise to litigated cases were handled when the court was not used. The insights derived from the community observer interviews thus provided a broader social and cultural context for the insights derived from the court-based research.

Personal injuries were one of four major substantive topics selected to receive special attention in this study.[10] It soon became apparent, however, that personal injuries were viewed quite differently from the other topics, and the differences appeared to be related to the fundamental social changes that were taking place in Sander County. Focusing on personal injuries in this chapter makes it possible to examine the role played by formal law in mediating relationships between different groups in a changing society and to consider why the rare use of formal legal institutions for certain purposes can evoke strong concern and reaction in a community. The answer, I shall suggest, lies in the ideological responses of long-time residents of Sander County whose values and assumptions were subjected to profound challenges by what they saw as the intrusion of newcomers into their close-knit society.

INJURIES AND INDIVIDUALISM

For many of the residents of Sander County, exposure to the risk of physical injury was simply an accepted part of life. In a primarily agricultural community, which depended on hard physical work and the use of dangerous implements and machinery, such risks were unavoidable. Farmers in Sander County told many stories of terrible injuries caused by hazardous farming equipment, vehicles of different kinds, and other dangers that were associated with their means of obtaining a livelihood. There was a feeling among many in Sander County — particularly among those from a farming background — that injuries were an ever-present possibility, although prudent persons could protect themselves much of the time by taking proper precautions.

It would be accurate to characterize the traditional values associated with personal injuries in Sander County as individualistic, but individualism may be of at least two types. A rights-oriented individualism is consistent with an aggressive demand for compensation (or other remedies) when important interests are perceived to have been violated. By contrast, an individualism emphasizing self-sufficiency and personal responsibility rather than rights is consistent with the expectation that people should ordinarily provide their own protection against injuries and should personally absorb the consequences of harms they fail to ward off.[11]

It is not clear why the brand of individualism that developed over the years in Sander County emphasized self-sufficiency rather than rights and remedies, but with respect to personal injuries at least, there can be no doubt that this had occurred. If the values associated with this form of individualism originated in an earlier face-to-face community dominated by economically self-sufficient farmers and merchants, they remained vitally important to many of the long-time Sander County residents, even at the time of this study. For them, injuries were viewed in relation to the victims, their fate, and their ability to protect themselves. Injuries were not viewed in terms of conflict or potential conflict between victims and other persons, nor was there much sympathy for those who sought to characterize the situation in such terms. To the traditional individualists of Sander County, transforming a personal injury into a claim against someone else was an attempt to escape responsibility for one's own actions. The psychology of contributory negligence and assumption of risk had deep roots in the local culture. The critical fact of personal injuries in most cases was that the victims probably could have prevented them if they had been more careful, even if others were to some degree at fault. This fact alone is an important reason why it was considered inappropriate for injured persons to attempt to transform their misfortune into a demand for compensation or to view it as an occasion for interpersonal conflict.

Attitudes toward money also help to explain the feelings of long-time residents of Sander County toward personal injury claimants. Although there might be sympathy for those who suffered such injuries, it was considered highly improper to try to "cash in" on them through claims for damages. Money was viewed as something one acquired through long hours of hard work, not by exhibiting one's misfortunes to a judge or jury or other third party, even when the injuries were clearly caused by the wrongful behavior of another. Such attitudes were reinforced by the pervasive sense of living in what had long been a small and close-knit community. In such a community, potential plaintiffs and defendants are likely to know each other, at least by reputation, or to have acquaintances in common. It is probable that they will interact in the future, if not directly, then through friends and relatives. In these circumstances it is, at best, awkward to sue or otherwise assert a claim. In addition, in a small community, one cannot hide the fact of a suit for damages, and the disapproving attitudes of others are likely to be keenly felt. Thus, I was frequently assured that local residents who were mindful of community pressures generally reacted to cases of personal injury, even those that might give rise to liability in tort, in a "level-headed" and "realistic" way. By this it was meant that they would not sue or even, in most cases, demand compensation extrajudicially from anyone except, perhaps, their own insurance companies.[12]

Given the negative views that local juries adopted toward personal injury cases, terms such as "realistic" for those who avoided litigation were indeed well chosen. Judges, lawyers, and laypersons all told me that civil trial juries in the county reflected — and thus reinforced — the most conservative values and attitudes toward personal injury litigation. Awards were very low, and suspicion of personal injury plaintiffs was very high. A local insurance adjuster told me: "The jury will be people from right around here that are, a good share of them will be farmers, and they've been out there slaving away for every penny they've got, and they aren't about to just give it away to make that free gift to anybody." And one of the leading local trial lawyers observed:

> There's a natural feeling, what's this son of a bitch doing here? Why is he taking our time? Why is he trying to look for something for nothing? . . . So I've got to overcome that. That's a natural prejudice in a small [community], they don't have that natural prejudice in Cook County. But you do have it out here. So first I've got to sell the jury on the fact that this man's tried every way or this woman's tried every way to get justice and she couldn't. And they now come to you for their big day. . . . And then you try like hell to show that they're one of you, they've lived here and this and that.

The prospects for trying a personal injury case before a local jury, he concluded, were so discouraging that, "If I can figure out a way not to try a *pressure to settle.* case in [this] county for injury, I try to."

Where there was no alternative as to venue, potential plaintiffs typically resigned themselves to nonjudicial settlements without any thought of litigation. And, as I have already suggested, for many in the community the possibility of litigation was not considered in any case. One woman I spoke with had lost her child in an automobile accident. She settled the case for $12,000 without filing a claim, yet she was sure that this amount was much less than she could have obtained through a lawsuit. She told me that because she and her family knew they were going to stay permanently in the community, the pressure of the local value system foreclosed the possibility of taking the matter to court: "One of the reasons that I was extremely hesitant to sue was because of the community pressure. . . . Local people in this community are not impressed when you tell them that you're involved in a lawsuit. . . . That really turns them off. . . . They're not impressed with people who don't earn their own way. And that's taking money that they're not sure that you deserve."

Others had so internalized this value system that they followed its dictates even when community pressures did not exist. A doctor told me that one of his patients was seriously burned during a trip out of state when an airline stewardess spilled hot coffee on her legs, causing permanent discoloration of her skin. This woman refused to contact a lawyer and instead settled directly with the airline for medical expenses and the cost of the one-week vacation she had missed. Regarding the possibility of taking formal legal action to seek a more substantial award, she said simply, "We don't do that." The same attitude may help to explain the apparent reluctance of local residents to assert claims against other potential defendants from outside Sander County, such as negligent drivers or businesses or manufacturers.

Thus, if we consider the range of traditional responses to personal injuries in Sander County, we find, first of all, a great deal of self-reliant behavior. Injured persons typically responded to injuries without taking any overt action, either because they did not view the problem in terms of a claim against or conflict with another person or because membership in a small, close-knit community inhibited them from asserting a claim that would be socially disapproved. Some sought compensation through direct discussions with the other party, but such behavior was considered atypical. When sympathy or advice was sought, many turned to friends, neighbors, relatives, and physicians. The County Health Department, the mayor, and city council representatives also reported that injured persons occasionally sought them out, particularly when the injuries were caused by hazards that might endanger others. In such cases, the goal was generally to see the hazard removed for the benefit of the public rather than to seek compensation or otherwise advance personal interests.

INSURING AGAINST INJURIES

Persons who had been injured often sought compensation from their own health and accident insurance without even considering the possibility of a claim against another party or another insurance company. As a local insurance adjuster told me:

> We have some people that have had their kid injured on our insured's property, and they were not our insured. And we call up and offer to pay their bills, because our insured has called and said my kid Tommy cracked that kid over the head with a shovel, and they hauled him off to the hospital. And I called the people and say we have medical coverage and they are absolutely floored, some of them, that it never even crossed their minds. They were just going to turn it in to their own little insurance, their health insurance, and not do anything about it whatsoever, especially if [Tommy's parents] are close friends.

By moving quickly to pay compensation in such cases before claims could arise, this adjuster believed that she prevented disputes and litigation. It helped, too, that the adjuster and the parties to an accident, even an automobile accident, usually knew each other: "In Chicago, all those people don't know the guy next door to them, much less the guy they had the wreck with. And right here in town, if you don't know the people, you probably know their neighbor or some of their family or you can find out real quick who they are or where they are." The contrast between injuries in a face-to-face community and in a metropolis like Chicago was drawn in explicit terms:

> I think things are pretty calm and peaceful as, say, compared to Chicago. Now I have talked to some of the adjusters in that area from time to time and I know, well, and we have our own insureds that go

in there and get in an accident in Chicago, and we'll have a lawsuit or at least have an attorney . . . on the claim within a day or maybe two days of the accident even happening. Sometimes our insured has not any more than called back and said I've had a wreck, but I don't even know who it was with. And before you can do anything, even get a police report or anything, why you'll get a letter from the attorney. And that would never, that rarely ever happens around here.

This adjuster estimated that over the past fifteen years, her office had been involved in no more than ten automobile-related lawsuits, an extraordinarily low number compared with the frequency of such cases in other jurisdictions.[13] Of course, once an insurance company has paid compensation to its insured, it may exercise its right of subrogation against the party that caused the accident, and one might expect insurance companies to be unaffected by local values opposing the assertion or litigation of injury claims. It is not entirely clear why insurance companies, like individuals, seldom brought personal injury actions in Sander County, but there are some clues. This particular adjuster, who had grown up in Sander County, shared the local value system. Although she did not decide whether to bring suit as a subrogee, she may well have affected the decisions of her central office by her own perceptions and by her handling of the people and documents in particular cases. Furthermore, her insurance company was connected to the Farm Bureau, a membership organization to which most local farmers belonged. The evident popularity of this insurance carrier in Sander County (over 75 percent of the eligible farm families were estimated to be members of the Farm Bureau — it is not known how many members carried the insurance, but the percentage was apparently high) meant that injuries in many cases may have involved two parties covered by the same insurance company.

Occasionally, an insurance company did bring suit in the name of its insured, but given the unsympathetic attitudes of local juries, such lawsuits seldom met with success in Sander County. The adjuster mentioned above told me of a farm worker from Oklahoma who was harvesting peas for a local cannery. He stopped to lie down and rest in the high grass near the road and was run over by her insured, who was driving a pick-up truck and had swerved slightly off the road to avoid a large combine. When the fieldworker's insurance carrier sought compensation, the local adjuster refused, claiming that the injured man should not have been lying in the grass near the road and could not have been seen by her insured, who, she insisted, was driving carefully. The case went to trial, and a jury composed largely of local farmers was drawn: "I was not even in there, because our lawyers that represent us said, 'how many of those people do you know out there?' And I said, 'I can give you the first name of everybody on the jury.' He said, 'you stay over there in the library ... don't let them see you.' So I stayed out in my little corner and listened to what went on, and we won, we didn't pay 5 cents on it." Thus, even a lawsuit involving insurance companies on both sides was ultimately resolved in a manner that accorded with traditional values. The insurance companies' knowledge of jury attitudes in Sander County undoubtedly affected their handling of most injury cases.

LAWYERS AND LOCAL VALUES

Sander County attorneys reported that personal injury cases came to them with some regularity, although they also felt that many injury victims never consulted an attorney but settled directly with insurance companies for less than they should have received. When these attorneys were consulted, it was by people who, in the opinion of the attorneys, had real, nonfrivolous grievances, but the result was seldom formal legal action. Most personal injury cases were resolved, as they are elsewhere (Ross, 1970), through informal negotiation. Formal judicial procedures were initiated primarily to prod the other side to negotiate seriously or when it became necessary to preserve a claim before it would be barred by the statute of limitations. The negotiating process was, of course, strongly influenced by the parties' shared knowledge of likely juror reaction if the case actually went to trial. Thus, plaintiffs found negotiated settlements relatively attractive, even when the terms were not particularly favorable.

But expectations regarding the outcome of litigation were probably not the only reason that members of the local bar so seldom filed personal injury cases. To some extent Sander County lawyers, many of whom were born and raised in the area, shared the local tendency to censure those who aggressively asserted personal injury claims. One attorney, for example, described client attitudes toward injury claims in the following terms: "A lot of people are more conducive to settlement here just because they're attempting to be fair as opposed to making a fast buck." Yet, the same attorney admitted that informal settlements were often for small amounts of money and were usually limited to medical expenses, without any "general" damages whatever.[14] His characterization of such outcomes as "fair" suggests an internalization of local values, even on the part of those whose professional role it was to assert claims on behalf of tort plaintiffs.

The local bar was widely perceived as inhospitable to personal injury claimants, not only because there were few tort specialists but also because Sander County lawyers were seen as closely linked to the kinds of individuals and businesses against whom tort actions were typically brought. Although plaintiffs hired Sander County attorneys in 72.5 percent of all nontort actions filed locally in which plaintiffs were represented by counsel, they did so in only 12.5 percent of the tort cases.[15] One lawyer, who was frequently consulted by potential tort plaintiffs, lived across the county line in a small town outside of Sander County. He told me, "I get a lot of cases where people just don't want to be involved with the, they perceive it to be, the hierarchy of Sander County. . . . I'm not part of the establishment."

Thus, even from the perspective of insurance company personnel and attorneys, who were most likely to witness the entry of personal injury cases into the formal legal system in Sander county, it is clear that the local culture tended in many ways to deter litigation. And when personal injury cases were formally filed, it usually was no more than another step in an ongoing negotiation process.

Why was the litigation of personal injury cases in Sander County subjected to disapproval so pervasive that it inhibited the assertion of claims at all stages, from the moment injuries occurred and were perceived to the time parties stood at the very threshold of the formal legal system? The answer, I shall argue, lies partly in the role of the Sander County Court in a changing social system and partly in the nature of the personal injury claim itself.

THE USE OF THE COURT

In the recent literature on dispute processing and conflict resolution, various typologies of conflict-handling forums and procedures have been proposed. Such typologies usually include courts, arbitrators, mediators, and ombudspersons, as well as two-party and one-party procedures, such as negotiation, self-help, avoidance, and "lumping it" (see, e.g., typologies in Abel, 1973; Felstiner, 1974; Steele, 1975; Nader and Todd, 1978; Black and Baumgartner, 1983; Galanter, 1983). Analyses of these alternative approaches incorporate a number of variables that critically affect the ways in which conflict is handled and transformed. Such variables include, among others, procedural formality, the power and authority of the intervenor, the coerciveness of the proceedings, the range and severity of outcomes, role differentiation and specialization of third parties and advocates, cost factors, time required, the scope of the inquiry, language specialization, and the quality of the evidence to be heard. When variables such as these are used to analyze various approaches to conflict resolution, the result is typically a continuum ranging from the most formal, specialized, functionally differentiated, and costly approaches to the most informal, accessible, undifferentiated, and inexpensive. The court as a forum for dispute processing and conflict resolution is typically placed at the costly, formalistic end of such continua.

Yet, common sense and empirical investigations consistently remind us that trial courts rarely employ the adjudicative procedures that make them a symbol of extreme formalism. Very few of the complaints filed in courts are tried and adjudicated. Most are settled through bilateral negotiations of the parties or, occasionally, through the efforts of a judge who encourages the parties to reach an agreement without going to trial. This was true of the Sander County Court, as it is of courts elsewhere, and it applied with particular force to the relatively infrequent personal injury complaints that were filed in Sander County. Adjudication on the merits was extremely rare. In my sample, only one of fifteen personal injury cases went to trial, and the judges and lawyers to whom I talked confirmed the generality of this pattern. Yet, the court did play a crucial role in the handling of personal injury conflicts. It did so by providing what was perhaps the only setting in which meaningful and effective procedures of any kind could be applied. To understand why this was so, we must examine some distinctive characteristics of the relationships between the parties in the personal injury cases that were litigated in Sander County.

Among the relative handful of personal injury cases filed in the Sander County Court, almost all shared a common feature: The parties were separated by either geographic or social "distance" that could not be bridged by any conflict-resolution process short of litigation.[16] In at least half of the fifteen personal injury cases in the sample, the plaintiff and the defendant resided in different counties or states. These cases were evenly split between instances in which the plaintiff, on the one hand, and the defendant, on the other hand, was a local resident. In either situation, geographic distance meant that the parties almost certainly belonged to different communities and different social networks. Informal responses by the injured party, whether they involved attempts to negotiate, to mediate, or even to retaliate by gossip, were likely to be frustrated, because channels for communication, shared value systems, and acquaintance networks were unlikely to exist. This is reflected in the disproportionate presence of parties from outside the county on the personal injury docket.[17]

A more elusive but no less significant form of distance was suggested by interviews with the parties as well as by the court documents in several personal injury cases. In these cases, it became apparent that "social distance," which was less tangible but just as hard to bridge as geographic distance, separated the parties even when they were neighbors.

Social distance could take many forms in Sander County. In one personal injury case, the plaintiff, who lived in one of the outlying towns in Sander County, described himself as an outsider to the community, although he had lived there almost all his life. He was a Democrat in a conservative Republican town; he was of German extraction in a community where persons of Norwegian descent were extremely clannish and exclusive; he was a part-time tavernkeeper in a locality where taverns were popular but their owners were not socially esteemed; the opposing party was a "higher up" in the organization for which they both worked, and there was a long history of bad blood between them.

In a second personal injury case, a Mexican immigrant and his family sued a tavernkeeper under the Illinois Dram Shop Act for injuries he had suffered as a bystander in a barroom scuffle. Latino immigration into the community had, as we have seen, increased greatly in recent years to the displeasure of many local residents. Cultural misunderstandings and prejudice ran high, and little sympathy could be expected for a Latino who was injured in the course of a barroom fight. Thus, the plaintiff's wife was quite worried about bringing the lawsuit. She feared that they would create more trouble for themselves and told me, "I was afraid that maybe they'd say our kind of people are just trying to get their hands on money any way we could." The decision to sue was made, because they believed that people behind the bar had contributed to the injury by passing a weapon to the man who had struck the plaintiff (although, under the Dram Shop Act, the tavern could have been found liable without fault) and because they saw no other way to recover the income they had lost when the plaintiff's injury had kept him from working.

The tavernkeeper, who considered herself a member of the social under-class (although in a different sense from the Mexican immigrants), was bitter about the case and about the Dram Shop Act. When I asked her how the plaintiffs had known that she was liable under the Act, she answered, "I haven't any idea. How do they know about a lot of things is beyond me. They know how to come here without papers and get a job or go on welfare. They are not too dumb, I guess."

In this case, then, the two parties were separated from each other and from the community by a great chasm of social distance. One person was set apart from the general community by ethnicity and was well aware that his injuries were unlikely to be regarded with sympathy. The other party was also, by self-description, a second-class citizen. As a tavern-keeper, she told me, "you come up against many obstacles, prejudices, and hard times, you wouldn't believe." Both descriptions of social alienation were accurate. Yet, the defendant had an established place in the traditional social order. She owned a small business in a town dominated by the ethos of individual enterprise. Her line of work was widely recognized and accepted, although not accorded great prestige, in a community where taverns were among the most important social centers. Her acquisition of Dram Shop insurance made her a "deep pocket" comparable to other local business enterprises that might provide substantial compensation in appropriate cases to injured persons. The plaintiffs in this case, far more than the defendant, were truly social "outsiders" in Sander County. For them, nonjudicial approaches appeared hopeless, and passively absorbing the injury was too costly. Only formal legal action provided a channel for communication between the two parties, and this ultimately led, despite the defendant's reluctance, to settlement.

Social distance also played a part in an action brought by a woman on behalf of her 5-year-old daughter, who had suffered internal injuries when a large trash container fell on her. The little girl had been climbing on the trash container, which was located in back of an automobile showroom. The plaintiff and her husband were described by their adversaries as the kind of people who were constantly in financial trouble and always trying to live off somebody else's money. The plaintiff herself stated frankly that they were outsiders in the community, ignored or avoided even by their next-door neighbors. As she put it, "Everybody in this town seems to know everybody else's business . . . but they don't know you."

Her socially marginal status in the community precluded any significant form of nonjudicial conflict resolution with the auto dealer or the disposal company, and the matter went to the Sander County Court, where the $150,000 lawsuit was eventually settled for $3,000. Since initiating the lawsuit, the plaintiff had become a born-again Christian and, from her new perspective on life, came to regret her decision to litigate. The little money they had obtained simply caused her to fight with her husband, who sometimes beat her. She came to believe that she should not have sued, although she did feel that her lawsuit had done some good. After it was concluded, she observed, signs were posted near all such trash containers warning that children should not play on them.

In my interviews with local residents, officials, community leaders, and legal professionals, I presented the fact situation from this last case (in a slightly different form, to protect the privacy and identity of the original participants) and asked them how similar cases were handled in the segments of the community with which they were familiar. From our discussion of this matter there emerged two distinct patterns of behavior that, the interviewees suggested, turned on the extent to which the aggrieved party was integrated into the community. If the parents of the injured child were long-time residents who were a part of the local society and shared its prevailing value system, the consensus was that they would typically take little or no action of any sort. Injuries, as we have seen, were common in a rural community, and the parents would tend to blame themselves for not watching the child more carefully or, as one interviewee put it, would "figure that the kid ought to be sharp enough to stay away" from the hazard. On the other hand, if the parents of the injured child were newcomers to the community, and especially if they were factory workers employed in the area's newly established industrial plants, it was suggested that their behavior would be quite different. One union steward assured me that the workers he knew typically viewed such situations in terms of a potential lawsuit and, at the least, would aggressively seek to have the auto dealer and the disposal company assume responsibility for the damages. Others described a kind of "fight-flight" reaction on the part of newcomers and industrial blue-collar workers. One particularly perceptive minister said, "Those . . . that feel put down perceive everything in the light of another putdown, and I think they would perceive this as a putdown. See, nobody really cares about us, they're just pushing us around again. And so we'll push back." He also noted, however, that it was equally likely that aggrieved individuals in this situation would simply move out of the community, the "flight" response.

There was, then, some agreement that responses involving the aggressive assertion of rights, if they occurred at all, would typically be initiated by newcomers to the community or by people who otherwise lacked a recognized place in the status hierarchy of Sander County. Such persons, in the words of a local schoolteacher, would regard the use of the court as a "leveler" that could mitigate the effects of social distance between themselves and the other side. Persons who were better integrated into the community, on the other hand, could rely on their established place in the social order to communicate grievances, stigmatize what they viewed as deviant behavior, press claims informally, or, because they felt comfortable enough psychologically and financially, simply to absorb the injury without any overt response whatever.

Interestingly, this was precisely the picture drawn for me by the evangelical minister who had converted the mother of the 5-year-old girl. Lifelong residents of the community, he told me, reacted to stressful situations with more stability and less emotion than newcomers to the community who were less rooted and whose lives were filled with pressures and problems and what he called, "groping, searching, grasping." For the minister, born-again Christianity offered socially marginal people a form of contentment and stability that was denied them by their lack of a recognized position in the local society. He argued that external problems such as personal injuries were secondary to primary questions of religious faith. He told me, "If we first of all get first things straightened out and that is our relationship with God and is our help from God, all of these other things will fall into order." This was precisely the message that the plaintiff in this case — any many other socially marginal people in the community like her — had come to accept. On this basis, many social outsiders in Sander County could rationalize passivity in the face of personal injuries, passivity that was at least outwardly similar to the typical responses of Sander County's long-time residents.

The picture of the Sander County Court that emerges from this brief overview of personal injury cases differs substantially from that which might be suggested by conventional typologies of conflict-resolution alternatives. In processual terms litigation, although rare, was not strikingly different from its nonjudicial alternatives. It was characterized by informal negotiation, bargaining, and settlement in all but the extremely infrequent cases that actually went to trial. Yet, these processes occurred only as a result of the filing of a formal legal action. Because of the distance separating the parties, nonjudicial approaches, even with the participation of lawyers, sometimes failed to resolve the conflict. Resorting to the Sander County Court could vest socially marginal persons with additional weight and stature, because it offered them access to the levers of judicial compulsion. The very act of filing a civil complaint, without much more, made them persons whom the other side must recognize, whose words the other side must hear, and whose claims the other side must consider. The civil trial court, by virtue of its legal authority over all persons within its jurisdiction, was able to bridge procedurally the gaps that separated people and social groups. In a pluralistic social setting, the court could provide, in the cases that reached it, a forum where communication between disparate people and groups could take place. In so doing, it substituted for conflict-handling mechanisms that served the well-integrated dominant group but that became ineffective for persons who were beyond the boundaries of the traditional community.

The communication that the court facilitated could, however, give rise to anger and frustration. Plaintiffs often viewed the process negatively, because even when they went to court, they could not escape the rigid constraints imposed by a community unsympathetic to claims for damages in personal injury cases. Thus, the plaintiff whom I have described as a Democrat in a Republican town told me that the experience of filing and settling a personal injury claim was "disgusting . . . a lot of wasted time." Low pretrial settlements were, not surprisingly, the rule.

Defendants viewed the process negatively, because they were accustomed to a system of conflict resolution that screened out personal injury cases long before they reached the courthouse. Even though settlements might turn out to be low, defendants resented the fact that personal injuries had in the first place been viewed as an occasion to assert a claim against them, much less a formal lawsuit. Being forced to respond in court was particularly galling when the claimant turned out to be a person whom the core members of the community viewed with dislike or disdain.

In short, the Sander County Court was able to bridge gaps between parties to personal injury cases and to promote communication between those separated by social or geographic distance. It did so, however, by coercion, and its outcomes (particularly when both parties resided in the community) tended to exacerbate rather than to ameliorate social conflict. In the court's very success as a mechanism for conflict resolution we may, therefore, find a partial explanation for the stigmatization of personal injury litigation in Sander County.

THE PRESERVATION AND DESTRUCTION
OF A COMMUNITY

In rural and archaic Japan . . . people used to believe that calamity that attacked the community had its origin in an alien factor inside the community as well as outside it. The malevolent factor accumulated in the community. It was related also to the sins committed wittingly or unwittingly by members of the community. In order to avoid the disastrous influence of the polluted element, it was necessary for the community to give the element form and to send it away beyond the limits of the village. However, the introduction of the alien element, which could turn into calamity at any time, was absolutely necessary for the growth of the crops. Thus the need for the alien factor had two facets which appear contradictory to each other on the surface; that is, the introduction of the negative element of expiation as well as the positive element of crop fertility.

— MASAO YAMAGUCHI,
"Kingship, Theatricality, and Marginal Reality in Japan"

The social and economic life of Sander County had undergone major changes in the years preceding this study, and the impact of those changes on the worldview of local residents and on the normative structure of the community as whole was profound. Small single-family farms were gradually giving way to larger consolidated agricultural operations owned by distant and anonymous persons or corporations. The new and sizable manufacturing plants, together with some of the older local industries, now figured importantly in the economic life of Sander County and were the primary reasons why the population had become more heterogeneous and mobile.

These changes had important implications for traditional concepts of individualism and for the traditional relationships and reciprocities that had characterized the rural community. Self-sufficiency was less possible than before. Control over local lives was increasingly exercised by organizations based in other cities or states (there were even rumors that local farmlands were being purchased by unnamed foreign interests). Images of individual autonomy and community solidarity were challenged by the realities of externally based economic and political power. Traditional forms of exchange could not be preserved where individuals no longer knew their neighbors' names, much less their backgrounds and their values. Local people tended to resent and perhaps to fear these changes in the local economic structure, but for the most part they believed that they were essential for the survival of the community. Some of the most critical changes had been the product of decisions made only after extensive deliberations by Sander County's elite. The infusion of new blood into the community — persons of diverse racial, ethnic, and cultural backgrounds — was a direct result of these decisions. The new residents were, in the eyes of many old-timers, an "alien element" whose introduction was, as in rural Japan, grudgingly recognized as "absolutely necessary" to preserve the well-being of the community.

The gradual decay of the old social order and the emergence of a plurality of cultures and races in Sander County produced a confusion of norms and of mechanisms for resolving conflict. New churches were established with congregations made up primarily of newcomers. Labor unions appeared on the scene, to the dismay and disgust of many of the old-timers. New taverns and other social centers catered to the newer arrivals. Governmental welfare and job-training programs focused heavily (but not exclusively) on the newcomers. Newcomers frequently found themselves grouped in separate neighborhoods or apartment complexes and, in the case of blacks, there were reported attempts to exclude them from the community altogether. The newcomers brought to Sander County a social and cultural heterogeneity that it had not known before. Equally important, their very presence constituted a challenge to the older structure of norms and values generated by face-to-face relationships within the community.

PERCEPTIONS OF CONTRACT AND
PERSONAL INJURY CLAIMS

The reaction of the local community to the assertion of different types of legal claims was profoundly affected by this proliferation of social, cultural, and normative systems. The contrast between reactions to claims based on breaches of contract and those based on personal injuries is especially striking. Contract actions in the Sander County Court were nearly ten times as numerous as personal injury actions.[18] They involved, for the most part, efforts to collect payment for sales, services, and loans. One might expect that concerns about litigiousness in the community would focus on this category of cases, which was known to be a frequent source of court filings. Yet, I heard no complaints about contract plaintiffs being "greedy" or "sue happy" or "looking for the easy buck." Such criticisms were reserved exclusively for injured persons who made the relatively rare decision to press their claims in court.

In both tort and contract actions, claimants assert that a loss has been caused by the conduct of another. In contractual breaches, the defendant's alleged fault is usually a failure to conform to a standard agreed on by the parties.[19] In personal injury suits, the alleged fault is behavior that falls below a general societal standard applicable even in the absence of any prior agreement. Both are, of course, long-recognized types of actions. Both are "legitimate" in any formal sense of the word. Why is it, then, that actions to recover one type of loss were viewed with approval in Sander County, but far less frequent actions to recover the other type of loss were seen as symptomatic of a socially destructive trend toward the overuse of courts by greedy individuals and troublemakers? The answer appears to lie in the nature of the parties, in the social meanings of the underlying transactions, and in the symbolism of individuals and injuries in the changing social order.

Most of the contract litigation in Sander county involved debts to businesses for goods and services. Typically, the contracts that underlie such debts are quite different from the classic model of carefully considered offers and acceptances and freely negotiated exchanges. Yet, many townspeople and farmers in the community saw such obligations as extremely important (Engel, 1980). They were associated in the popular mind with binding but informal kinds of indebtedness and with the sanctity of a promise. Long-time Sander County residents viewed their society as one that had traditionally been based on interdependencies and reciprocal exchanges among fellow residents. Reliance on promises, including promises to pay for goods and services, was essential to the maintenance of this kind of social system. One farmer expressed this core value succinctly: "Generally speaking, a farmer's word is good between farmers." Another farmer, who occasionally sold meat to neighbors and friends in his small town, told me: "We've done this for twenty years, and I have never lost one dime. I have never had one person not pay me, and I've had several of them went bankrupt, and so on and so forth. I really don't pay any attention to bookkeeping or what. I mean, if someone owes me, they owe me. And you know, I've never sent anybody a bill or anything. I mean, sooner or later they all pay."

In these interpersonal exchanges involving people well-known to one another there was, it appears, some flexibility and allowance for hard times and other contingencies. On the other hand, there was a mutual recognition that debts must ultimately be paid. When I asked people in the community about a case in which an individual failed to pay in full for construction of a fence, the typical reaction among long-time residents was that such a breach would simply not occur. Of course, breaches or perceptions of breaches did occur in Sander County, and the result could be, in the words of one farmer, "fireworks." I was told stories of violent efforts at self-help by some aggrieved creditors, and it was clear that such efforts were not necessarily condemned in the community (Engel, 1980: 439–40). A member of the county sheriff's department observed that small unpaid debts of this kind were often viewed as matters for the police:

flexibility of implicit contracts between farmers.

> We see that quite a bit. They want us to go out and get the money. He owes it, there's an agreement, he violated the law. . . . You see, they feel that they shouldn't have to hire an attorney for something that's an agreement. It's a law, it should be acted upon. Therefore, we should go out and arrest the man and either have him arrested or by our mere presence, by the sheriff's department, a uniformed police officer, somebody with authority going out there and say, hey, you know, you should know that automatically these people give the money and that would be it. So therefore they wouldn't have to go to an attorney. Boy, a lot of people feel that.

Other creditors, particularly local merchants, doctors, and the telephone company, brought their claims not to the police but to the Sander County Court. In some cases, contract plaintiffs (many of whom were long-time residents) appeared to litigate specifically to enforce deeply felt values concerning debt and obligation. As one small businessman explained:

> I'm the type of a person that can get personally involved and a little hostile if somebody tries to put the screws to me. . . . I had it happen once for $5, and I had it happen once for $12. . . . I explained to them

carefully to please believe me that it wasn't the money, because it would cost me more to collect it than it'd be worth, but because of the principle of it that I would definitely go to whatever means necessary, moneywise or whatever, to get it collected. And which I did.

Even those creditors for whom litigation was commonplace, such as the head of the local collection agency and an official of the telephone company, shared the perception that contract breaches were morally offensive. This view appeared to apply to transactions that were routinized and impersonal and to the more traditional exchanges between individuals who knew each other well. As the head of the collection agency said, "When you get to sitting here and you look at the thousands of dollars that you're trying to effect collection on and you know that there's a great percentage of them you'll never get and no one will get, it's gotta bother you. It's gotta bother you." Certainly, business creditors felt none of the hesitancy of potential tort plaintiffs about asserting claims and resorting to litigation if necessary. Equally important, the community approved the enforcement of such obligations as strongly as it condemned efforts to enforce tort claims. Contract litigation, even when it involved "routine" debt collection, differed from tort litigation in that it was seen as enforcing a core value of the traditional culture of Sander County: that promises should be kept and people should be held responsible when they broke their word.

CONCLUSION

In Sander County, the philosophy of individualism worked itself out quite differently in the areas of tort and contract. If personal injuries evoked values emphasizing self-sufficiency, contractual breaches evoked values emphasizing rights and remedies. Duties generated by contractual agreement were seen as sacrosanct and vital to the maintenance of the social order. Duties generated by socially imposed obligations to guard against injuring other people were seen as intrusions on existing relationships, as pretexts for forced exchanges, as inappropriate attempts to redistribute wealth, and as limitations on individual freedom.

These contrasting views of contract and tort-based claims took on special significance as a result of the fundamental social changes that Sander County had experienced. The newcomers brought with them conceptions of injuries, rights, and obligations that were quite different from those that had long prevailed. The traditional norms had no doubt played an important role in maintaining the customary social order by reinforcing long-standing patterns of behavior consistent with a parochial worldview dominated by devotion to agriculture and small business. But the newcomers had no reason to share this worldview or the normative structure associated with it. Indeed, as we shall see, they had good reason to reject it.[20] Although they arrived on the scene, in a sense, to preserve the community and to save it from economic misfortune, the terms on which they were brought into Sander County, as migrant or industrial workers, had little to do with the customary forms of interaction and reciprocation that had given rise to the traditional normative order. The older norms concerning such matters as individual self-sufficiency, personal injuries, and contractual breaches had no special relevance or meaning given the interests of the newcomers. Although these norms impinged on the consciousness and behavior of the newcomers, they did so through the coercive forces and social sanctions that backed them up, not because the newcomers had accepted and internalized local values and attitudes.

Indeed, it was clear that in the changing society of Sander County, the older norms tended to operate to the distinct disadvantage of social outsiders and for the benefit of the insiders. Contract actions, premised on the traditional value that a person's word should be kept, tended to involve collection efforts by established persons or institutions[21] against newcomers and socially marginal individuals. Such actions, as we have seen, were generally approved by the majority of Sander County residents and occurred with great frequency. Personal injury actions, on the other hand, were rooted in no such traditional value, and, although such claims were infrequent, they were usually instituted by plaintiffs who were outsiders to the community against defendants who occupied symbolically important positions in Sander County society. Thus, a typical contract action involved a member of "the establishment" collecting a debt, but the typical personal injury action was an assault by an outsider on the establishment at a point where a sufficient aggregation of capital existed to pay for an injury. The distinction helps to explain the stigmatization of personal injury litigation in Sander County as well as its infrequency and ineffectiveness.[22]

Yet, personal injury litigation in Sander County was not entirely dysfunctional for the traditional social order. The intrusion of "the stranger" into an enclosed system of customary law can serve to crystallize the awareness of norms that formerly existed in a preconscious or inarticulate state (See Fuller, 1969:9–10, and Simmel, 1908 [1971]). Norms and values that once patterned behavior unthinkingly or intuitively must now be articulated, explained, and defended against the contrary values and expectations of the stranger to the community.

In Sander County, the entry of the stranger produced a new awareness (or perhaps a reconstruction) of the traditional normative order at the very moment when that order was subjected to its strongest and most devastating challenges. This process triggered a complex response by the community, a nostalgic yearning for the older worldview now shattered beyond repair, a rearguard attempt to shore up the boundaries of the community against alien persons and ideas (compare Erikson, 1966), and a bitter acceptance of the fact that the "stranger" was in reality no longer outside the community but a necessary element brought in to preserve the community and, therefore, a part of it.

Local responses to personal injury claims reflected these complexities. In part, by stigmatizing such claims, local residents were merely defending the establishment from a relatively rare form of economic attack by social outsiders. In part, stigmatization branded the claimants as deviants from the community norms and therefore helped to mark the social boundaries between old-timers and newcomers. Because the maintenance of such boundaries was increasingly difficult, however, and because the "alien element" had been deliberately imported into the community as a societal act of self-preservation, the stigmatization of such claims was also part of a broader and more subtle process of expiation (to borrow Yamaguchi's [1977] term), a process reminiscent of rituals and other procedures used in many societies to deal with problems of pollution associated with socially marginal persons in the community (Douglas, 1966; Turner, 1969; Perin, 1977:110–15).

Local residents who denounced the assertion of personal injury claims and somewhat irrationally lamented the rise in "litigiousness" of personal injury plaintiffs were, in this sense, participating in a more broadly based ceremony of regret that the realities of contemporary American society could no longer be averted from their community if it were to survive. Their denunciations bore little relationship to the frequency with which personal injury lawsuits were actually filed, for the local ecology of conflict resolution still suppressed most such cases long before they got to court, and personal injury litigation remained rare and aberrational.

Rather, the denunciation of personal injury litigation in Sander County was significant mainly as one aspect of a symbolic effort by members of the community to preserve a sense of meaning and coherence in the fact of social changes that they found threatening and confusing. It was in this sense a solution — albeit a partial and unsatisfying one — to a problem basic to the human condition, the problem of living in a world that has lost the simplicity and innocence it is thought once to have had. The outcry against personal injury litigation was part of a broader effort by some residents of Sander County to exclude from their moral universe what they could not exclude from the physical boundaries of their community and to recall and reaffirm an untainted world that existed nowhere but in their imaginations.

[handwritten marginal note:] Drawing on Geertz's sense of symbolic action.

CHAPTER TWO

Making Law at the Doorway

The Clerk, the Court, and the Construction of Community in a New England Town

BARBARA YNGVESSON

This chapter describes the negotiation of meaning in neighbor and family conflicts brought to a western Massachusetts criminal court.[1] The process used to handle these conflicts, known as a "show cause" or "complaint" hearing, marks the earliest phase of the criminal procedure in cases in which there has been no arrest.[2] This hearing is one of the least visible of court processes because complaint hearings are private and occur prior to the formal issuance of a criminal charge. They are conducted by the court clerk, who has the discretionary power either to allow a complaint application and issue a criminal charge or to deny it and handle the matter "informally" in the hearing itself. Thus, in local conflicts the clerk acts both as gatekeeper, keeping what is "not legal" out of the court proper, and as a peacemaker. The clerk's position at the court also allows him to play what one clerk defined as a local "watchdog" role, controlling "problem" people and "brainless" behavior in the communities in the court's jurisdiction.

My analysis focuses on the way exchanges between clerk and citizens produce legal and moral frameworks that justify a decision to handle a case in a particular way. The clerk plays a dominant role by controlling the language in which issues are framed, the range of evidence presented, and the sequence of presentation. He silences some interpretations and privileges others, constructing the official definition of what constitutes order and disorder in the lives of local citizens. But the definition of events during a hearing is also shaped by these working-, middle-, and lower-class people, using this arena with varying degrees of sophistication to structure the political and moral contours of their families and neighborhoods. Thus, it is through interaction between the clerk and citizens that court and community are mutually shaped.

Empirical literature provides a familiar portrait of courts as bounded and set apart, a domain of specialists controlled by an elite, or forums of "rough justice" with their own subculture and behavioral routines, distant from the practices and values of those who are judged there (Emerson, 1969; Abel, 1973; Robertson, 1974; Eisenstein and Jacob, 1977; Mather, 1979). This representation of a distant and, for ordinary people, impenetrable legal system is mirrored in theory that explains the role of modern law in terms of its control and imposition "from above" in the stratified settings of the industrialized world (Black, 1976; Unger, 1976; Cain and Hunt, 1979). At the same time, ethnographic study of conflict management "from below" suggests a more complex portrayal of law and of courts in shaping and reflecting local practices and understandings (Engel, 1984; Merry, 1985; Yngvesson, 1985a; Greenhouse, 1988). These studies point to what Sugarman (1983:2) describes as the "complex, semiautonomous coexistence" of state law with local processes and to the interpenetration of our most fundamental cultural assumptions with legal ones (Thompson, 1978; Gordon, 1984).

Studies of police, of lower-court judges, and of other local officials involved in the administration of justice (Bittner, 1969, 1974; Feeley, 1979; Harrington, 1985; Wilson, 1970) suggest that these actors play a key role in pulling the court into processes that maintain local order, because they keep a peace defined in local terms but imposed from without by officials of the state. In this chapter, I argue that it is through the interaction of criminal justice officials with local citizens that "the practical meaning of law" (Bourdieu, 1987:217) is shaped and that patterns of dominance in court and community are reproduced and occasionally challenged.

My analysis draws on an understanding of law and of the state that is grounded in the theory of practice (Bourdieu, 1977, 1987; Taylor, 1985; Skocpol, 1987). For Bourdieu (1987:217) the meaning of law is determined in "the confrontation between different bodies . . . moved by divergent special interests," but for Skocpol (1987:26) the state is "not just a set of formal offices, but . . . sets of relationships among all who participated in some identifiable interaction connected with state actions."[3] In earlier work I have examined this interaction, focusing on how the meaning of events and relationships is negotiated during the disputing process, and the implications of this for the reproduction and transformation of social order (Mather and Yngvesson, 1980–81).

This framework provides the context for my analysis of complaint hearings. In particular, I examine the delicate balance of coercion and complicity, conflict and cooperation that secures the clerk's dominance in shaping citizen complaints and that is central to an explanation of the exercise of power in this arena.[4] It is dependent on the legal construction of the clerk as both of the law and "not legal," a transitional figure linking court and community; it also hinges on the construction of the hearings as occurring "out of court" in a transitional space that allows the clerk and citizens to participate in producing the law while reproducing patterns of dominance at the courthouse and beyond. In this way I argue that the construction of "court" and "community" are part of the same moment and that complaint hearings reproduce the paradox at the heart of modern law: that it is "characterized by an independence achieved in and through dependence" (Bourdieu, 1987:225). It is neither "from above" nor "from below" but simultaneously separate and immanent, imposed and participatory.[5] Thus, in this chapter I seek to build on and go beyond the dichotomies inherent in previous literature about this process.[6]

THE COURT IN JEFFERSON COUNTY

The Jefferson County District Court is located in Riverside, Massachusetts, a town of 20,000 and the county seat. Its jurisdiction includes the town of Riverside and eighteen other villages and towns ranging in size from 200 to 8,000 people. The courthouse, an imposing red-brick building with white columns, sits at a major intersection just beyond the town center, which separates the town's elite residential neighborhood from its business district to the south and divides the "transitional" and slum areas that spread out to the east and west around the former sites of two of the town's major industries.

Like other district courts in Massachusetts, this one is closely tied to the communities it serves.[7] Most of its personnel are residents of Riverside, and many were raised there.[8] Court staff are connected to the business and professional communities in Riverside by ties of kinship, school attendance, and membership in social clubs. Today, as in the past, its presiding and other regular justices are prominent citizens, known for their strong community orientation. The present presiding justice grew up in a working-class neighborhood in the town, served on the legislature, and was a member of one of the town's prominent law firms before he became a judge. The other regular judge and the assistant clerk at the court grew up on what they describe as "the other side of the tracks" in Riverside. The judge became a partner in a local law firm and has served on the board of one of Riverside's major financial institutions. The assistant clerk served as a town policeman for twenty-one years, and in consequence not only knows a broad range of residents but also continues to have close ties with the police department. One of the assistants in the clerk's office is the daughter of a former Riverside police chief. The head clerk, born in a neighboring town, is one of the few "outsiders" at the court, a term he used to describe both himself and an African-American Riverside resident recently hired to work in the clerk's office.

Court staff share concerns expressed by others in Riverside and articulated on a daily basis in the county paper regarding the changing face of the town in the past decade or two as represented by loitering youth, runaway teenage women, and more serious juvenile crime; vacant buildings left as the major employers moved to other regions; and neighborhoods where there is "nothing that pulls people together." An imagined community of people who "go where they belong," avoiding the need to confront different ways of life, is perceived as being threatened by "scum" moving in from nearby cities. In the downtown area, transients and other "undesirables" roam the streets, a reminder of the proximity of nearby Milltown, whose "downstreet" neighborhood epitomizes the disintegration of community and defines chaos for the working-class residents of Riverside.

Although citizens have a variety of means for handling people and behavior that are defined as appropriate for public complaint,[9] they turn to the police and ultimately to the court for more authoritative intervention. The police, familiar figures in all but the most elite neighborhoods of the county, are typically called first, but they rarely make an arrest or file a complaint with the court. Only when repeated calls to the police have failed to resolve a problem do people turn to the court themselves.[10]

"GARBAGE" CASES AND THE LEGAL CONSTRUCTION OF THE CLERK AS NONLEGAL

If we arbitrarily granted all the complaints, we'd have a whole bunch of garbage.

— ASSISTANT CLERK, JEFFERSON COUNTY COURT

The clerk's office, where citizens and police must apply for issuance of a criminal complaint, is located just inside the doorway to the courthouse and marks the entry point to the court system for all nonarrest cases in the county. Private citizens filed 293 applications for issuance of a criminal charge with the clerk between June and December 1982. During this period, police brought 324 additional applications in response to citizen complaints.[11] Citizen complaints are loosely termed "garbage" at this court and others[12] as an implicit contrast to "serious" complaints brought by the police. A "garbage case" describes a conflict that is "everyday," a "shoving match in which somebody threw the first punch," "kids pushing kids," or a "lovers' quarrel." Initial sifting of these complaints in the field by police, who call them "kidstuff," points to their subsequent definition as "garbage" at the court. Court staff describe them as "private" matters that require a referee, a sounding board, or advice but do not view them as appropriate for a criminal charge. The presiding judge describes them as "little problems" in which people need "to be heard," so they "don't take it into their own hands if they can't resolve them." The assistant clerk simply says, "A lot of it is, people want to come to the courthouse. That keeps things out of court. They need a third party, and they don't have one available." The outcome of hearings on "garbage" cases confirms their representation by court staff as nonlegal matters.[13] By contrast to the complaints filed by police, which are issued in 82 percent of the cases, citizen complaints tend to be dismissed by the clerk or withdrawn by the complainant; only one-third become formal criminal charges in court.[14]

The clerk's role at the court is defined by his involvement with citizen complaints. As an official who deals with cases that are "not really law," he becomes, and is officially defined as, "not really legal" (McBarnet, 1981), a lay magistrate who is urged to act as a mediator and to "refrain from initiating criminal proceedings where the conflict can be fairly resolved by something less" (Committee on Standards, 1975:3:00). In keeping with this, the clerk is instructed to base decisions on "practical considerations of every-day life on which reasonable and prudent men, not legal technicians, act" (Commitee on Standards, 1975, 3:08). At the same time, the hearings are officially represented as a mechanism for enforcing the law, for determining "whether it appears that a crime has been committed" (*Mass. Gen. Laws Ann.*, 1979, ch. 276, §22) and whether there is "reasonable belief that the accused committed the crime in question" (Committee on Standards, 1975:3:17). The hearings are also described as a form of due process that protects the persons against whom a complaint is sought by permitting them "an opportunity to be heard personally or by counsel" prior to issuance of a criminal charge (*Mass. Gen. Laws Ann.*, 1979, ch. 218, §35A: 55).

The flexible official construction of the clerk's role as both law enforcer and peacemaker allows for wide leeway in how individual clerks choose to conduct a hearing. Styles of the clerks I observed ranged from distanced and formal decision making in a trial-like atmosphere, to forms of participatory decision making in which disputants were actively involved in constructing a solution to a case, to informal, but unilateral decision making by the clerk. Variation in style is affected somewhat by the style of the court and its local (as versus more professional) orientation; but the style of a hearing is shaped as well by the identities of the participants and their response to one another.[15] Thus, although some clerks were more comfortable with distanced decision making and others sought consensus, the style of proceedings and the construction of events in a case were shaped by the particular combination of participants, the knowledge that separated or linked them, and the implications of this for the exercise of power in a hearing. Which clerk, parties, and other professionals participated in a hearing affected the discourse used, the distribution and patterning of talk, the structuring of social space, and ultimately the meanings imposed on events.

At the Jefferson County Court, the styles of the two clerks differ markedly.[16] The head clerk, a man in his mid-thirties, is restrained and formal in both the hearings and his relations with colleagues and others who come to the clerk's office for assistance. With a graduate degree in education from the state university, he has more formal education than others in the office, but he is not legally trained. In hearings he carefully attends to correct procedure, relating his decisions to legal definitions and statutory sources and preferring to take cases under advisement rather than announcing a controversial decision during the hearing itself. Thus in an assault complaint, in which an attorney argued for issuance because there had been unpermitted touching, the head clerk denied the complaint a week later, after consulting the Massachusetts General Laws, on the grounds that criminal assault requires intent to cause physical harm, "not simply touching with intent." In another complaint of assault and battery, brought by a woman against a neighbor for stepping on her daughter's toes, the head clerk argued that issuance was inappropriate, saying, "I don't believe this comes to an assault. Assault and battery has to be an intentional striking, a threat to do bodily harm and the means to carry it out. Battery is striking with intent to do bodily harm."

The head clerk's control over the hearing is intimately tied to the implied control of the court setting and to the threat inherent in bringing a criminal charge. Although he does not hesitate to address problems of neighborhood relations and family structure during a hearing, he carefully keeps these "local" matters separate from the determination of probable cause. Thus, it is the head clerk, more than his assistant, who stands for what is most "legal" about the complaint procedure at this court.

The assistant clerk, a man in his late fifties, presents quite a different image, and it is primarily through him that the interdependence of court and community is played out in hearings on citizen complaints. A native of Riverside and a town policeman for twenty-one years before becoming a clerk, he is familiar to many of the parties who approach the court with complaints (he estimates that he knows at least 50 percent of them), and is known to colleagues in the community by his nickname. The middle-class complainant who comes to him because "he used to bust me when I was a teenager," the alcoholic who has faced him on repeated complaints of disturbing the peace, and the transient who lumbers regularly into the courthouse or a church coffee hour demanding advice and reassurance, all accept his judgment and counsel; indeed, the assistant clerk describes his efforts to handle many local conflicts not as judgments but as "little sermons," and he is successful in using these to forge a consensus among participants in a hearing.

His manner in hearings combines wry humor with a down-to-earth, no-nonsense approach, which allows him to cut through the complexities of relationship and intense emotions the proceedings may evoke. He never hesitates to interrupt, to call, "Time!" when things seem to be getting out of hand, or to order people to pay attention to what is going on. Unlike the head clerk, who relies on legal technicalities to control proceedings, the assistant clerk uses his knowledge of local communities and his personal authority to structure the hearings in ways that suit his own ends. Through skillfully timed questions, some of which probe beyond the events described in a complaint, he controls the range and sequence of information presented. Using what Santos (1977:14) terms "rhetorical reasoning," he draws on familiar imagery and everyday analogies to frame the behavior of participants as "brainless," "like children," or appropriate "in the ghetto." In this way he constructs commonsense interpretations of events. For example, in a case involving a charge of property destruction (damage to a "Big-Wheel" toy) by the father of an 8-year-old against a 14-year-old living on an adjacent street, the assistant clerk directed his attention to the father:

Clerk: He's a bit young to be playing with a 14-year-old.
Father: He's not out of my sight for long.
Clerk: If you're at 134 [Mayfield Street] and he's over there on Pine Street, he's out of your sight. The wrong guy comes cruisin' along, he's gonna be goin' for a ride. There's not much evidence to issue a complaint.

In this case, the clerk's familiarity with the neighborhood where the conflict took place made it possible for him to transform a complaint against one person into a "moral lapse" on the part of the complainant. He denied this complaint on probable cause grounds but implicitly supported his denial by reprimanding the complainant for his failure in adequately supervising his child.

In another case, a neighborhood fight in which parents and children in several families were involved, he concluded with a "little sermon," saying,

We have a case where the adults have to start acting like adults here. Probably, there's been a lot of discussion about these problems in front of the kids. Then the kids think they have to take up the fight for their parents. If there's a problem between the families, don't talk about it in front of them, so they don't think they have to take up the sword for you. Generally, if the parents don't get involved, the kids can settle these things themselves.

Use of technical language by a complainant may elicit more formal definitions from the assistant clerk as well. For example, in a complaint described as "threat to commit a crime, to wit murder," brought by a young man against his former girl friend's father, the assistant clerk argued that the incident was not criminal because there was no "intent." For intent to be present,

he [the father] would have had to take positive action, like chasing you out of his yard with a hammer or something. That would be an attempt. . . . Threat to commit a crime is a crime, and it isn't a crime.

It comes under a set of statutes where the judges are charged with keeping the peace. Then, they may have to put a surety on someone to keep the peace. It could be a threat to commit an assault and battery; and it could be a threat to commit murder. From what I've heard, the proper disposition here would be to just continue this case under the condition that he doesn't have anything to do with you and you don't have anything to do with him.

In this case, as in others, the clerk drew on implicit cultural stereotypes: that a "threat" to kill is not a crime in the context of a heated exchange involving intimates and that physical abuse is "discipline" if it is carried out by parents on children. These stereotypes were contrasted with legal definitions to justify denial. At other times, actions framed in legally grounded arguments about rights were redefined in a discourse of shared responsibility to construct images of everyday expectations and of mundane "trouble" (Emerson, 1969:83–100).

Although the head clerk seems uneasy with the tension between claims of rights and assertions of customary moral obligation that complaint hearings constantly evoke, the assistant clerk skillfully manipulates this, saying that this "middle area between them is where I want to stay. Sometimes I'll move as far as possible to one side or the other in order to accomplish what I need to." His decisions are made during the hearing and sometimes evoke open anger in the courtroom or provoke renewed arguing or fighting in the hall or the parking lot. He seems relatively undisturbed by this and remarks that some cases "will never be resolved." Nevertheless, he does not discourage people from bringing complaints, and it is through cases such as these that the limits of law are shaped and the contours of a moral community surrounding the courthouse etched.

A key feature of the assistant clerk's skill is the "personalized and far-reaching control" (Bittner, 1969:183) that he established as a former policeman. Like a policeman, his intimate acquaintance with local persons, places, and histories (Bittner, 1974:32) enables him to situate particular conflicts in particular settings and suggest solutions that reflect local expectations. In this way he avoids an overtly coercive role while defining local conflicts in terms of his own concerns about levels of risk in an area and the implications of this for public order. Thus, his handling of the complaint process subtly blends consensus with coercion, merging imperceptibly into what Bourdieu (1977:191–92) terms "disguised domination," the "gentle, invisible form of violence which is never recognized as such, and is not so much undergone as chosen." The assistant clerk's practice thus represents the delicate balance between law as imposed and law as shared at this court.

Next, I discuss the handling of "garbage" cases, focusing on struggles over issuance and on strategies used by the clerks to control the development of a case. These include the construction of a hearing as a formal legal event, the manipulation and control of silence (determining what can and cannot be said and at what times), and the interweaving of distinct discourses to control the meaning of persons and relationships.[17] In this way the clerks construct imageries of order and of relationship that make "common sense" and justify a decision to handle a complaint in a particular way.

CONSTRUCTING THE COMMUNITY AT THE COURTHOUSE

The bourgeois subject continuously defined and redefined itself through the exclusion of what it marked out as "low" — as dirty, repulsive, noisy, contaminating. Yet that very act of exclusion was constitutive of its identity

— PETER STALLEYBRASS and ALLEN WHITE
The Politics and Poetics of Transgression

Different strategies for resolving conflict convey different ways of imagining the self, and these different forms of self-definition suggest different ways of perceiving connection with others

— CAROL GILLIGAN, "Remapping the Moral Domain"

The hearings I discuss in this section involve problems of neighborhood life-style and family order in three Jefferson County neighborhoods. These make up almost one-third (95 cases, or 32 percent)[18] of citizen complaints and include the most stereotyped "garbage" cases brought to the clerk. They involve conflicts about noisy motorcycles and fighting children, burned pies and ruined clothes, overgrown trees and borrowed rings, matters termed "ridiculous" and "brainless" by the clerks. At filing, they are transformed into complaints of "assault and battery," "threats," and "disturbing the peace" and become vehicles for talking about legal rights and local morality, joining the language of law with the "common sense" of custom to shape notions of the good neighbor, the bad daughter, and the dutiful parent and to construct different images of the self in relationship. By pulling the court into the most mundane areas of daily life, these hearings become forums for constructing the separateness of law while transforming the courthouse into an arena for "thinking the community," for constituting what the local community is and who is not of it, even as they involve the local community in defining the place of law.

The clerks generally try to resolve these matters without issuing a complaint. They are constrained, however, by the capacity of complainants and others, whose position in the local community and knowledge of the law empower them to manipulate the complaint procedure to achieve their own goals. In the forty-seven neighbor and family complaints I observed, previous experience with the court system, ongoing connections with court staff, and ties to the professional and business community in Riverside were factors affecting capacity; these cases also suggested a tentative relationship between class and the capacity of users. As members of the local community, the clerks too may use issuance as a tool for controlling particular conflicts and those involved in them.

I explain negotiations over issuance in the context of cultural assumptions shared by court staff and other local officials about "normal trouble" in particular settings or relationships and of contemporary political and cultural issues in Riverside and the county as a whole. Quantitative analysis suggests that the relationship of the parties is of some significance in affecting the decision to issue and that family problems with runaway teenagers are of particular concern to the court, while neighbor cases are more typically dismissed. But analysis of the hearings indicates that even conflicts that are understood as "kidstuff" by the court staff may be constructed as serious problems of public order through the exchanges of the clerk with other participants in the proceedings.[19] To explore these issues, I present four extended cases, drawing on eighteen of the thirty-one hearings that I observed involving neighborhood conflicts and on two of the sixteen that I observed on family conflicts.

Forging a Compromise: The Good Neighbor and the Ethic of Responsibility

I begin with a hearing that illustrates the dynamic in neighbor complaints where the clerk successfully mediated the positions of the parties prior to dismissing the case.[20] The complaint, which involved a conflict over neighborhood noise, is similar to others, in which a localized nuisance (the children of "scum from Eastville," motorcycles, or a barking dog) became a vehicle for discussing changing ways of life in Riverside and surrounding towns. The clerk approached these problems by framing them in terms of interconnected lives and the need to be responsive to neighbors ("What you do is other people's business, because it affects them"). Complainants and attorneys, by contrast, discussed them in terms of rights and competing claims of self and other ("He's got the right to use the property for his business, and Jack's got a right to live there in peace"). These differing constructions of events suggest two conceptions of responsibility, reflecting what Gilligan (1986:239) has described as "different images of the self-in-relationship." In the one construction, "neighbor" implies a dynamic relationship in which each person's world is transformed by the presence of the other; in the second, the identity of each party is protected in a discourse of rights that maintains the equality and separateness of each individual.

The complainants in these conflicts were inexperienced and only used the courthouse as a last resort.[21] Once there, they did not press for issuance but looked to the clerk for assistance in resolving their conflict. As one complainant said, she was there because she hoped that "if [the defendant's] father and the police couldn't make him behave . . . the courthouse people could." The presence of a lawyer did not change this pattern. In the hearing that follows, for example, the lawyer for the complainant joined with the clerk in defining conditions for compromise rather than pressing for issuance.[22] Thus, the clerk was given broad scope in these conflicts and drew on his knowledge of local life and his skill in constructing an imagery of interdependence to resolve them. But as I will suggest, the use of this imagery was most successful when participants were relatively powerless and less adept in mobilizing a discourse of rights to frame their position.

CASE 1: *"The Noisy Motorcycles."* This complaint was brought from a neighborhood to the east of Riverside where several small businesses and some larger ones are gradually replacing a region of farmland and farm stand. A few private residences are interspersed with a dress shop, a restaurant, an auction gallery, a foreign car company, and a motorcycle business. The complaint, for "assault" and "disturbing the peace," was brought by a 60-year-old working-class man against his neighbor, the owner of the motorcycle business. The businessman allowed clients to test-run motorcycles behind his shop, and he also allowed his son to ride there after school and on weekends. His neighbor was bothered by the noise, and during the eighteen months since the shop had opened had complained to the businessman, had called the police on numerous occasions, and had also gone to the town meeting to complain; none of these efforts, however, had resolved the matter. Finally, after a call to the police one Saturday, the officer suggested the complainant go to the court clerk.

The assistant clerk opened the hearing with the following statement:

> For the record, this is a "show cause" hearing scheduled on behalf of —— on a complaint application by ——, alleging assault and battery and disturbing the peace. This is not a trial; it is not a minitrial. You will not be found guilty or not guilty. I do not have to have evidence beyond a reasonable doubt: just evidence enough to make a reasonable person believe that you could have done it. You do have a right to have an attorney. I cannot, at this stage, appoint an attorney for you, but you may obtain one at your own expense. Would you like time to obtain recounsel? . . . Do you have any questions? First I'll hear from —— [the complainant], and then you —— [the defendant] will have a chance to tell your story.

This introduction, repeated at all the hearings I attended, establishes the official quality of the proceedings while underscoring their nonlegal character. It also establishes the clerk's role as decision maker. Although the hearings are represented as nonlegal, they are held in the juvenile courtroom, which is smaller and more intimate than the regular courtroom but arranged so that the clerk sits at a raised bench, with the parties facing him at a table below. Proceedings are recorded, and the clerk is in control, directing questions to each of the parties in turn, so that he can elicit the type and sequence of information he wants and exclude what he defines as inappropriate. The style of the hearings typifies that described by Atkinson and Drew (1979)[23] for courtroom examination:

> *Clerk* [to complainant]: Where do you reside? Where's your property in relation to his?
> *Complainant:* It's right next door.

Clerk: Is that your home?

Complainant: Yes.

Clerk: What happened?

Complainant: It started on Saturday.

Clerk: What time of day?

Complainant: In the afternoon. . . . I just kept hearing that awful noise of motorcycles. He's going around and around the track, and it just got on my nerves. . . . I walked over and I said, "Andy, I'd like to talk to you." And he poked me in the chest. So I called the police. I asked the police about it, and they told me to fill out a complaint for assault and battery.

Clerk: What time of day do they ride out there?

Complainant: All day long.

Clerk: Where's this track?

Complainant: Right behind my house.

Lawyer for the complainant: How long has this been going on?

Complainant: About a year or so. . . . If they see me in my garden, they go right by. If I'm not there, they come right in.

Clerk [to defendant]: Andy, what do you have to say?

Defendant: For the past eighteen months, I've been running my business there. We use the field behind the building to test the motorcycles. He's complained eight or ten times. Much of the time it's other people who get onto the property through the railroad tracks. If people come onto my property by way of the railroad tracks, they are trespassing on my property as well as the railroad's. If people are on my property when I'm not there, what can I do about it? It's a commercially zoned piece of property. He brought a complaint to the town meeting, and all they did was tell me to cooperate. We never run a motorcycle more than five or ten minutes at a time.

Clerk: Do you have your land posted where they come off the tracks?

Defendant: Yes. Not only that, but they have a fence. I have a friend whose father's high up in the railroad. He's going to check about the railroad fencing it off.

Clerk: If it came to that point, would you have any objection to fencing in the property?

Defendant: I don't see why I should have to go to the expense.

Clerk: It may seem like a burden to you, but you say you've been there eighteen [to complainant] months. How long have you lived there?

Complainant: Six or seven years.

Clerk: See, when he moved there, he didn't have any problems with noise. More of us have had problems in Plainfield with kids racing up and down the road with trail bikes.

Lawyer: We just hoped perhaps something could be worked out. We realize that he has a right to do testing and that his kid has a right to ride there. He's got the right to use the property for his business, and Jack's got a right to live there in peace.

Clerk: I could issue a complaint for disturbing the peace. But as far as him poking you in the chest with his finger — he wasn't really threatening you bodily harm.

Complainant: He poked me! I'm not lying!

Clerk: But you weren't hurt. There was no hospitalization, and you weren't really threatened. So that's not the problem. The problem is the other people that come on the property.

Defendant: I still feel like I'm the one being picked on. It's my property!

Clerk: There's a limit to things you can do on your property.

Defendant: Where I live in Sayre, I have a nice home in farm country. When they harvest tobacco, there's three generators going all night long. But what am I going to do about it? Complain that they're disturbing the peace?

Clerk: But that's the way of life in Sayre. You could move down to New York City and there'd be nothing you could do about the noise either. He was living there quietly before the motorcycle shop moved in.

Defendant: I'm just going to continue doing what I can do. There has to be some proof that it's noisy.

Clerk: You know, people with a swimming pool have to fence it in. There are limits to what is safe and legal, even on your own property.

In this hearing the clerk used procedural formality to control the development of the case, while drawing on his knowledge of the neighborhood and of criminal law to construct events in a particular way. He rejected the notion that poking constituted assault, thus setting the limits of court intervention in the case, although he indicated that he could issue a complaint for disturbing the peace. He supported this, however, not in a discourse of rights but by portraying a "way of life" that both the businessman and the older resident were creating. The noise was excessive because it was occurring in an area where the "way of life" had been "quiet" until the motorcycle shop moved in. But as he noted later, "It's a tough thing. He's trying to run a business down there, and his neighbors are all upset because of the noise." The lawyer for the complainant argued that the rights claim of the businessman to "continue doing what I can do" on his own property was balanced by the rights of residents in the neighborhood to "live there in peace," underscoring the equality of the parties, but the clerk emphasized their interdependence, phrasing his arguments as "little sermons" (or what Schorske, 1981:69, in quite a different context, has referred to as "integrating myths"): "The only thing I can say is you've got to learn to be considerate of your neighbors. You've got to live with them. . . . It's not that simple. . . . That reminds me of a story. All these people were in a lifeboat, and one guy's huddled down there in a corner, and he won't have anything to do with anybody. All of the time he was saying, 'It's none of your business what I'm doing,' but he was steadily digging a hole in the bottom."

This construction justified a solution in which each made changes in life-style in response to the presence of the other. With issuance as an implied threat, the businessman agreed to investigate the fencing of his land so that only those with his permission could ride there, and he was to restrict motorcycle riding to fifteen minutes at a time. The complainant had to tolerate some noise because of the presence of the motorcycle business next door. By defining the issue in this case as one of neighbors-in-relationship rather than as one of rights, the clerk's proposed solution required a transformation in the world of each because of the boundary they shared.[24]

This type of solution, which Gilligan (1986:242) has termed "inclusive" rather than "fair," was characteristic of the assistant clerk, who frequently lamented that today there are "all these people wandering around with all these rights." It tacitly recognized that although "way of life" is shaped by tradition, it is constantly changed by the arrival of new neighbors. The clerk's solution limited the place of the criminal procedure in the construction of neighborhood life, and his participation actively involved the courthouse in what Bourdieu (1987:234) has called "the practical activity of worldmaking." The complainant's inexperience also contributed to the way this complaint was handled, as he emphasized what the clerk perceived as a "frivolous" assault charge and did not follow through on the clerk's suggestion that the nuisance complaint could be issued. He had come to the courthouse for assistance, and once there allowed the clerk and the attorney to shape the meaning of this case and the way in which the courthouse was used to influence it.

"Getting Rid of Someone Legally," Community Politics, and the Ethic of Rights

Unlike the last case, in which the clerk underscored the interconnection of the parties and sought a compromise, hearings in the next case, "The Expanding Tree," developed as straightforward proceedings for determining probable cause. Like "The Noisy Motorcycles," this case was related to problems of neighborhood life-style and was brought to the clerk as a charge of disturbing the peace. But here the identity of the parties, their greater sophistication in mobilizing the law, and the broader political meaning of the case in the town defined the clerk's role quite differently and shaped the imagery in which this case was framed at various legal levels.

There were no sermons about shared responsibilities in "The Expanding Tree," although everyone involved with the case agreed that it was specifically about "the end of a driveway" and more generally about the presence of "these kind of people" next door to an established Riverside family. The criminal complaint served as a vehicle for pursuing these problems, which were defined by a political and economic conflict that had polarized Riverside for years, following an exodus of major industry in the 1970s and 1980s. This conflict split its more conservative citizens, who worried about the "quality of life" in the town from those who advocated "progress": a new form of town government, new and alternative forms of business, and by implication the "alternative" ways of life that might accompany these.[25] The relationship of "The Expanding Tree" to this broader conflict transformed the role of the clerk from mediator of a "garbage" quarrel between neighbors to an advocate for one side in an issue that epitomized the struggle between old and new in the town.

CASE 2: *"The Expanding Tree."* The case involved a dispute between two families in a "transitional" neighborhood over a right of way straddling the boundary of their land. A large maple tree had grown into the right of way, forcing one of the parties to trespass slightly on the land of the other when it was used.[26] The families involved were an older man of Italian descent and his siblings (the Busonis), who had lived in the neighborhood all their lives. The man was a retired civil engineer, and his parents had purchased their house in 1917. The other family, a couple with three children (the Smiths), had moved into the house next door to the Busonis four years previously.[27]

The contrast in the houses of the two families was striking. The Busonis' house was an unremarkable white-frame structure, the property neat and well maintained. The Smiths' house, by contrast, was dominated by a turret, had been painted in unusual colors, and was surrounded by a tall fence hung with extraordinary masks. The Smiths, who describe themselves as "former hippies," were coowners of a small crafts store in town. In addition, Rick Smith was vice-chairman of the local merchants' association and chair of a citizens' committee to oversee the spending of a federal block grant for downtown renovation. He was an active supporter of efforts to encourage greater economic development in Riverside.

The Busonis objected to having the Smiths as neighbors and according to the Smiths had begun various forms of harassment to drive them out as soon as they moved there: shouting at them or their friends if they "blocked" the driveway; complaining to the building inspector about the Smiths' swimming pool; and protesting to the town planning board, to a Massachusetts state senator, and to the Department of Housing and Urban Development in Washington that Rick Smith was misusing funds from the federal grant. The Smiths were equally determined to stay in the neighborhood but chose to make life as miserable as possible for the older family, parking cars in the right of way, so the Busonis could not get by, putting up a "spite fence" between the two properties,[28] and finally erecting a granite hitching post on the contested triangle of land, so that it was impossible for the Busonis to use it. One night this occasioned a public confrontation in the driveway involving Rick Smith and a friend on one side and several Busoni siblings on the other. Rick Smith described it as follows:

> They had picks and shovels. I sat on the post, four of them dug around me, and I pushed it back in. They were leveling abuse at me. The next night I shipped my wife and kids out and we got feeling drunk and nasty. I've refused violent confrontation all along because

. . . he's trying to provoke that. We put the post back in again, they came and dug it out, and we sat back and called them words I'd never heard before. Then we dug a hole. Then his lawyer called and asked if there wasn't some way we could work it out—which is what we wanted.

Smith explained that "for years [he had] been trying to find a legal way to get rid of this guy," but that he had been "over a barrel" until he read the deed and discovered that Busoni was illegally trespassing on his land. He erected the post, he said, to force Busoni to initiate legal proceedings, and this strategy was successful. Busoni filed a suit in the superior court, requesting an injunction that would prevent the Smiths from using the triangular piece of land and force them to remove the granite post. In addition, a friend of the Smiths, and subsequently Rita Smith, brought criminal complaints against Busoni for disturbing the peace to the court clerk. Rick Smith had known the clerk since he was a teenager, when the clerk, who was then a policeman, "used to bust me." The Smiths were also known to other court staff, including the presiding judge, through their involvement in political and other town activities.

The first of the complaints, brought by the Smiths' friend when Busoni yelled at her for parking in the driveway and then followed her in his car as she drove away, was (in the words of the assistant clerk) "issued technically" but dismissed after six months when no more trouble was reported by the woman. A second complaint was filed some months later against Busoni by Rita Smith, who claimed he followed her and her children in his car when she was driving to a nearby beach. The assistant clerk again heard this complaint and devoted the hearing to a detailed reconstruction of the sequence of events. He asked Rita Smith about the route she had taken, questioned the children carefully as to whether they had seen Busoni following them, and checked to be sure Rita Smith had identified Busoni correctly:

Clerk: When you drove in [at the beach] did you look at Mr. Busoni?
Rita Smith: Yes. I looked at him and said, "You've had it now." And he took off.
Clerk: When you turned around and came back out, you caught up with him?

Rita Smith: Yes, he was driving slowly.
Clerk: What you're saying is that he made a U-turn and ended up following you?
Rita Smith: I had the green. He got the red, but I saw the signal which indicated he was going over the bridge.

Busoni denied that he had been following Rita Smith, and he explained that all of this was "the result of a driveway suit." The clerk responded, "I'm sure it's a dispute about the end of the driveway. I don't think Mrs. Smith would dispute that, and you wouldn't dispute that. The whole thing is the result of that." Nevertheless, the clerk concluded, "As far as this hearing is concerned, I believe there is probable cause to have a complaint issued. You'll have to go to court." Busoni's sister, who attended the hearing with him, objected to the clerk's decision:

Sister: Then it's her word against ours?
Clerk: I guess it is.
Sister: Should we have had a lawyer, sir? I'm really terribly concerned.
Clerk: This is not a trial. We don't have to have evidence beyond a reasonable doubt. I don't have to explain this to you. . . . But you both started at the same time. . . .
Busoni: Right.
Clerk: Going in the same direction. . . .
Busoni: No.
Sister: One doesn't have the right to go up the street? How can my brother go and hear her yelling?
Clerk: No, she said her kids yelled at her.
Sister: How should my brother hear this? You're establishing he heard this?

At this point the exchange between the Busonis and the clerk was becoming heated, and the clerk called, "Time!"

Sister: So whoever puts in this complaint is likely to have the complaint issued?
Clerk: Not exactly. It's kind of a one-sided hearing. Like a grand jury, I'm the grand jury.

In conducting this hearing, the assistant clerk assisted Rita Smith in developing an argument for probable cause through his detailed questions while allowing Busoni to present an incoherent, rambling account of his actions. When the Busonis objected to the outcome, he asserted his authority as decision maker by drawing on a legal analogy to describe the hearings and his role. This strategy silenced the Busonis, and the imagery suggested one of the poles of meaning in terms of which the clerk's practice is constructed. In cases with other participants, hearings became "little chats" with the assistant clerk as counselor, rather than legal proceedings with the clerk as jury.

A week after this complaint was heard by the clerk, the superior court considered the suit filed by Busoni for a temporary injunction against the Smiths. Busoni was represented in the case by a prominent local attorney. The Smiths represented themselves, but they were assisted in preparing their defense by the court librarian, by a friend who was a local attorney, and by experience Rita Smith had gained when she helped her ex-husband through law school. They were also supported in pursuing this case, as they were during the complaint hearing, by advice and reassurance from the assistant clerk.

In the superior court, the case was even more narrowly defined by the judge, who stated that "the only thing at issue is a triangular piece of land." The Smiths argued that by installing the post they were "exercising our rights of property in the only legal way we knew," not blockading the driveway. Busoni's attorney argued that the triangular piece of land no longer belonged to the Smiths because a maple tree had grown in the driveway, forcing the Busonis and their tenants to use this land for several years. Thus, he concluded, the Busonis were entitled by right of adverse possession. The judge ruled in favor of the Busonis. In her conclusions, the judge noted that "this is a neighborhood dispute, and in general the court is not the place for these problems. But if they get to the point where this one is, it is best to come to court with them." She also asked the Busonis to be "considerate" in their use of the triangle, thus alluding to an imagery of neighborhood that was eclipsed in this conflict yet had played such a dominant role in those discussed above.

Shortly after the injunction hearing, Busoni was arraigned in district court on the criminal charges brought by Rita Smith. This charge was ultimately "continued without a finding" for a year, with a view to dismissal if there was no more trouble. But Busoni's appearance as a defendant in criminal court was reported in the local newspaper and constituted a public sanction for his behavior. The outcome of the injunction hearing was also covered by the news media, which described it as a case about "cutting down a tree." Rick Smith was quoted as saying that "whoever wrote the right of way should be shot" and that their objective in the conflict was to prevent their property from being eroded by the roots of the maple tree and by the cars that drove to the Busoni house. In a written response a friend of Busoni suggested that, "perhaps one reason [the right-of-way] . . . was written as such is to be protected from these . . . kind of people. . . . Surely a man's home is his castle, but let me ask you as a taxpayer, would you want to live like that? Take a look and see what land is being eroded. . . . Is this the way to repay a family who has lived in the same spot for almost seventy years?"

This letter identified the fundamental social and cultural issues surrounding this case, which were not found in the legal discourse that shaped it in court. It was a case about protection from "these kind of people," about the erosion of the community by alien life-styles, and about the dangers this posed to families who have "lived in the same spot for almost seventy years." It was also a case about the social and cultural space separating Riverside's newer businesses and their owners from its more established merchants and professionals. The arena for the conflict was not simply a transitional neighborhood or the courthouse but downtown Riverside, where a number of alternative shops with "a flavor of their own, such as the Book Swap Cafe, a video arcade, a record shop, the Scorpion Karate Academy, crafts shops such as that owned by the Smiths, and a natural food store, have been established in recent years. Community bulletin boards post notices "for upcoming protest marches, yoga lessons, tractors for sale, people looking for apartments." While some reports in the newspaper endorse these efforts to reconstruct the life and image of Riverside's business district, others voice concerns about some of the businesses and the kinds of people who frequent them.[29]

The meaning of the conflict between the Smiths and the Busonis over "The Expanding Tree" was shaped by this broader debate, and particularly by Rick Smith's prominence in town affairs. The complaint hearing and the criminal court appearance by Busoni that followed were arenas in which this conflict was waged, and its outcome there was surely influenced by the connection of this case to local fears and hopes about the changing face of the town. As in "Noisy Motorcycles," however, its main significance was less in its outcome than in its use as a "text" through which the changing identity of the town and its residents could be constructed at the courthouse.

Bringing the Neighborhood to the Courthouse:
Controlling "Garbage People" in Milltown

The next case, "The Bad Neighborhood," involves fifteen complaints of neighborhood fighting brought to the courthouse from "downstreet" Milltown, a six-block, densely populated area of mixed tenement and row housing on Riverside's eastern boundary. As in "The Expanding Tree," the interpretation of incidents in "The Bad Neighborhood" was influenced by local social and economic change, in this case the construction of a low-income housing complex and a possible shift in the ethnic identity of the area. These fears transformed complaint hearings into neighborhood battlegrounds, pointing once again to the political and cultural complexity of the interpersonal conflicts brought to the clerk and its effects on the way a case is handled. Unlike the previous cases, however, this one reveals the different meanings of the same conflict for various participants and suggests the diversity of stances taken by the clerks over a series of hearings. In this case, as in "Noisy Motorcycles," arguments about neighborhood life-style were used to shape understandings about behavior and to justify the clerk's suggestion that complaints be "held at the 'show cause' level" rather than issued as criminal charges. But as complainants continued to come from the same area, the clerks' roles became more aggressive, and ultimately two complaints were issued because of pressure brought by those involved. In this sense it illustrates, in quite a different way than the last case, the power of local audiences in shaping the meaning and outcome of a complaint and in affecting the role played by the clerk. In "The Expanding Tree," it was the social embeddedness of middle-class parties to the case that structured the clerk's approach; in "The Bad Neighborhood," experienced and persistent low-income court "regulars" adapted the hearing process to their own political ends and pushed the clerk into action that would support these.[30] At the same time, the clerks used hearings on "The Bad Neighborhood" to construct their own vision of order in the "good neighborhoods" of middle-class Riverside and to underscore the boundaries between the "way of life" there and the social "chaos" of the bad neighborhood next door.

Finally, this case once again points to the ways in which different models of relationship and social order inform the arguments and outcome in complaint hearings. Unlike "Noisy Motorcycles," in which the imagery of neighborhood as overlapping ways of life framed a compromise, in "The Bad Neighborhood," interconnectedness was defined as "chaos," and efforts by complainants to define neighborhood conflicts in terms of "rights" were dismissed as irrelevant. Rather, court staff reshaped "vicious" actions as "normal" behavior in a chaotic environment and issued complaints only when this behavior threatened to spill over into the more bounded spheres of middle-class living in Riverside.

CASE 3: *"The Bad Neighborhood."* The fifteen complaints in this case were linked in complex ways. There were charges and countercharges, which reflected shifting ties of enmity and friendship between complainants and defendants; several complaints were brought by individuals on different blocks against the same defendants. Of the fifteen complaints, I observed eight as they were heard. All dealt with neighborhood fights, most of which were concentrated on two streets described as "bad" by participants: Middle and Fitch streets. They focused on incidents involving children: children ruining each other's clothes, setting fires, hitting each other, destroying each other's toys, chasing each other with knives, or pushing each other into buildings or trees. In addition, there were incidents of adults hitting children and of parents fighting with each other. The police were called first but advised complainants to go directly to the clerk. They described the incidents as "kidstuff" that required a "referee," a job suitable for the clerk but not for them. The fights occurred, according to the police, because of "the psychology of the people." The clerks in turn described the complainants as "brainless," as having "no moral sense," and as acting "like children." Fighting, I was told, is a "way of life" in Milltown; the job of the clerk and the police was to contain this.

Other agencies were involved in "containing" Milltown people in various ways. All of the people involved in neighborhood fights were also monitored by social workers through "C & P" or "CHINS" orders brought to oversee the behavior of children or the ability of the family to care for children.[31] In this area, according to social workers, home situations are "unstable," family boundaries are permeable,[32] and children are subject to neglect or abuse. The involvement of Milltown complainants in the social service network is significant in explaining the perceptions and actions of court staff and other local officials in handling these cases. Like the outpatients "of no known address" who wander Milltown's streets and appear repeatedly in the police station and the court, Milltown parents and children also were perceived as needing the intervention and supervision that social services and the court could provide.

. The roles assumed by the two clerks in handling these Milltown complaints evolved over the course of several months from a more straightforward "gatekeeping" role, in which issues of social order were addressed, to a more aggressive role in monitoring and challenging "downstreet" morality. During the earliest hearings, both clerks defined the fights as everyday behavior. In one complaint brought by the mother of 8-year-old Petra against a 10-year-old for "willful destruction of property," the head clerk argued against issuing the application, "since what is involved is two girls here swapping clothes."[33] A complaint brought two weeks later by the same woman for assault and threats by another child on her daughter was heard by the assistant clerk, who again defined the actions as acceptable behavior among children:

> *Clerk:* Petra, do you want to tell me what happened?
> *Petra:* We went to school before they. They were waiting at the corner. Marie tried to slice Jane's head off. I got pushed into a tree and hit my head.
> *Clerk:* You were going to school at the time?
> *Petra:* Unhuh.
> *Clerk:* How old are you?
> *Petra:* Eight.
> *Clerk:* She pushed your head against a tree?
> *Petra:* She pushed me!
> *Clerk:* She said she was going to slice the other girl's head off. Did you believe her?
> *Petra:* Yes, because she had a jackknife.

The mother of the accused child did not deny the accusation but explained that the incident occurred because, "Middle Street is a bad street. It's a violent street. Children on that street are apt to be violent. I don't know what it is. When I lived on Main Street I didn't have these problems. Ask any Milltown police officer, and he'll say Middle Street is a bad street."

Like other hearings, this one was quite formal. The assistant clerk directed the questioning, focusing on the details of events and underscoring the "official" logic of complaint hearings: that events (acts) determine outcome and that the aim of the hearing is to determine probable cause. Finally, he agreed that the complaint was justified:

> Technically, I can issue it. [But he asked,] Would you be satisfied if we issued it technically but hold it at the "show cause" level? It's not a real vicious thing, it doesn't appear. We won't have another hearing, but we'd issue it if there was more trouble. Kids push kids. [And he counseled,] One thing parents should be sure they don't do is discuss their problems in front of their kids. The kids watch TV, they want to protect the parents, they take up your fight, and first thing you know, kids 8 or 10 or so are fighting, and their fathers are slugging it out.

Here the clerk used familiar imagery ("Kids push kids") and the suggestion that the root of the problem lay in the quality of parenting to ground his decision that the complaint should not go to court. He conceded, however, that it could be "issued technically," implying that matters such as these belonged at the courthouse.[34] In this way he kept the matter out of court but within his control. He encouraged complainants to use the courthouse as a forum in which particular "commonsense" assumptions about life in "downstreet" Milltown were articulated and reinforced: that violence there was "normal trouble" and that it could be tolerated by the court as long as it was sufficiently contained. The mother's suggestion that the neighborhood, and not the children, were "bad" drew on this same logic, one implicitly shared by the clerk and others. What "went without saying" for all participants in these hearings was that in "bad" neighborhoods, "vicious" behavior is' not "vicious" but "normal" exchange and that the clerk's role was that of keeping people in line through sermons and the monitoring implied by "holding" a case at the show cause level. The hearing reinforced these assumptions about the order of things in Milltown and the courthouse's role in maintaining that particular order. The clerk simultaneously shaped and supported a legal complaint. He also constructed a solution that drew on meanings that were "known" by all and thus made "common sense." But the issue that brought complainants to court (efforts by new homeowners to change the "bad" neighborhood to a "good" one) was not resolved, and the same people reappeared at the courthouse door.

Later complaints involved homeowners using the court as a weapon in ongoing fights with renters or other "undesirable" residents next door. Some of these were phrased as boundary disputes; others were brought to the clerk as assault cases. In all of them, the complaint procedure was used by Milltown residents to voice concerns about the social and moral order of their neighborhood. As one complainant, who had bought a house on Fitch Street four years previously, said about the Hispanic neighbors who had just moved in,

> We own our own home, and when you have a house, and there's kids next door setting fires! . . . They say it's because we're prejudiced. It ain't that! If it was white kids setting fires, we'd feel the same way. . . . She complains that my kids call her kids "niggers." [But] there's one "nigger" that means "color" . . . then there's another "nigger" that means "people that lie and steal and cheat." That's the true meaning of the word! They can claim it's discrimination because they're colored.

The head clerk conducted three of the hearings involving ethnic and other issues of social identity on Fitch Street. The immediate participants in these complaints were five adults and six children: a Hispanic woman and her four children, a man of Polish ancestry and his wife and their two children, and a man and woman of English ancestry. The Hispanic and Polish families were renters in the same building; the family of English descent owned the house next door. In two of the hearings, the English family had brought the Polish family to court; in a third one, the Polish and English families were allied against the Hispanic woman.

This series of complaints illustrates how the meaning of events develops through several related hearings and points to the role of participants, especially an organized and vocal audience (Mather and Yngvesson, 1980–81), in shaping the way meaning is construed. At one hearing, the courtroom was filled with residents who had been involved as either participants or witnesses to a fight involving the Polish and English families. They testified to assaults by the women against each other and to threats by the Polish man against the English woman. An effort by one complainant to frame these problems in terms of property rights simply elicited a comment from the clerk that "rights of way often cause problems between neighbors."

The clerk dismissed these complaints, which he later described as "frivolous" problems involving "poor people, both monetarily and intellectually." But at a hearing involving the same parties and others four months later, his approach shifted. This conflict involved accusations against the child of the Hispanic woman for chasing other children with a knife; cross-complaints of assault by the adults; and a complaint by the Hispanic woman that one of the adult men threatened to "crush her face." The police once again described this conflict as "kidstuff." The clerk as usual conducted it formally, asking for details of who was struck, receiving witness testimony, and attempting to restrict the range of information presented:

> *Hispanic woman:* How far back should I start?
> *Clerk:* I think we should restrict it as narrowly as possible. . . . If you want to start at the beginning of the day . . . what precipitated the incident?

In spite of the clerk's efforts to narrow the conflict through repeated comments that certain information had "nothing to do with the complaint," testimony aired a range of concerns about the Hispanic woman's behavior, her ways of minding her children, her job, and her children's behavior. Finally, the clerk turned off the tape recorder and said:

> *Clerk:* I'm going to go off the record here. What are you folks going to do about this problem with the children?
> *Hispanic woman:* I'm moving! Because of the area, because of the people who live here!
> *Polish complainant:* My children are getting abused too! It seems to be the neighborhood. Even the school says our neighborhood is bad.
> *Hispanic woman:* She doesn't control her daughter. She sticks out her tongue at us, sticks up her middle finger. . . . She calls us spics and niggers.
> *Clerk:* You know, if this goes to court, none of the peripheral issues — about noise, disturbances, disagreement — are going to be admitted into evidence.

Hispanic woman: Nobody's going to do anything to just leave me alone? We can't even go outside without them calling us spics and niggers!

After listening to this exchange, the clerk admonished the parties to "begin acting like adults and not like children," but he decided to issue two of the complaints. He noted later that this series of events had gone beyond an ordinary neighborhood quarrel and "needed a more formal setting." The extent of the fighting and the presence of knives concerned him, and he added that "the people involved lack a sense of right and wrong and of conforming to neighborhood standards. Their behavior possibly would not be tolerated even in Eastfield or New York." Social workers involved with participants through "C & P" or "CHINS" orders, who had attended the hearings at the request of the complainants, also agreed that the fighting in the neighborhood was getting out of hand and was preventing children from attending school because of concerns about violence.

The final phase of this conflict involved an exchange between the Hispanic woman and the Polish man in the corridor of the courthouse after one of the hearings. As a result of the exchange, the Polish man filed a complaint application against her for "threats," accusing her of coming at him with sticks. The hearing on this application was conducted by the assistant clerk and included the Polish man and his wife and the Hispanic woman. This hearing, like others, was carried out as an examination. But unlike others, the clerk assumed a far more aggressive role as it evolved:

Clerk: What were you afraid for?
Polish man: Because my wife got me on "A & B" [assault and battery], and I just got off probation.
Clerk: You don't understand what I'm saying.
Polish man: I was afraid because she [the Hispanic woman] knows karate.
Clerk: [with a half-smile and considerable skepticism] Was she in a karate stance? You weren't afraid she was going to hurt you. You were afraid you were going to violate your probation by hitting her.
Polish man: I was afraid she was going to knock the shit out of me, and I couldn't hit back. She's hit me a few times in the house, and I had to take it.
Clerk: You don't look like you could be pushed around.

Wife of Polish man: She made the threat when she had the sticks.
Clerk: My only concern is to have this stop. I'm sure that's what you all want.
Wife of Polish man: I want justice done.
Polish man: I want it so a female can't beat up on a guy and get away with it.
Wife of Polish man: [shouting] If I hadn't gone between those two there would have been a fight because she was furious!
Clerk: You mean you stopped him from fighting.

In contrast to the head clerk's earlier approach to this Milltown conflict (issuing complaints, so that the court could act as a moral monitor), the assistant clerk denied the application but used the hearing to challenge fundamental "myths" around which social relations in Milltown are played out: assumptions about strong women and weak men ("I was afraid she was going to knock the shit out of me and I couldn't hit back"); about powerful "spics" and weak whites ("I was afraid because she knows karate"); and about the rational and moral superiority of local whites over foreign "niggers." (Clerk: "I'm not going to argue about this. The two of you if you have any brains will stay away from each other.") The assistant clerk not only challenged these myths but also in effect "disintegrated" (Eco, 1976:80) the imagery used by the disputants and substituted his own middle-class meanings for theirs: that men are more powerful than women ("You don't look like you could be pushed around") and that people who become involved in fights of this kind are brainless and irrational.[35] The extent to which this hearing threw into relief the fundamental incompatibility of the life-style and values of the middle-class clerk from Riverside with those of the lower-class residents of Milltown was dramatically stated in the fury with which the wife of the Polish complainant left the courtroom, spitting on the floor and screaming her frustration at the clerk, drawing the attention of everyone in the immediate area.

The intensity of hostility that emerged in this hearing is in part explained by a broader controversy in the "downstreet" area regarding a new apartment complex. A meeting between townspeople and members of the Board of Selectmen aired concerns that the new project, which was federally subsidized, would be "filled with a lot of Puerto Ricans." Anxiety about this issue was repeatedly expressed in interviews with "downstreet" residents, and complaint hearings served as another, more authoritative setting where these concerns were given voice, with the neighborhood itself appearing at the courthouse to fight its battles with outsiders. As in earlier hearings, this conflict was not "about" children or the assaults, threats, malicious destruction, and trespassing charges filed with the clerk. Rather, it dealt with the struggles of "downstreet" residents to define appropriate boundaries for their neighborhood, boundaries that would keep out people they defined as dangerous.[36] They achieved some limited success in this, since the Hispanic woman and her family moved from Milltown shortly after the last hearing described here.

For the clerks and other local officials, the hearings provided an opportunity to keep an eye on the disorder characterizing Milltown life, to take action when it threatened to get out of hand, and to highlight dramatically the boundaries between this way of life and their own. Milltown complaints were perceived as "kidstuff," and complainants were described as acting "like children." Their perceived similarity to children defined Milltown people as polluting and as potentially threatening to the orderly life of its more "rational" middle-class neighbor.[37] At the courthouse, Riverside people not only monitored Milltown "kidstuff" but also defined their own identity by contrast to the "brainlessness" next door. It is worth noting, however, that confrontations with the "otherness" of Milltown took place in a setting where accounts and people "don't count," thus reproducing not only the definition of Milltown people as "garbage" but also the role of the clerk and complaint hearings as the appropriate means for containing this.

Private Conflict, Public Danger: Controlling Teenage Runaways

In concluding this section, I briefly discuss the use of the complaint procedure for handling problems involving runaway or abusive teenage women.[38] These hearings provided some of the most intense struggles over definition and issuance, struggles in which local attorneys challenged the definitions proposed by the clerk and the court. All involved acts that in other contexts would be constructed as "kidstuff" — swapping, shoving, or "nothing real vicious" — yet, all were issued as charges of assault, larceny, or malicious destruction by the clerks, who encouraged social workers and others to bring such complaints. In some, it was the clerk, not the complainant, who pressed for issuance.

CASE 4: *"The Stolen Rings."* One such case was brought by a Milltown woman alleging the theft of three rings by a 15-year-old Riverside teenage girl who had been living with her. She also complained of damage to her apartment by the teenager and her boyfriend, who was also living there. Discussion during the hearing revealed the alleged theft to be a case of "borrowed" rings. Another Milltown woman, an experienced court user who had accompanied the teenager to the hearing, argued that the rings "were lent, not stolen. The two of them used to exchange jewelry all the time! It was just that she had forgotten!" She also urged the complainant to drop the charge: "Why make everybody keep coming back to court, when [the boyfriend] says he'll pay you? You'll get the same thing, and the kids won't end up with a record and having to come in for probation every week!" But a friend of the complainant urged her not to withdraw the complaint, reminding her of the damage that had been caused and describing for the clerk the teenager's sexual behavior, which she defined as promiscuous: "The next thing you know [the boyfriend] will be wanting to make it with the little girl across the street." The complainant decided against pressing formal charges, on the understanding that the teenager would return the rings and pay for the damages. But the clerk, who had determined early in the hearing that the teenager was unsupervised by a parent and was living openly with her boyfriend at the complainant's house, was reluctant to dismiss this case. The hearing continued into the hall and eventually into the clerk's office as he sought to persuade the complainant to change her mind about dropping the charge, saying, "If you withdraw the complaint, you won't be able to come back in and have it issued later. Your only option would be small claims. . . . And it will be expensive for you to file a small claims case, and the judge can't or usually won't order them to pay you if they don't have a job. Or he might order them to pay over a six-month period. Even then, it's hard to collect. . . . I'm not trying to dissuade you."

In spite of his efforts, the complaint was withdrawn. The complainant changed her mind, however, and returned two days later; the clerk agreed to issue the complaint, although he had said earlier that he could not do so. At the arraignment hearing, a $500 bail was set, and in spite of the efforts of a court-appointed attorney to have this reduced, the teenager was sent to a detention center pending trial.[39]

Events surrounding the bail hearing and subsequent hearings were tense, with emotional exchanges between the prosecutor and the attorney representing the young woman. One of the judges who heard the case responded to the attorney's suggestion that the defendant was "effectively an emancipated minor" by shouting, "Well, you can argue until you're blue in the face, but I'm not going to let a 15-year-old girl go out and roam the streets, living with some 23-year-old kid with no job!"

This case was finally settled informally, and the teenager moved in with her sister in Riverside. But it illustrates well the collaboration between clerk, other court staff, social workers, and private citizens in sketching particular images of danger in Riverside. The teenager in this complaint was both "endangered" (Donzelot, 1979:109) and "endangering" (Perin, 1977:120). Although they were identified not by a police arrest procedure but by a member of the community, the clerk determined that the defendant's health, safety, and morality were at risk. Equally important to the way this case was handled, however, were assumptions about the risk she posed to the community at large, related to what Perin (1977:119) has called the fear of "out-of-bounds sexuality."

Donzelot's (1979:112) suggestion that juvenile law occupies a "pivotal position . . . between an agency that sanctions offenses (the retributive justice of ordinary law) and a composite group of agencies that distribute norms" could be applied equally well to the role of clerk's hearings in these cases. Social workers were eager to control the women involved in these complaints, but their efforts to do so were hindered by the rebelliousness of the teenager and by the constraints of Department of Social Service (DSS) policy. In a complaint and cross-complaint for assault and battery brought by a foster mother against her foster daughter and by the daughter against her foster parents, the clerk had to decide whether the daughter's action of grabbing her foster mother in a neck hold and the foster father's action of dragging the girl along a sidewalk constituted probable causes for criminal complaints. At the hearing on the teenager's complaint, her attorney argued that the actions of the foster parents were criminal:

Lawyer: I think this complaint should be issued. . . . Mr. D did say he dragged her, and Mrs. D said she had her hand on [the complainant's] hair and arm. Any touching can be assault and battery — any touching done with intent.
Clerk: But they didn't cause her physical harm.
Lawyer: But it was touching with . . . there was intent in the touching.

Clerk: What should they have done?
Lawyer: Call DSS. If it were permissible to use physical force [Mrs. D] should anticipate a response, and she shouldn't have filed charges.

The clerk denied this complaint on the grounds that the foster father's actions constituted appropriate discipline, illustrating the use of the hearing for transforming what DSS policy defined as "unprivileged touching" into acceptable behavior by a parent.[40] By contrast, the complaint by the foster mother against the daughter was issued over the counter without a hearing, demonstrating the use of the complaint procedure to transform grabbing into a crime.

CONCLUSION

My goal has been to point to some of the more subtle ways in which law and society come together by discussing the practice of a "marginal" official in the lowest echelon of our legal system, the criminal courts. Occupying a role that lacks even the requirement of legal training, the clerk is a lay magistrate, assigned to hear cases too trivial for the court proper and defined by the seriousness of the cases he handles. Citizens and police must apply to the clerk for issuance of a criminal complaint when an allegedly criminal act has occurred but there has been no arrest. Although the court views police cases as legitimate problems of public order, citizen complaints are defined by trial court policy as "minor" matters, domestic and interpersonal conflicts that call more on the court's "sense of the community . . . than on the adjudication of facts and the application of abstract principles of law" (Committee on Juries of Six, 1984:74). Clerks themselves describe these conflicts as "garbage cases" that do not belong in court. It is their job, like that of the police and prosecutor in trial courts elsewhere, to protect the legal system from such matters.

But I argue that to classify such complaints as "garbage" and to view the clerk as simply a gatekeeper who dismisses (and may informally resolve) "private" conflicts is to disregard the uses of the complaint procedure for maintaining a moral order that the courthouse itself represents. Prominently placed at the cultural and political center of New England towns, the courthouse seems to stand guard. In Riverside, as elsewhere, it recalls a colonial republican tradition in which virtuous, public-spirited citizens keep watch, protecting the "community of visible saints" from corrupt forces within and beyond its boundaries.[41] Like magistrates in seventeenth- and eighteenth-century Massachusetts, staff in district courts today are intimately linked to communities surrounding the courthouse and use their legal roles as vehicles for local governance (Hartog, 1976). Thus citizens are encouraged to bring "private" quarrels to the courthouse, where charges of assault, threats, or disturbing the peace are used to structure neighborhood political confrontations and influence their outcome.

The clerks used two distinct images of order and relationship to develop the meaning of events in a complaint and to argue for issuance or denial. One image portrayed order as based on the interconnections of neighbors and on shared meanings emerging from a customary way of life. The other represented order as based on balanced claims between individuals whose relationship is defined by rights to property, privacy, and to live in peace. The clerks used assumptions about customary life-style to distinguish "normal trouble" from potential crime in particular areas, linking acts with relational contexts to justify a particular definition of events or a decision about issuance. By controlling the discourses in which these definitions are framed, the clerks serve as key operators effecting the transformation of "kidstuff" into crime or vice versa. The hearings thus become arenas where particular notions of order and rights are articulated and reinforced: concepts of the good neighbor, the responsible parent, or the brainless "downstreet" person; ideas about vicious and everyday behavior; and beliefs about the kinds of settings where brainlessness, threats, and other behavior that "lacks moral sense" are tolerated by the court.

The clerk describes his role in handling "garbage" as that of a "watchdog." But my analysis suggests, that although he is the dominant figure in the hearings, his power is contingent, dependent not only on his authority as a legal official but also on his knowledge of, stature in, and connections to the local community, and his rhetorical skill in using these to define conflicts in particular ways. Paradoxically, then, the clerk is most powerful when he is most connected, and this explains why it is the assistant, rather than the head clerk, who is the key figure in complaint hearings at the Jefferson County court.[42]

Although these connections are empowering for the clerk, they also constrain him in subtle ways. This constraint is central to the politics of issuance in complaint hearings and underlies the tension between imposition and sharing that is their most characteristic feature. Fundamental to this tension is an ambiguity in the meaning and implications of "knowledge" as both empowering and subjecting. The one who "knows" has "a practical understanding of or thorough experience with" and is thus more powerful, but "to know" is also "to be subjected to" and thus in a sense "controlled by."[43] The clerk's local knowledge empowers him but also, although to a lesser degree, empowers those through whom he comes to define a situation as needing more formal court intervention. This is revealed at times (as in "The Expanding Tree") without any overt struggle during the hearing itself, emerging rather as a tacit understanding that is the outcome of interactions in other arenas. At other times (as in "The Bad Neighborhood" or "The Stolen Rings") the struggle is explicit and is shaped by the experience and persistence of knowledgeable court regulars, who construct particular situations as "serious" or "trivial" and use the law to accomplish interpersonal and political goals of their own. This struggle does not in any obvious way alter the structure of power in the hearings, at the courthouse or in the society surrounding it. But it both reflects and contributes to the tension that underlies the structure of power and suggests some of the "points of resistance" (Foucault, 1990 [1968]:96) through which challenges to relations of power emerge.

From this perspective, the boundaries that separate "serious" from "garbage" matters, public from private, or law from community at one point in time and that are objectified in statistics about issuance are seen to be shifting and "live" (Mensch, 1982), suggesting the socially constructed nature of these categories and their dependence on particular relations of dominance and subordination at particular historical periods. The practice of the court clerk, located in a space that "connect[s], by separation, classes and discourses" (Stalleybrass and White, 1986:194), reveals this contingency in negotiations that contribute to the construction of the court and of the community it is intended to protect. In a setting that is literally at the doorway to the courthouse, the hearings both underscore and question the differences between "real law" that belongs in court and "garbage" that belongs in the community; they also point to the permeability of the boundaries between "brainless" people whose chaotic lives require the monitoring of the courthouse and the more "rational" and bounded spheres of middle-class life-style that the courthouse was established to uphold. In a system that is constructed around the tension between an imposed law and one that is constituted from within, the clerk acts as a kind of "good" khadi (Weber, 1967:350–56), fashioning the law into an instrument for the use of particular local communities to construct themselves and impose their order on others in the jurisdiction of the courthouse.

CHAPTER THREE

Courting Difference

Issues of Interpretation and Comparison in the Study of Legal Ideologies

CAROL J. GREENHOUSE

LAW, INTERPRETATION, AND COMPARISON

Current interpretivist approaches in sociolegal research represent a relatively recent branch of an old intellectual genealogy in the social sciences.[1] At the branching point, social scientists question natural science models as representations of human experience and, in different ways, embrace the premise that the meanings of cultural and social forms are constituted in their use (Skinner, 1985:7). This chapter examines two major implications of the multifaceted interpretive approach in law and society research.[2]

First, any interpretivist stance implies the importance of what anthropologists call *difference*. This term refers to the social and cultural processes by which people come to be recognized as differentiable (as genders, races, individuals, nations, and so on). The cultural premises that establish criteria of "like" and "unlike" are embedded in symbols and the relationships among symbols. "Difference" in this sense is fundamental to the reproduction of social forms and values. "Difference" refers not (or not only) to the "fact" that societies, regions, communities, and small groups might have different "cultures" but, rather, to the questions of why and how categorical distinctions are drawn in the first place. In other words, the interpretivist's starting premise is that differences of any kind are not intrinsic but are culturally defined according to extrinsic criteria of representativeness. Difference is in the eye of the beholder, and when an interpretivist looks at difference, he or she does not look at any particular distinction but at the whole system of values and meanings by which distinctions are drawn, symbolized, defended, reproduced, and modified.

Second, the view that difference is constructed or invented in the course of social experience requires the examination of (among other things) the symbolic processes by which arbitrary distinctions become legitimate "givens" of public life. If symbols have no intrinsic meaning (Schneider, 1968), they can be useful in communication only to the extent that they relate to other symbols. Indeed, to be effective, symbols must mark both what they represent and what they do not represent; this double-sidedness is crucial to their meaning. Thus, an interpretivist project is inevitably comparative in that its very subject (symbolic representations of difference) is itself comparative.

This chapter clarifies the connections between the comparative and symbolic dimensions of interpretivism through a selective examination of a particular legal ideology's criteria of difference. Geertz's (1973:220) reference to ideologies (the plural form is significant) as "maps of problematic social reality and matrices for the creation of collective conscience" serves well as an orientation point in the discussion that follows. The criteria of difference I discuss emerge from people's efforts to portray the world they live in and to juxtapose and reconcile that world to the worlds they imagine might have been in the past or might become in the future. Most of what follows consists of ethnographic data from a suburban town in the United States, a place I call Hopewell.[3] That research centered on local cultural conceptions of law in both broad and narrow senses, in that I was interested in Hopewell's court as an institution, particularly as a symbol in local systems of meaning. The court is an important symbol in Hopewell in that it marks the convergence of multiple lines of differentiation: between past and present, insiders and outsiders, harmony and trouble, and more. (Parallel concerns are expressed elsewhere; see Engel, 1987, and Yngvesson, 1988.) As this complex of meanings converges in questions of law and social order, I refer to them together as the local legal ideology.

As Hunt (1985:33) states, legal ideologies are not meaningful in and of themselves but become meaningful in context. This proposition draws on principles of semiotics, specifically, the arbitrariness of signs and their meaning in relation to other signs. A related proposition is that legal systems are systems of knowledge inseparable from other local systems (Geertz, 1983). Putting these two ideas together, one can say that legal systems are meaningful in local terms.[4]

In addition, norms and rules do not necessarily account for behavior; instead, they represent different sorts of claims to legitimacy by speakers of various sorts (Greenhouse, 1982b, 1985). Thus, legal ideologies and ideologies in general involve conventionalized invocations of norms and rules that simultaneously suggest and eliminate competing ideologies by elaborating locally significant categories of meaning. Ideologies represent strategic claims concerning the nature of normative orders. It follows that any reference to ideology in the singular is a concession to a particular set of claims (i.e., by its adherents) concerning that ideology's truth value.

The ethnographic material presented tells the following story. Residents of Hopewell explain the court's role by drawing on their understandings of the basic terms of their social existence: personhood, way of life, harmony, conflict and change, to list some examples. Local speakers use these terms to mark the boundaries among locally constructed social categories. (These in turn represent symbolic resolutions of important local struggles that lie outside the scope of this chapter; see Greenhouse, 1986.) Thus, the ideas Hopewell residents hold concerning the nature of social order are not merely epiphenomena of some underlying social process; they themselves constitute the very terms of local social organization. More important, these are the same terms in which even very personal quests for meaning are expressed. Informants present such terms as absolutes (e.g., insider vs. outsider, saved vs. damned), but in practice they are highly flexible idioms of negotiation and concern.

My major ethnographic argument is that, although people claim to *thesis* evaluate the newcomers to their town in terms of their reputation as conflictful and litigious, in fact, their ideology works the other way around. Local understandings of conflict and the court depend on prior assessments of the town's social groups and its patterns of change. I base my argument on an analysis and comparison of two sorts of data: interviews with key informants on the nature and causes of change in Hopewell, and observations of court cases. It is the pervasiveness of a few social distinctions and their invocation by local people as explanations of conflict across the interviews and the cases that are particularly compelling. My purpose is not to suggest in any way that people in Hopewell misperceive their social reality and construct an ideology to accommodate those mis-perceptions but the opposite: The nature of ideology, at least a successful ideology, is to be self-fulfilling.

THE IDEA OF COMMUNITY IN HOPEWELL

The town I call Hopewell is now a suburb firmly adjoined to a major southern metropolis, but at the time of my research there, it still stood apart within the boundaries of the small rural market town it had been for most of its history. Hopewell is the county seat, with a population of about 4,000 in a county of about 100,000 (as of 1970). Beyond Hopewell at the time of my research, the town quickly faded into farmland or just wasteland where farms had been before World War II spelled their col-lapse. The city, not more than 30 miles away, was booming. The town and the city are an important polarity for Hopewell residents in both practical and symbolic terms.

Townspeople express and demonstrate a profound ambivalence toward the city. On the one hand, they recognize it as the keystone of the local economy: Almost two-thirds of the workers from Hopewell and Hope-well county commute there daily. But the city also looms as a menace to an ill-defined but nonetheless valued way of life. It is unclear whether people from Hopewell would be conscious of this way of life in the absence of the city's burgeoning growth. Indeed, Hopewell is in the midst of very rapid and profound social change. On the one hand, people welcome change; on the other, they dread what it might mean for the future of their commu-nity, as they call it (see Varenne, 1977 and 1986, for a discussion of community as an American cultural construction emergent in contexts of perceived social change). Given its rapid growth and proximity, the city stands in rather easily for the local people's sense of their town's future, as if Hopewell were somehow destined to evolve into its twin.

In rather specific ways, when Hopewell residents talk about what the growth of the county will mean for their town, *harmony* is an important word, as is the phrase *way of life*. Indeed, both ideas consolidate complex issues of local identity in a single temporal and spatial framework. What-ever harmony means in Hopewell (more on this later), its antithesis is the specter of a faceless suburb, whose residents are merely occupants of their private dwellings, with no commitments to each other, their neighbors, or their town.

It is in this context that the local court acquires its symbolic meanings.

Relative to local visions of the future, the town's past is thought of as harmonious. The future is defined as conflictual; conflict augurs the loss of a former way of life defined as harmonious.[5] People assume both that the court regulates the community for its own good and that use of the court is a signal of the town's decline.[6] Such reasoning makes the present the test of both the past and the future. Hopewell Past and Hopewell Future are two towns; they exist side by side in the minds of Hopewell's residents. People who think of themselves as being from Hopewell try to assure themselves that the future will reflect the past. They fear an unfamiliar future, in which harmony and Hopewell's way of life will be forever lost. Such thinking symbolically divides insiders from outsiders — "we" would pass the test of change if "they" had not intervened. The question of how the relationships among these categorical distinctions (of past and future, insiders and outsiders) are organized offers the main theme of the ethnographic data. The stakes in maintaining these categories are high. They constitute a worldview and, as such, the tools with which Hopewell's people shape their public and private futures.[7]

COURT AND COMMUNITY IN HOPEWELL: LOCAL VIEWS

When people discuss the role of the court in Hopewell, their common keynote is change.[8] For the judge and clerk of the Superior Court, the talk of change is very specific, focusing on the kinds of cases the court hears, the nature of the community, and, more broadly, human nature. For others, the question of the role the court plays in town evokes general statements concerning the growth of the town and its relatively urban atmosphere compared to some undefined point in the past. In this section, I focus on local meanings of change in Hopewell and the values implicit in conventional representations of change. My key informants on these issues are the judge and the clerk, both of whom are considered local experts on questions of the state of Hopewell's current social order.

The clerk of the court began his service in the early 1950s. He is the son of the former judge and is the descendant of a long line of active Hopewell citizens. This man began his commentary on the court by observing that twenty-six years before, the civil and criminal dockets combined totaled not more than fifty cases; now there are over 1,500 civil cases filed. In the old days, he says, the only defendants were either outsiders or "village characters," that is, known deviants such as "moonshiners." Today, he says, the town's problems are different, the "color" is gone, and he maintains, the court reflects as no other public institution does the impact of Hopewell's proximity to the city. The clerk describes the new role of the court in terms of changes in the kinds of suits filed. He cites three sources of change in the court's docket; explanatory notes in each category paraphrase his remarks:

1. Changes in the law: Divorces once required three jury verdicts before separation was final; now, no jury is necessary, and a divorce can be obtained in thirty days.
2. Technological change: The extension of the interstate highway near Hopewell and the increase in the number of cars have, in the clerk's view, generated an increase in the number of property damage claims.
3. Social change: The influx of outsiders has, according to the clerk, led to a decline in trust and a resulting change in credit relations. He says that this trend is manifested in an increase in collection cases. In his view, urbanization has also eliminated the market for moonshine and increased the market for illegal drugs.

According to the clerk, the single most important source of change in town is the rise in its population. For him, increased population density is both problematic in itself and exacerbates whatever negative developments relative crowding might bring. He attributes local growth to "white flight" from the metropolis to the suburbs. Hopewell is 98 percent white, and its residents are predominantly moderately affluent and college educated. The proximity of the city makes parts of Hopewell County a bedroom community; however, it is not only newcomers who commute to the city. In Hopewell County, abundant land and low property taxes now encourage residential development, as did an ample water supply and sewerage facilities in the early years of the town's postwar growth (water and sewerage are severe problems today). The clerk says that the absence of a zoning ordinance provides for unrestricted opportunities for speculators and developers whose new high-density subdivisions and apartment complexes lured outsiders (and the implication here is undesirable outsiders) into the county and town. Things might be different, he suggests, if the growth were due to local births, rather than an influx of newcomers.

The clerk's analysis of the town's recent changes involves several lines of differentiation. First, he distinguishes between insiders and outsiders and attributes the changes in the court's role to the outsiders. This is clearly a negative development in his view, because he sees any increase in the use of the court as a signal of social fragmentation. Legal and technological change provide the basic material for such fragmentation, but such changes would not themselves be problematic if people were inclined to "get along" rather than litigate.

For the clerk, change in itself is negative, if inevitable, in Hopewell. His own vantage point daily confirms his view that social life has lost some of its value: "I think that people are being thrown together more now, and they are quicker to go to court. People with good neighbors don't need courts — people just don't *want* to get along now" [his emphasis]. He adds that the result of this situation is more regulation: "There is a lot of law being made." He offers this observation as one measure of the losses imposed by the town's recent changes.

For the clerk, the heart of those losses is revealed in the implicit contrast he draws between people who live in Hopewell as families and neighbors and others who live in Hopewell alone, without primary bonds in the town. I take this to be the referent of his contrast between actual sources of growth from ex-urbanites and the hypothetical growth from increases in the local birthrate. This is not merely a comment on birthrates but on gender and the impact on families of women in the workplace. For many people, the new meanings of womanhood entail risks, for marriage, children, and generally, the quality of life. Many people in Hopewell worry aloud about the social significance of the isolation of the thousands of single people or childless couples in the county.

Everyone realizes that the patterns of change they witness are also widespread beyond Hopewell, but the issue of family provides the idiom with which people express other sorts of changes. For example, they recognize the realities of life and the need for occupational mobility; on the other hand, they are ambivalent about a society made up of people, who, necessarily or not, place income above family ties. They tend to define newcomers as isolated salary earners, and local people as family breadwinners. Thus, issues of change become bound up in the idioms of gender, family, and interpersonal conflict, because these constitute the symbolic boundary between the past and the future. People imply that one role the law should play is to provide some countervailing force when the family begins to break down. For example, the clerk says that the net effect of the change in the divorce law is to make divorce too easy; divorce would not be so commonplace today if the legal process itself were cumbersome enough to provide some time and incentive for an unhappy couple to "work things out." The cases described offer various contexts for elements of these ideas.

The judge has a somewhat different view of the current scene. Although he has spent all of his life in town, he views Hopewell with somewhat more detachment than the clerk. Indeed, local people say that "he is not from here," meaning that his parents were not from Hopewell, but this in no way discredits him. Perhaps they notice that he does not talk about Hopewell in terms of its past. His observations on the changing role of the court focus less on local changes than on recent developments connecting Hopewell and national trends. He, too, articulates these changes in terms of new litigation:

1. Illegal drugs: All first-time offenders are prosecuted in the lower court, where a year of unviolated probation erases the record. Even so, the judge reports that the court is flooded with drug cases involving high school and college students using substances that are increasingly available from the city nearby. The county's undercover narcotics squad and the school board's newly purchased drug-sniffing dog are aimed at deterring drug use.

2. Consumer suits: The judge reports a large number (unspecified) of consumer suits against manufacturers for faulty items. He interprets such litigation as a sign of social change, in that in the past, consumers in Hopewell did not use manufactured items from "anonymous" dealers. Furthermore, he adds, if they did purchase manufactured goods, the vendor was a local retailer (more than likely a friend or a relative, according to the judge) who was readily responsive to complaints.

3. Malpractice suits against professionals: The judge interpreted this development as a sign of declining trust in contemporary American society.

4. Suits against judges under federal law for denial of civil rights by virtue of or during imprisonment: The judge explains this category of litigation in the same terms as professional malpractice suits. Both categories reflect his concern with national litigation trends and their social implications.

5. Damage suits resulting from increased automobile use and accidents.

As does the clerk, the judge expresses his ideas concerning change in terms of family. Although divorce is by no means a new area of litigation, the high divorce rate is a particular concern for the judge. He attributes the divorce rate to couples whose economic needs require both spouses to work. When a glassworks plant operated in the county a generation ago, he says, most of the divorce cases were between glassworks employees working incompatible shifts. At that time, Hopewell County was (according to the judge) the only county in the nation in which divorce suits outnumbered applications for marriage certificates. Comparing the present profile of divorce litigants with the workers of a generation ago, the judge focuses on the marital problems of today's two-income white-collar couples. He implies a difference between Hopewell's stable "traditional" families (the term is not his) and the socially isolated newcomers who live in the new developments on the edge of town near the highway that links Hopewell to the city.

Despite their differences, both the clerk and the judge see the amount of litigation in the Hopewell court to be a source of concern, not only because litigation presses the courthouse personnel to their limits but also because it is a sign of social decline. They represent the changes that threaten the town's future as coming from outside of Hopewell: new technology, new law, new residents, new problems, and new social orientations. They describe, again in family terms, the worldview of the future as one besieged, that is, isolated individuals or nuclear families living without social resources and without trust. Their lack of trustworthiness makes trust unprofitable for everyone else; hence, the aggregate loss of community, the new litigiousness, and the critical inability to resolve problems through negotiation or with the aid of traditional third parties outside the court (e.g., vendors).

The judge interprets these changes as the result of Hopewell's integration into the regional and national economy. He does not focus on the loss of a way of life but on external sources of social change. The clerk, on the other hand, sees Hopewell as the victim of internal changes, essentially generated by an influx of a "kind of person" (this is not his language but a commonplace local usage) not suited to community life. He defines a harmonious community beyond which social life has perilously little meaning. It is important that both men see the court as the vanguard of the new Hopewell, the gateway beyond which the future waits.

The clerk's view — of Hopewell lost — is widely shared by others who identify with the town's past. They express concern about the state of contemporary values in general or the values of newcomers to Hopewell. One woman says, "They just came to take our money and make trouble." Another woman refers to the people "with dollar signs in their eyes." A frequent theme in church sermons is avoidance of the temptations of the city; indeed, most young people I knew visited the city only under the most carefully controlled circumstances: never alone, always for some structured activity, planned well in advance.[9]

The judge's view of, in a sense, Hopewell gained is echoed by the many people interested in the town's development. Long-time residents of Hopewell can cite ample evidence of the town's growth. The term *growth* has positive connotations fully intended, I believe, by those individuals who welcome the new capital and the new sophistication of the town. I do not recall meeting anyone who was nostalgic about the town's past, even though some might relish talking about the old days. In this one respect, the clerk's lament is distinctive; when he talks about the current state of things, it is with evident sadness. The more usual tone is one of bemusement, that change should have come so quickly — and to Hopewell. For many people, whatever the future might bring, the present town is a source of pride, even relief. Women in particular cite the extent to which the old days were confining; they welcome the relative social freedom of the modern town.

Still, the clerk's fears for the future are widely shared. People generally recognize that Hopewell will have to pay a price for its development; when the payment is to be due and who will set the price provide the substance of much of the informal talk about Hopewell and its prospects.

THE IDEA OF COMMUNITY IN COURT: SIX CASES

The themes of conflict, change, insiders and outsiders, and family life constitute important criteria of difference in Hopewell. They are significant in many domains; their significance is highly visible in the daily activity of the courtroom.[10] The following case descriptions show how evaluations of litigants are shaped by the generic differences defined by townspeople, as described by the judge and the clerk. These generic interpretations of litigants work to define important aspects of litigants' courtroom experiences. In more general terms, the cases show how such differences reproduce themselves in social experience.[11]

CASE 1: *Simple Battery.* This case came up on appeal from the court of the justice of the peace, which consistently refers its cases to this court. The plaintiff was a woman who filed a charge of battery against her son-in-law. They were both present in the courtroom, as were the woman's daughter and a neighbor who was witness to the incident. The defendant was represented by an attorney. After the daughter and neighbor were sworn in, they were escorted to the witness room and told not to discuss the case. The plaintiff was questioned at length over exactly where on her body she had been struck; she answered vaguely and complained that no one believed her when she said she had been struck. Then she was asked whether or not she had provoked her son-in-law, to which she also answered vaguely. A long argument followed between the solicitor (prosecutor) and the defense attorney over how much evidence was admissible before the court, an argument in which the judge did not participate. They resolved the debate by proceeding with the questioning, because, as the solicitor said, "The court will listen to what it wants to."

There were three versions of the events in question. The plaintiff claimed she was struck by her son-in-law when she berated him for his continual unemployment. The defendant claimed he struck her because she swore at him. The neighbor, a witness for the defense, claimed that the plaintiff simply fell. She came to the house when she heard shouting, because she thought the defendant and his wife were having one of their frequent arguments. The neighbor said, "I'm a good Christian woman, and if I could help bring them together, I would." Under questioning, it appeared that her efforts at reconciliation consisted of pulling the telephone off the wall when the defendant's wife reached for it to call the police. The defendant then said that the plaintiff's charges grew out of an accumulation of past incidents. There had been many earlier arguments and beatings. The defendant said, "A man can take just so much," to which the solicitor responded, "Yes, I understand that." The judge explained that, although under state statute, foul language constitutes provocation in simple battery cases, in this case, he found the defendant guilty and fined him $50.

At three points in this case, the action of the courtroom was explicitly focused on the issues of difference that are central to Hopewell's legal ideology: the sources of conflict outside the community of Hopewell; the special salience of gender; and the social inadequacies of litigants. First, the plaintiff is required to respond to the question of whether she provoked her son-in-law to violence. Indeed, we have seen that plaintiffs are predefined as troublemakers with inadequate skills of self-mastery or reconciliation. Second, the special nature of women as an integrating force in the community emerges in the neighbor's defense of her proactive intervention in the dispute. Third, she invokes the idea of conflict as sin in the same statement: "I'm a good Christian woman, and if I could help bring them together, I would." It is the first of these distinctions that predominates in the next case.

CASE 2: *Simple Battery and Assault.* In this case, a woman complained that her husband had beaten her. She claimed he was drunk at the time and that in the course of an argument he had thrown her down onto their couch. When she fell, she burned herself with her lighted cigarette and, to protect herself from further abuse, threw their son's roller skate at him. At that point, the husband reached for his gun and withdrew only when their 16-year-old son intervened. The husband and wife had been in court under similar circumstances twelve times before, according to the solicitor. The solicitor said to the judge: "They've been at this for twelve years, and can't end it — I think we ought to go in and end it for them." The judge responded that the couple belonged in domestic relations court, not in his criminal court. Finally the judge turned to the husband and said, "I can understand people not getting along and fussing and fighting, but if there's anything I despise, it's a sloppy drunk." The defendant was fined $100 and sentenced to twelve months in jail.

The solicitor's and judge's remarks in this case reiterate both specific and general versions of the idea that litigants are inadequately or inappropriately socialized. When the solicitor says of the litigants that "we ought to go in and end [their marriage] for them," the context is his observation of the long troubled history of their "way of life." The judge speaks in more general terms: "[If] there's anything I despise, it's a sloppy drunk." In both instances, the attribution of excess (conflict, drunkenness) is used to characterize the litigants in contrast to the speaker himself. Another dimension of the generic litigant is suggested in the following case.

CASE 3: *First-Offense Drug Charge.* All first-time violators of the marijuana and narcotics laws in this county are treated as misdemeanor cases. (Second offenses are classed as felonies and are heard in the Superior Court.) The Inferior Court judge customarily delivers a stern lecture on the effects of drugs and of a prison term on a person's life. In this case, the young man involved was sentenced to two weekends of janitorial duty in the jail and was required to attend a class on the dangers of drug use. If the defendant were to be arrested a second time, he was told, he would receive full sentences for the first and second offenses. If he fulfilled the terms of his probation, then his record would be cleared. The defendant's wife was called forward to stand with her husband while the judge pronounced his verdict and sentenced him.

The judge's calling the defendant's wife forward to hear the sentence with her husband suggests that she is, in effect, sentenced with her husband. Two cultural issues are involved in this moment. First, we have already seen that women are assigned (and, as in Case 1, sometimes assign themselves) special responsibilities for keeping the peace. Perhaps, the judge called the defendant's wife forward as an ally of the court, a potential agent of her husband's rehabilitation. On the other hand, we have also seen that families, like individuals, are evaluated as being predisposed to getting along or making trouble and that family provides essential elements of the local discourse of conflict and change. If litigants as a category are generically flawed, then the extension of that genre to include their families is not surprising. In local terms, the appropriate social field for rehabilitation (in this case, sentencing) should be the family, because the family is regarded as the first source of personal values. People express doubt that an individual can transcend his or her family's "type." The idea that litigants reflect the social incompetence of their families concludes the next case.

CASE 4: *Abandonment.* The young, unmarried, pregnant woman in this case was living with her mother, who was collecting welfare for her support. Together, they sued the young woman's boyfriend for support. All three were present, and he confirmed that he was the father of the unborn child. The judge told him that he must pay something toward the care of his child's mother or go to jail. The judge then turned to the pregnant woman and said: "It's his job to support you, not me. I contribute to welfare." He fined the young man $59.75.

Speaking in the first person, the judge suggests that these litigants would not be in court if they knew what their responsibilities were. The judge assumes that personal effectiveness in mobilizing and sustaining a harmonious family life would preclude litigation, as would more general forms of social competence. One important implication of this assumption is that conflict is described as a matter of maturity and choice. The following case develops this idea.

CASE 5: *Custody*. This case began as an argument between divorced spouses over who was to take care of their son on a particular day. The husband, who was a policeman in Hopewell County, arrived to take him for the day against the wishes of the child's mother. Their case was dismissed after the couple's anger toward each other flared up in front of the judge. The judge admonished the husband for not being in uniform during the day (he was in court in civilian dress) and then said to the couple: "This is the end of it — I don't want to see you down here anymore. There ain't going to be any more trouble. You're both grown, and the child belongs to both of you."

Although this case certainly provides the judge with an opportunity to contrast mature family life with litigation, he suggests that this couple might be an exception to the generic negative type: "This is the end of it." Moreover, he seems to believe that they can avoid future trouble because they are both "grown" and connected through their child. One aspect of their maturity will be their ability to set aside their differences.[12]

CASE 6: *A Continuing Saga*. In the morning's final case, the female defendant presented the court with what its "back benchers" suggested to me was a continuing and entertaining melodrama. She was middle-aged and made a dramatic entrance in a bright pink wool suit, her bleached-blond hair fashionably styled but in disarray. She had obviously been crying. She was in court to ask that her case be put off another month. She had kidnapped a member of her family in an attempt at self-help in a situation so complex that I was not able to deduce it from the hearing, nor could the clerk's staff make it clear to me. She had been in court many times before as her situation unfolded. This time, she had hidden her relative in her apartment; when he was found, criminal charges were filed against her.

The defendant had been in court so often before that she was on a first-name basis with court staff. When she entered the courtroom, the staff people and the regular spectators, such as policemen waiting to testify in other cases, rolled their eyes in mock despair, laughing silently. According to staff members, she came to court so often, both as plaintiff and defendant, that the court considered her part of its standing business. She also seemed to enjoy some special privileges, evidenced in the unusual informality of her relationships with the court personnel and an exceptional permissiveness that left her monologues uninterrupted until she had fully vented her complaint. One courthouse secretary explained that any attempt to contain her speech would lead her to protest so strenuously that "we'd never hear another case all week." The consensus around the courtroom seemed to be that this woman was harmless and that the courtroom sessions provided her with some necessary therapy.

The court personnel and habitual spectators visibly relaxed as they watched this case unfold as a spectacle before them. To some extent, the fact that the defendant was to them a figure of comedy can be seen as a twist on the cultural distinctions that otherwise make her situation parallel to that of the other litigants I have described: the implications of gender, her ineptitude, her lack of self-control, her endless family troubles — all of these were grist for commentary by people around the courtroom. Although the therapeutic dimension of her case might seem to represent a departure from the earlier cases, the description of her as a litigant differs only in degree from that of the others.

The cases described in this section offer important parallels to the local view expressed by the Superior Court judge and clerk that court users are people who lack essential social and personal resources. In general, the assumption of most people who are interested in the current court is that its dockets are filled by newcomers, because only newcomers could be so dependent on third parties for the resolution of interpersonal disputes. Whereas general evaluations of insiders and outsiders are expressed in terms of their associations with conflict, the cases show that assessments of the positive or negative aspects of conflict and court use are contingent on prior evaluations of social groups.[13] The categorical differentiation of these symbolic groups and behaviors takes precedence over the content of the categories.

My aim in presenting data from various sources in Hopewell has been to set different canvases side by side and to show the consistent cultural techniques that define their respective images. People might differ in the degree to which they evaluate change as positive or negative, but the canvases reveal a shared and coherent set of representations that substantiate such evaluations:

(1) The cultural category of community draws on a fundamental distinction between a past predefined as harmonious and a future defined as

perilous. Current concerns about the role of the court and the nature of disputing in Hopewell emerge out of this temporal framework. The temporal framework is itself rooted in valuations of social groups. This view is more explicit in the interview data, but it is implied in the judge's, attorneys', and litigants' suggestions that overt conflict is a sign of social inadequacies of various kinds.

(2) Those valuations, in turn, distinguish people who can handle conflict on their own from people who cannot. In expressing concern over the durability of the town's way of life, local people devalue conflict and its expression. In expressing their concerns about Hopewell's future, local people focus on the future of interpersonal relations. They assume that if the courts are crowded, it is because individuals choose not to get along. Whether or not this is the case, the local interpretation and representation of litigiousness in this way are culturally significant.

(3) In conferring approval on people who can get along, and withholding it from people who do not want to get along, local views distinguish between overt and felt conflict. Value accrues to demonstrations of self-control and self-mastery. Avoidance, silence, prayer are remedial strategies that not only satisfy people's criteria for assessing the costs and benefits of open dispute (see Baumgartner, 1984) but also are culturally preferred.[14]

(4) One's capacity for self-mastery is related by local people to further social distinctions: "belonging" in Hopewell, belonging to a community, and belonging to a family. One group of Hopewell residents, the Southern Baptists, see belonging to a church as the definitive criterion of community (see Greenhouse, 1986). Baptists and others point to the quality of family life as one measure of Hopewell's social health. Family ties are positively valued, even when they are not happy ones. The widespread distinction drawn between insiders and outsiders, or newcomers, includes the assumption that insiders live in families, and outsiders live alone (a married couple or an isolated nuclear family do not automatically meet the criteria of belonging). The ability to maintain the family bond centers on the contractual ties that are believed to constitute society itself (Greenhouse, 1985).

Although courts, then, are widely understood in Hopewell as legitimate institutions of the state, they stand outside the community of meaning that, however indeterminately, defines Hopewell in the view of its residents. Courts, in other words, symbolically guard the gates of Hopewell.

In the case of Hopewell, the cultural understanding of conflict, that is, what conflict is and what it means to people, focuses on conflict's anti-social aspects. Conflict emblematizes the negative meanings of individualism. The symbolic role of the court is relevant not as an agency that can "do" anything about the encroachments of change, but as one that marks and measures those encroachments. If, as local people claim, newcomers in Hopewell are without the kinds of social ties that make other people prefer getting along, the court cannot change that situation in any fundamental way. The court reaffirms and sees reaffirmed the important distinctions out of which the local view is constructed. Court personnel emphasize the failures of individuals in interpersonal conflict. They paint a portrait of individualism unchecked, but they add a temporal dimension that disaggregates the characteristics of individualism and associates them with different moments in time. The positive meanings of individualism are associated with the mythical representation of the community's past. The negative meanings of individualism are associated with the representation of the community's future, that is, with the antithesis of community, whatever that will be.

CONCLUSION

In turning from Hopewell to the rest of the world, one is tempted to ask what Hopewell's legal ideology, or any ideology, is about. Hunt (1985: 18–19) warns against too literal an effort along these lines: Although metaphors of "reflection" are "ubiquitous," they "[import] a dubious epistemology derived from a naive materialism." Certainly, it is appropriate to stress that ideologies are fundamentally about themselves, yet some ideologies succeed, and some fail. How do adherents of ideologies defend their beliefs against their own inevitable openness, against the skepticism of which they define themselves as free?

The defense of ideology lies in its symbolic distinctions. In Hopewell, the social logic I have presented asserts a distinction between newcomers and locals in both spatial (from there to here) and temporal (past and future) terms. Arguably, a second distinction divides the putative materialism of newcomers from more cooperation, even more spirituality, among the locals. A third distinction defines disputing as a newcomer's trait and contrasts it with the cooperative or, failing that, restrained interactions of the insiders. In the local view, these three distinctions are causally connected. The newcomers constitute a relatively marked category, and the insiders a relatively unmarked category. The newcomers' mark, in the local view, is their highly individualized pursuit of material gain; its corollary is newcomers' stereotype as having deficient family lives. To local people, these are not merely labels or attributes of social groups in Hopewell; they are explanations of change and the groups themselves.

The importance of maintaining these temporal and sociological distinctions is that they expand the repertoire of social strategies available to insiders. Insiders acknowledge the importance of being able to defend themselves against the newcomers and so justify an individualistic and materialistic discourse even as they devalue it. Insiders, then, can live in two value systems simultaneously: one (ours) that emphasizes affective ties and cooperation, the other (theirs) that centers on competitive self-interest. They defend their legal ideology as the expression of their way of life; however, it is more accurately understood as an appropriation (albeit in the negative) of what they claim are their competitors' values. From one perspective, this might be seen as a functional adaptation to change. Perhaps it is; however, I want to stress another perspective, from which social change is understood as predefined in the arrangement of the cultural categories out of which local people construct their sociology.

Hopewell's ideology of law provides the symbols in terms of which people comprehend the widening, and to some extent displacement, of their former social hierarchies. Until World War II, Hopewell was a small commercial center in what had been an agricultural area for more than a century. With postwar development, the old agrarian elite lost its status as farming collapsed and new economic ventures and newcomers took control of the management of local capital. Sustaining interpersonal relations in the midst of this process of social transformation is awkward. These changes certainly make it increasingly difficult for people to maintain the old local brand of populism that gave Hopewell's public life its traditional character. I am not proposing that Hopewell's ideology of law causes or reflects the shifting patterns of haves and have-nots (and the goods in question might be material or intangible) but, rather, that it is in itself an acknowledgment by (self-defined) insiders of the dwindling efficacy of the worldview they characterize as their particular tradition.

In other words, the assiduous marking of the rather hypothetical categories of "insider" and "outsider" and the elaboration of the perils of the influx of newcomers in effect gives "insiders" permission to abandon or supplement their old egalitarianism for or with a more individualistic stance. This, I think, is the implication of their view that once materialistic newcomers gain a foothold, "insiders" feel they must become materialistic, too, however reluctantly, in order to defend what is theirs. This motive is no less a construction than some of the more abstract dimensions of local ideology; however, it signals the sorts of social processes that sustain this ideology over time.

Finally, turning from Hopewell and the terms of its social assessments to the larger problem of the significance of difference, a few points remain. First, ideologies are about differences. If any particular ideology claims to exist apart from the cultural and social machinery that defines and sustains the systematization of differences intrinsic to it, then its claims to autochthony or autonomy must be examined as cultural facts that relate to the law's enduring capacity to create myth. Ideology is a set of representations of differences and their meanings; any analysis of a particular ideology must take these contingent competitors into account.

This leads to a second, methodological point. If interpretive approaches offer an appropriate set of tools for sociolegal research, it is because the basic premises of social life are invented, negotiated, and reproduced in the context (they are the context) of everyday life. I have argued that, taken together, these two points suggest that an interpretive project is inevitably a comparative one.

Finally, the significance of systems of differentiation (such as we have been exploring in Hopewell) is that they reveal the terms in which a society organizes its own contests over the universe of its imagined alternatives. Because ideologies imply each other and the boundaries around social systems are themselves ideological constructs, the differences among sociocultural systems should be approached in the same terms as the differences within systems. Once ideology is understood as entailing an interpretive project, then the internal and external audiences of any particular ideology are inextricably linked.

POSTSCRIPT

This chapter was written in 1988, in an ethnographic present that described Hopewell as I knew it in the mid-1970s and in 1980. I visited Hopewell very briefly in 1991, after eleven years' absence, but also after a year or so of renewed correspondence with some of the people I had known best during my residence there. Although I did not resume my formal study of Hopewell — nor is this the place for detailed documentation of the intervening years — it is clear that Hopewell has changed dramatically since that earlier period. It is now a modern suburb, even more a bedroom community for the nearby city than it was ten years ago. The county has more than doubled its population, which is now considerably more diverse and cosmopolitan than it was fifteen years ago. According to its minister, the Southern Baptist church in Hopewell now has an ethnically and nationally diverse fellowship of over 10,000 people from the United States and 26 other countries. The Historical Society is now primarily under the leadership of "insiders" — the daughters and wives of some of the men whose business acumen changed the face of the town twenty and thirty years ago.

With the exception of the Historic District in downtown Hopewell, the county seat is literally unrecognizable from the days when I knew it. Whatever fork in the road people felt they faced a decade ago, it has now been successfully navigated, in the views of the people I was able to consult recently. Their view of the town's past remains one that makes the stewardship of local historical consciousness a special responsibility, but they also view participation in that stewardship as a collective and inclusive enterprise that can socialize newcomers to the local "way of life." This proposition is among the issues we discuss in Part II.

PART TWO

Law, Values, and the Discourse of Community

When we first began the conversations that led to this collaborative project, we were struck by the points of contact among our three research sites and our individual interpretive problems. Eventually, distrusting the relative ease with which we could move the conversation from one town to another, we began to explore why these three places might have so much in common. Superficially, the settings look (and are) different, and people in all three places consider themselves to be typical of their respective regions. Not coincidentally (as this book aims to explain), people in each place put similar value on their (or others') engagements with law. We also sought to understand the differences among our findings; those are also part of the discussion in the text.

The major link among these towns with such distinctive pasts is the nature of their common worries about the future. If our separate groups of interlocutors could meet — and we hope that this book will give them some sense of having met — we suspect that shared concerns about the future would be among the subjects about which they could most easily converse. Sander County and Hopewell were, until relatively recently, rural centers in areas dominated by agriculture and small business. Riverside was always more of a commercial center. All three places have now been overtaken (to embrace the local point of view) by the suburban, commercial and industrial reach of the growing metropolises that now overshadow them. At one point, we began to consider that the evident urgency local people bring to distinguishing insiders from outsiders is, in ways that are not obvious, about the direction, pace, and ownership of these trends.

While pursuing these possibilities, we realized that local constructions of identity are contingent on the relationship of elites and former elites to such large-scale processes of change and, as such, are relatively detailed commentaries on them. Recent local developments connect specific, although generic, "others" with the transactions that now tie the towns to their regions, nation, and world. The shared concerns of the three sets of town residents include the troubling ambiguities of these relationships that, in local memory, have acquired neighbors' faces.

Although people in all three settings invoke some local variant of the notion of "traditional values" and portray the present and future as departures from them, local social life in the past was divided in important ways. People's characterizations of the past are interestingly double, multiple, or contradictory. In Hopewell, for example, historical myths emphasize both rural *and* urban images of the past. In Riverside and Sander County, people assert both the local *and* regional "character" of the community. Although celebrations of the past portray a less divided American society, historical narratives and contemporary rhetoric preserve the lines of division that had particular relevance to local concerns. Indeed, it appears to be what they see as the forced abandonment of such distinctions — a "melting pot" created by law and multinational capital — that people resist.

Attitudes toward law and law use thus encode local analyses and critiques of major institutions and developments well beyond the towns' boundaries. Whereas insiders stress the positive value of restraint in conflict situations for the sake of the "community," the available discourse for expressing this value by its very nature preserves the outlines of important tensions: past and present hierarchies, contested centers of power, rival meanings of community, and so on. We explore these commentaries in detail, relating them to local experience.

The notion of community in these three towns is a paradoxical one in that democratic values, community, and selflessness are invoked in ways that preserve hierarchy, individualism, and competition. Insiders associate "culture" and civility, self-restraint and moderation with their own preferred values. The values they reject are those they associate with outsiders, whom they easily dismiss in the abstract as self-indulgent, immature, or incompetent. They connect their preferred values with the practices and beliefs of their own local power elites.

Part II begins in the convergence between attitudes toward law and understandings or characterizations of the sociological dynamics that constitute local life in Sander County, Riverside, and Hopewell. Chapter 4 examines this nexus of ideas for the deeper meanings people import to avoidance and involvement as alternative modes of social participation. These appear to be primarily about people's values with respect to the nature of their "communities" as places. "Place" means somewhat different things in the three ethnographic contexts we studied; however, their common theme is the positive value people place on local identity. There is a tension that follows from this high value; sometimes what people value is the local or separate character of their town; sometimes, on the other hand, it is the connection to the state and nation that they value, *through* their town. The social tensions that are evident in the oppositional terms that make up people's social vocabularies in these towns reflect this ambivalence. Chapter 5 examines the symbolic struggle between local autonomy and the state, as well as the social processes through which this struggle is manifested in modern times.

In the course of exploring the struggle between local and national visions of community life, another fundamental set of meanings emerges from the concept of "place" itself. When local identity is positively valued, "place" seems to stand in for historical processes; it is knowledge of and participation in these processes that constitutes "being from" Hopewell, Riverside, or Sander County. Chapter 6 examines local constructions of the past in the three towns. Although their pasts are different, the common thread that links them now is their highly selective and mythicized constructions of a past "way of life" and its values. We interpret these as a critique of modern processes of change. In the Conclusion, we consider further what we believe are local critiques of the more substantive aspects of change, in particular, multinational capitalism and the melting pot.

CHAPTER FOUR

Avoidance and Involvement

Here, happily, unoppressed with any civil bondage, this society of fishermen and merchants live, without any military establishments, without governors or any masters but the laws; and their civil code is so light that it is never felt. A man may pass (as many have done whom I am acquainted with) through the various scenes of a long life, may struggle against a variety of adverse fortune, peaceably enjoy the good when it comes, and never in that long interval, apply to the law either for redress or assistance. The principal benefit it confers is the general protection of individuals, and this protection is purchased by the most moderate taxes, which are cheerfully paid.

HECTOR ST. JOHN DE CRÈVECOEUR,
Letters from an American Farmer

In the late twentieth century as well as in the late eighteenth century, the mythology of a happy community may be founded on the ideal of law avoidance. The fishermen and merchants of Nantucket, according to Crèvecoeur (1926 [1782]), relied on the law to protect the citizenry (presumably from criminal misconduct) but otherwise refrained from legal involvement, even in times of adversity or misfortune. In his narratives of life in America that he constructed for English readers, like some of the narratives constructed in communities today, Crèvecoeur drew distinctions between proper and improper law usage that helped to define the sort of community he wanted and, to some extent, the sort of community he actually observed.

For Crèvecoeur, as for many in the 1970s and 1980s, it was the assiduous avoidance of law that symbolized and, in a sense, constituted the community. Unlike those who lived in "populous towns" (140) already troubled by the corrupting influence of lawyers and by a "spirit of litigiousness" (143), Nantucket residents according to this mythology still dwelt in peace and harmony. It was this aspect of their lives that was to be emphasized to English readers so that they might appreciate the virtues of community life in America.

Our three American studies, in Riverside, Hopewell, and Sander County, suggest that in the twentieth century Crèvecoeur's myth of harmony is still widely shared, even in locales that differ in many other important ways. At the outset of our three-way collaboration, we anticipated that residents of towns in New England, the South, and the Midwest would have very different ideas about community, conflict, law, and law avoidance. Yet we found it surprisingly easy to draw comparisons. Regional and local differences both mattered and did not matter. Each of the elements we wished to compare was embedded in the particularities of local ways and traditions. Yet local specificity, when examined closely, actually helped us to perceive and understand that which we came to believe was common to the experience of community in American society.

The locale (Massachusetts, Georgia, Illinois) is indeed a source of variation; yet, the very notion of locale is what is most shared among these three communities. Local traditions may differ from place to place, but they reveal common concerns about the composition and boundaries of the community, about the negative aspects of conflict and its association with newcomers and "undesirables," about the passage of time and an uncertainty as to whether the future will bring progress or disintegration, about local autonomy and the loss of control to external political and economic power.

Our three studies were conducted during an era in which it was widely perceived that American society had become excessively "legalized" and its people litigious. However, the narratives of law avoidance and of law involvement were still told by some members of these three communities in ways that did not differ significantly from Crèvecoeur's account. A pervasive norm of nonlitigiousness was apparent in many of these narratives, contrary to popular perceptions that American society had become completely enamored of litigation. Although law and order were highly valued in all three towns, so was the ethic of rejecting law and of embracing forms of social order based on self-discipline and tradition rather than legal enforcement.

Such were the values expressed by many people we knew in Hopewell, Riverside, and Sander County. Nevertheless, the ethic of law avoidance bore no direct relationship to the actual behavior of those who espoused it. The "narratives of avoidance" that were recounted in all three settings were not necessarily descriptions of typical, everyday behavior but were ideological statements whose purpose and function within the community were both important and complex. They were a means by which some attempted to create or impose order within the community, to define or deflect change, and to articulate a philosophy of individualism and equality that could also be reconciled with their tenacious defense of the status quo.

It must be emphasized that, despite the importance of law avoidance as a cultural norm, law and legal institutions were central to the culture of the three towns and, therefore, had their own place in the mythology of the happy community constructed by residents. In each setting, the courthouse itself occupied a symbolically prominent position in the town square. The courthouse buildings and their occupants figured importantly in local histories of the communities. There were, in fact, some valued forms of litigation that partook of the symbolic centrality of the courthouse in the community. Energetic enforcement of the criminal law was strongly supported by those who decried litigiousness in general terms and was not viewed as evidence of excessive legalization of the society. On the contrary, the criminal justice system was thought to embody many of the community's most fundamental values and beliefs and, in Crèvecoeur's terms, to secure "the general protection of individuals." There was little sympathy for those who violated the criminal law, and there was no sense that a proliferation of arrests or criminal prosecutions indicated a legal system that had gone out of control.

Other forms of law invocation were also deemed appropriate by those who were otherwise suspicious of court use: actions by landlords to collect rent or to evict tenants who were in default, debt collections and other forms of contract enforcement, the enforcement of child-support obligations, and even divorce actions were all considered consistent with the culturally central role of the court in the community. Although the underlying social causes of such litigation might be regretted, the invocation of law was not condemned in itself.

Avoidance of and involvement with the law thus carried complex and variable cultural meanings. "Litigiousness" was indeed of great importance in all three settings, but its importance lay chiefly in its role as a signifier. Attempts to study litigiousness in particular communities or societies have always been problematic precisely because there are so many questions of meaning embedded in the processes of disputing and litigation themselves. We chose to approach this issue not by converting questions of meaning or signification into questions of frequency but by exploring how interpretations of the meanings of litigiousness are negotiated and deployed by different groups in the community.

What was consistent in all three communities was the selectivity of popular understandings as to the occasions on which law was to be invoked or avoided. Among different groups in these communities, certain kinds of litigation were highly valued; other kinds were devalued. Much depended on the nature of the social relationships underlying the different types of cases. In their narratives of law and conflict management in the community, residents created and reinforced distinctive categories of appropriate and inappropriate court use. These categories became a part of the cultural fabric of the community itself.

LAW AND THE MARKING OF SOCIAL BOUNDARIES

Residents and legal actors in the three towns expressed firm ideas about what persons and conflicts should be in or out of the court. The clerk in Riverside spoke of "ridiculous" and "brainless" matters and of "frivolous" problems involving "poor people, both monetarily and intellectually." Baptists in Hopewell spoke of the litigation of interpersonal disputes as a failure of religious faith and conviction. Long-time residents of Sander County viewed the litigation of personal injury claims — but not contract actions — as symptomatic of a selfish and destructive search for "the quick buck" that threatened to undermine the foundations of their rural community.

If "dirt is matter out of place" (Douglas, 1966), then litigiousness is not so much an excess of litigation as it is a sense that the wrong cases, the "garbage" cases, are polluting the courts simply because they are where they should not be (even though their presence may be valid in narrow legal terms). But this sense of the appropriate "place" for particular forms of conflict also expresses understandings of other kinds of social boundaries and other notions of where things and people should be. In all three settings there were people who were perceived as "out of place" in the community. To condemn their legal claims was to reaffirm their status as outsiders and to mark the social boundaries that excluded them from a legitimate role in the community. On the whole, perceptions of excessive litigation appear to be associated with perceptions of certain people as "outsiders"; affirmations of the ethic of avoidance appear to be part of a process by which insiders reaffirm their own status and identity.

Viewed in this way, in the three settings discourse concerning litigiousness and the virtues of avoidance becomes part of a more general process of establishing and maintaining social boundaries. Condemnation of certain types of litigation almost immediately transforms itself into degradation of the plaintiffs themselves as poor, uncultured, ethnically undesirable, or unchristian. By contrast, praise of avoidance becomes the chorus in a hymn to the virtues of community insiders: rooted, established, selfless, "good neighbors," religiously and ethnically acceptable, and respectful of traditional ways. Of course, those who are condemned as "litigious" may hold different ideas about good neighbors and the boundaries of the community. For ethnic outsiders or blue-collar workers, avoidance may be a less salient value than acceptance, and "litigiousness" may be a lesser evil than discrimination or economic exploitation. For them, the attempt to negotiate a niche in the community involves asserting claims to fair treatment and, in some instances, compensation, in the face of the broadly stated denunciation of litigiousness.

By associating a particular set of traits with those they define as longtime or elite insiders, or by defining themselves as such, some residents of the three towns express their sense of "place," of what it means to belong to the community. At the same time they express a sense of those who are "out of place," who are physically there but do not "belong." It would be difficult to draw specific boundaries around these groups, that is, between the people who feel entitled to claim a certain stewardship for the towns' way of life and those whose participation takes other forms. As is already clear, our study emphasizes the perspective of people who make such claims of stewardship and concern. Although their rhetorics differed in some ways, there were surprising similarities in the mythology of "insiders" and "outsiders" and in the traits that were valorized in all three settings. It was these similarities, in fact, that led us to pursue the comparative project, intrigued as we were by what appeared to be a common lexicon of difference in three superficially unrelated locales.

In Hopewell, the legal ideology expressed by court personnel and townspeople (see Chapter 3) was also articulated, although in different terms, by the town's Southern Baptists. For them, the distinction between insiders and outsiders involved not only a sociological distinction but also a theological one, dividing the "saved" from the "unsaved." The main theme of Greenhouse's original study was the connection local Southern Baptists drew between avoiding overt expressions of conflict, their faith as Christians, and the local way of life. Their sacred concerns had a historical dimension; withdrawal by Baptists from situations of conflict was consistent with a series of historical experiences stretching back to the mid-nineteenth century. Finding themselves internally divided or in a minority position on a number of issues important to the region (Cherokee removal, populism, antiabolitionism) the Baptists constructed a concept of social harmony and opposition to conflict that drew on both religious and political symbolism. They came to value those who accepted the transcendence of God's law over human authority and rejected those who engaged in interpersonal conflict, which was thought to threaten the collective good. Persons who were admired among Hopewell's Baptists were thus the individuals who "turned the other cheek," who yielded what was demanded, and left all judgments to Jesus. They were the individuals who sought salvation in prayer and in the fellowship of the church. By contrast, persons who were not admired and who were marked as outsiders to the Baptist community were the individuals who carped, complained, and objected to what they perceived as infringements of their individual interests. It was Christian as well as politically expedient within the community to refrain from disputation. Transcendence of conflict was a quality associated with individuals who were saved and with a community that had endured.

In this mythology of insiders and outsiders there were also some curious silences. African Americans, for example, were omitted from local talk about the driving forces of Hopewell's way of life, as if they lived beyond the margins of Hopewell literally as well as figuratively. "City folks," too, were regarded as a social type wholly distinct from Hopewell residents, although many in Hopewell might be identified by origin, inclination or employment as urbanites. At the time of Greenhouse's fieldwork, there were very few foreign-born individuals in Hopewell County; ethnicity, too, was not a dimension along which local people described their town. Thus, by their silences as well as by their narratives of belonging and not belonging, residents of Hopewell defined themselves and their community.

Insiders in Sander County expressed values similar in many ways to those found in Hopewell but described them in rather different terms. An understated interpersonal style was, perhaps, a quality the Scandinavian and German immigrants brought with them when they first settled there. Yet, the most respected individuals were not merely those who rejected glib self-promotion. They were those who understood the importance of social interdependence in a community where farmers cooperated to harvest crops and assisted one another in times of illness or injury. To be a member of the community — an insider — was to accept the fact that one's interests were not entirely one's own, that one's needs were tied to the needs and capabilities of others.

The traditional farming community of Sander County thus valued those individuals who, in word and deed, affirmed the necessity of preserving cooperative relationships. Petty claims, self-interest, and conflict were viewed as dangerous and undesirable qualities among local residents. They threatened the economic and social foundations of the community. People who were primarily concerned with protecting their own interests failed to recognize the linkages between individual and group survival and success. They were condemned as "outsiders" and stigmatized by the traditionalists of Sander County.

As was the case in Hopewell, there were significant silences in these narratives of insiders and outsiders in Sander County. Although much was made of lower-class outsiders who had entered the community in recent years (African Americans, Latinos, southerners, and even Indochinese refugees) one seldom heard discussion of the fact that some key political and administrative positions were held by newly arrived individuals associated with management-level positions in externally based businesses established in Sander County over the past ten or twenty years. The active civic role played by these newcomers was not mentioned often, although they tended to displace incumbents who were farmers and other old-timers. Nor was there much talk about persons reared in traditional Sander County families who "defected" to management positions in the new industries and businesses and thus withdrew, at least in part, from the older network of interdependence and reciprocity.

In Riverside, insiders defined good citizens and good neighbors by contrast to "garbage people," "scum," and ethnics — stereotypes of chaotic and violent lives threatening to the civic order. To some extent, the distinction between good and bad citizens was localized in the neighboring communities of Riverside and Milltown. Undesirable people in Riverside were associated with the disorder and decay of nearby Milltown, which served as both a negative example for Riverside residents and an imagined source of social pollution that threatened their own community.

Those who brought cases to the court clerk's office helped the insiders of Riverside to reaffirm these distinctions. The domestic and neighborhood dramas of irrational and violent behavior provided an occasion for ritual denunciation of people who lacked the civilizing traits of self-control, rationality, civility, responsibility, and concern for others. The very fact that these conflicts were brought to court was itself a matter to be deplored, for it suggested a failure to deploy social skills in nonjudicial contexts. Thus litigants in Riverside served as negative examples not only because of the disreputable nature of their private affairs displayed in this public forum but also because their resort to the formal legal system in itself revealed a lack of astuteness, a social ineptitude associated with the "other half" of society.

What was not often mentioned in these mythical narratives of insiders and outsiders in Riverside was the fact that, despite the town's image of pastoralism and tranquillity, it contained its own economic underclass. Attempts to locate such persons entirely in Milltown were a form of collective denial that Riverside itself contained those deemed "scum" and ethnic outsiders. At the same time, there were also silences concerning the presence in Riverside of very wealthy bankers and business people, whose attributes clashed in a rather different way with the myth of the sturdy New England small-town resident.

Thus, local constructions of "community" in the three settings in Georgia, Illinois, and Massachusetts drew selectively on different images and symbols to characterize the personality traits people associated with outsiders. But the similarities are striking. In all three settings, the self-designated mainstream members of the community praised those who withdrew from conflict, who valued group interests over individual interests, who recognized the interdependencies of neighbors and the fragility of the civic order that was continually threatened by unpredictable, violent, and self-centered "others." In all three communities, the good citizen was defined by negative reference to the bad citizen, whose failures were most obviously apparent in the public conflicts and lawsuits he or she brought. Such lawsuits were of critical importance, for they were often interpreted and represented as occasions when "outsiders" engaged in characteristic efforts to press alternative visions of the community and its norms and thus to manipulate their own social status in self-serving ways. Such talk about litigation provided one of the most important occasions in all three communities for articulating, negotiating, and redefining the personal qualities and behavior that were most highly valued and disvalued.

As the inappropriate use of law was an important part of the constellation of undesirable characteristics associated with "outsiders" in all three communities, we should ask why local people invoked the law in these ways and how such invocations reinforced the negativity with which some of them were viewed. Three different forms of law use were locally viewed as evidence confirming the negative stereotype of litigants as a class.

The first involved conflicts among "them": domestic fights, drunken brawls, violence, and threats of violence. When such matters reached the court they were said to exemplify the disorder and danger associated with racial, ethnic, or religious outsiders or with the lower classes in general. Indeed, in these contexts litigation was viewed as part and parcel of the lack of self-control and the irrationality of such people. In the same view, litigiousness also confirmed the absence of "civilizing" (read "middle-class") institutions and norms of dispute settlement within their social groups.

A second form of law use involved litigation against people identified (by themselves or by others) as mainstream members of the community. Tort actions were the paradigmatic cases of this type. People often became plaintiffs in such cases for the same reasons they were marked as outsiders: They had less money and less adequate medical care, and they were more frequently endangered by illness, accident, poor-quality goods and housing, or industrial hazards. When such persons were injured and sought recourse against a wealthy local person or organization, there was a sense that the established community had been invaded by litigious outsiders. The fragility of traditional norms, relationships, and institutions was emphasized by such "invasive" litigation. In contrast, plaintiffs typically viewed this form of litigation as no more than an effort to avoid economic exploitation by shifting the cost of injuries onto the shoulders of those who could and should have prevented them. The plaintiffs' view was not shared by most people who thought of themselves as insiders. There were long-established procedures for gaining acceptance in the community and achieving success (although sometimes actual birth in the community was required). This type of litigation seemed to be an effort to circumvent such procedures and to enable outsiders to reap the benefits of the traditional community without the proper initiation rites and without shedding the traits that defined them as different and undesirable.

A third form of law use identified with "outsiders" involved assertions of civil rights. Here the primary purpose of the litigation was not to obtain compensation but to enforce constitutionally sanctioned entitlements. Rather than seeking money from establishment institutions or individuals, plaintiffs in such actions attempted to obtain access to the rights and privileges of "citizenship" within the community. A Sander County boy who was expelled from school for smoking sought reinstatement on the grounds that his procedural rights had been denied. His suit — ultimately unsuccessful in the Sander County court — was widely viewed as an effort to force acceptance of the individual on the community, rather than trying to reform the behavior (disrespect for authority, persistent rejection of "law and order" within the school) that led to his expulsion. This form of litigiousness, then, was just as threatening as that aimed at "the quick buck." If litigants could, through manipulation of the legal system, obtain citizenship in the community without adopting the "community values," then traditional conceptions of "place" and social order would be hopelessly confused and the very foundations of the community might crumble.

These three types of litigation all involved claimants who were people stereotyped as outsiders, but what about comparable claims by people who are locally viewed as insiders? Did "insiders" never suffer injuries? Did they never fight among themselves? Did their children never get in trouble in the schools? Although (by definition, if for no other reason) accidents and conflicts may have been somewhat more prevalent among those who were considered outsiders, it would be absurd to maintain that "insiders" did not encounter similar situations at times. By virtue of their public identity as insiders, however, they were able to handle such matters without recourse to law in many cases. A discreet phone call, a conversation at the club, a discussion over the back fence could provide a smooth and private resolution. "Citizenship" has its privileges, and one of them is the ability to deal with potentially conflictual situations while still maintaining one's posture as a reasonable, self-denying, nonlitigious person. For outsiders, who lack the channels through which their interests might be represented in a less confrontational manner, open conflict and sometimes litigation are the only alternatives to "lumping it." Lumping may be the more frequent choice for outsiders, but the occasional decision to assert their interests exposed them inevitably to accusations of litigiousness. Such accusations, in a sort of vicious circle, reaffirmed the very status (as outsiders) that forced them to resort to public conflict or litigation in the first place.

There is another sense in which the "restraint" of insiders and the "litigiousness" of outsiders were used to mark boundaries within the "community." In all three locales, people who claimed the sort of diffuse stewardship that interested us were preoccupied by issues of social change and the loss of valued traditional ways. We will comment on this preoccupation at greater length in the next sections. But it should be noted at this point that the inappropriate public claims and conflicts associated with outsiders were also perceived as threatening, because they possessed the potential to force change on the community. Personal injury claims suggested threats of redistribution of wealth and the destruction of traditional values. Lawsuits against schools suggested challenges to educational authority, the socialization of young people, and local control over key institutions. Claims by motorcycle shop owners (even as defendant) suggest rights to new forms of land use that could change the character of the community and the quality of life for long-time residents.

Thus, people who used the law were not only (by their mere presence) symptomatic of undesired social transformations but also instrumental in producing them. Ironically, they were able to do so by manipulating institutions and symbols that were central to the traditional order: the courthouse on the town square and the laws that should have guaranteed order rather than disorder.

In conversation, avoidance and litigiousness were, therefore, linked to the processes by which people sought order and "place" in social relationships and to the processes by which the identity and direction of those relationships were determined and defined as "community." Praise for the farmer who demonstrated forbearance when his neighbors needed extra time to make payments; praise for the landlord who sued to evict his undesirable tenants and collect back rent; blame for the minister who sought compensation in a slip-and-fall case. These seemingly inconsistent judgments on local citizens and on litigation all can be reconciled in terms of overarching concerns about community order in the face of changes that threatened traditional ways and values. Avoidance can preserve order, but so can litigation. It all depends on who the parties are and how the courts are being used. When the court was used to steer the community toward changes that seemed disordered, chaotic, and threatening to established institutions or practices, then one could see a convergence of insiders' concerns about persons who were out of place and about the future of the community as it had come to be defined.

INDIVIDUALISM AND COMMUNITY

Although the rhetoric of avoidance was not always consistent with the behavior of people who used it (those who, as we have observed, favored some forms of law use), it did provide an important means of delineating desirable social traits, such as reasonableness, self-mastery, respect for traditional ways and authorities, and selflessness. In addition, avoidance had ethical dimensions that served to reconcile certain tensions between values associated with individualism on the one hand and community solidarity on the other.

We have suggested that individualism may assume different forms in different situations. As discussed in Chapter 1, there is an individualism that emphasizes rights and entitlements and a rather different version that emphasizes self-reliance and independence. The first is consistent with claims against others, when claims are necessary to protect one's interests; the second is consistent with self-sufficiency, even in the face of rights deprivation. The ethical justifications of avoidance that we encountered in people's narratives of their own and others' troubles tap into the second of these two forms of individualism. Very often, people's stories about their (or others') grievances took the form of explaining what the narrator had endured, perhaps silently, rather than what he or she had expressed as an overt complaint. We call these stories "narratives of avoidance."

Narratives of avoidance are a form of praise for individual autonomy. They reinforce the type of individualism that appears most likely to minimize conflict in the community. Their implicit suggestion is that the good citizen tends to remain stoic and impassive in the face of "petty" conflicts. They confirm the virtues of those whose material and social achievements are not obtained at the expense of others; yet, at the same time they validate the rewards of strenuous competition in the marketplace. Such competition, unlike rights-based claims, is understood to support the values of community, not to undermine them. It is one thing to try to get ahead by suing when one is injured, but it is quite another to compete vigorously against one's neighbors in the commercial arena. People imply that self-interest in the marketplace ultimately advances the collective good rather than undermining it. As such, it is not selfish and greedy in the same way that litigation is said to be. Those who would consider litigation, it is believed, should practice avoidance and redirect their energies to fair and open competition in the marketplace.

By extolling avoidance as an *ethical* position, one can pursue self-interest and yet remain selfless, struggle for success and yet exhibit self-restraint and control, seek individual rewards and yet sustain the values of community solidarity. As an ethical position in contexts such as these, an avoidance stance asserts (without actualizing) the disengagement of the person from society even while pointing to a social structure based on interests and instrumentalities. The ethical dimension of avoidance can be recognized in narratives that do just this.

Avoidance narratives allow a speaker simultaneously to invoke culturally preferred solidarities (of family and town, for example) *and* to distinguish individual interests within those social fields. In this way, avoidance emerges as a culturally appropriate means of resolving some of the contradictions between self-interest and the collective good. Its counterpart, confrontation, which is derived from conceptions of individualism based on rights and entitlements and is associated with the stereotype of the outsider, utterly fails this test. Confrontation, viewed from this perspective, appears to pit the individual irreconcilably against the collectivity. From the same perspective, whatever gains an individual may obtain by invoking law are at the expense of the community.

EGALITARIANISM AND HIERARCHY

Narratives of avoidance, as we have seen, help to establish two important and related sets of public symbols: community boundaries, and the distinction between "insiders" and "outsiders." They also reinforce a version of individualism founded on self-reliance and independence and make it possible to reconcile some of the contradictions between self-interest and solidarity or collective good. Avoidance, understood as an ethical stance based on self-restraint, also enables people to resolve, or at least to moderate, a tension between egalitarian and hierarchical conceptions of community and society. The tension between these two perspectives has been familiar to observers of life in the United States at least since the time of Tocqueville, and its resolution has always been problematic. Avoidance proves useful in maintaining hierarchy while espousing egalitarian values.

We have suggested that the forms of litigation that are disvalued in the three communities are those associated with individuals who are categorically stigmatized as outsiders. Indeed, the discourse used to denounce such litigation becomes an important instrument for marking the boundaries that the "outsiders" are supposed to have transgressed (or, in their own view, challenged and attempted to renegotiate). The potential for social change implicit in such litigation worried people who were already concerned for the future of the social order itself. From their perspective, although the Bible may have promised that the last shall become first and the meek shall inherit the earth, this did not mean that litigation was an appropriate means to achieve the biblically sanctioned end. Its potential powers of social transformation were quite apparent. Litigation, as they saw it, promised wealth without work, power without respect, and inclusion without acceptance. In social contexts where people perceived their interests as requiring a struggle to maintain their position and ward off threatening changes, opposition to "litigiousness" was a helpful strategy.

People opposed to the influx of ethnic outsiders, to members of the lower social classes, or to those who refused to be "saved" had to be cautious in the rhetoric they employed. Democratic traditions precluded them from resorting to explicitly antiegalitarian forms of discourse. One could not openly denounce the egalitarian norms underlying the invocation of law on behalf of the poor or oppressed. But one could oppose the propensity to assert the right — as contrasted with the right itself. Once the premise is granted that society as a whole is racked with litigiousness and that litigation fundamentally undermines traditional notions of individualism and communitarianism, then the door is opened widely enough to criticize even those forms of litigation that promote basic norms of equality and justice. This transforms what would otherwise be a defense of hierarchy in opposition to democratic values to a defense of community in opposition to selfishness and anarchy. It also introduces a basic ambiguity into the very notion of community, as we shall see when we consider the inclusive and exclusive elements of this concept.

Observers of American society over several decades have suggested that the cultural meanings of nature and culture are important for understanding social stratification in the United States and the differentiation of the higher from the lower social classes (Dollard, 1957; Warner, 1962 [1953]; Wallace, 1978; Greenhouse, 1992). The implication — at least for some Americans — is that the continuum of lowest to highest class is also a continuum of nature to culture. Hierarchy in American communities is not simply a matter of status and material wealth, but also of character — upper-class restraint, civility, and moderation as opposed to lower-class self-indulgence, laziness, loss of self-control, sexuality, temper, and irrationality. The chapters in Part I offer numerous examples of the specific characteristics some residents of Riverside, Sander County, and Hopewell ascribe to their neighbors. Open disputing is, in effect, a form of pollution from this perspective, as it disperses the negatively viewed "natural" elements of social life across the social landscape. Pollution is at the symbolic heart of the question of why conflict is not only undesirable but also repugnant.

This view of the social universe has larger implications in terms of its logic of local-state relations. If the basic struggle for upward mobility is culturally understood as the struggle to transcend nature, then self-mastery becomes highly charged as a positive cultural value. At the top of the hierarchy, social life can be assumed (in this worldview) to be self-regulating, because it is cultural and therefore successful. In theory, the "lower orders" lack this self-mastery and are therefore failures. By definition, conflict is assumed to flow up the social scale; it is presumed to originate primarily at the lower end and it debases those whose lack of self-mastery causes them to engage in it. Whether it is expressed through family violence, barroom brawls, or inappropriate use of the legal system for "garbage cases," conflict is the outward token of those essentially moral traits that are said to differentiate persons who are acculturated from those who are somehow outside (or below) culture.

We have suggested that not all forms of conflict or litigation are condemned; nor are the elite the only ones who can practice avoidance. Both law use and law avoidance are open and available to those at all social levels, but the cultural signs must be read with care. Indeed, it is through the narratives of avoidance and involvement that people in American communities continually negotiate the categories of approved and disapproved legal behavior and behavior generally.

By participating in these narratives of avoidance and involvement, individuals have an opportunity to associate themselves with elite values and with the virtues of (selective) self-restraint. Such associations, whether through generalized discourse or actual conduct in conflict situations, can enhance the status of certain individuals and provide evidence of cultural proficiency that might justify upward movement in the social hierarchy. In this way, self-denial can, at least in theory, become self-advancement, and short-term losses can become long-term gains. By forsaking conflict in a particular encounter, and by foregoing the benefits that might have been obtained, one may seek a more generalized form of advancement: a recognition that one is among the "saved" and therefore worthy of respect and prestige.

Through its openness, its sense that "all can play," the avoidance ethic superficially appears to conform to egalitarian values consistent with the American tradition. Anyone, at least hypothetically, could convert individual instances of self-restraint into the general currency of social ascension; however, the narratives of avoidance and involvement have important underlying antiegalitarian implications. Hierarchy is preserved when those who are most disadvantaged and most susceptible to the deprivation of rights are told that any attempt to assert their interests will be interpreted as evidence that they are neither saved nor civilized and that their "litigiousness" is reprehensible. They are given a Hobson's choice. For those who occupy the lowest position in the social hierarchy, the decision to resist will be condemned, but realistically the decision to avoid conflict and accept the status quo is more likely to perpetuate their problems than to solve them.

Avoidance both creates hierarchy and is its outcome. It is an index of civility and cultural astuteness, separating those who are saved from those who are not, but it also involves an ethic that tends to preserve the existing status system and suppress challenges and conflict from below. Avoidance thus reproduces existing patterns of class and ethnic division, which in turn become a framework of potential conflict that explains and justifies avoidance. Even as the happy community (like that described by Crèvecoeur) defines itself, it constitutes a worldview in which challenges to the established order are most likely to fail and those defined as outsiders are least likely to usurp the position held by the local elite.

CHAPTER FIVE

Connection and Separation

In the preceding chapter we discussed the ways in which identity, specifically for culturally, politically, and economically powerful groups in each of the three locales, is created through opposition to the secular and conflict-ridden world of the bad neighbor or the sinner, to ethnic "outsiders" and other recent arrivals who lack deep roots and an accompanying concept of collective interests, and to "brainless" people whose repeated appearances in court are taken as evidence of their lack of self-restraint. We argued that narratives of avoidance and involvement construct these oppositions and the hierarchies they encode, positioning people within them in particular ways: as high or low, as restrained or uncontrolled, as included or excluded.

In this chapter, we again take up the theme of inclusion and exclusion but from a different perspective, examining the dependence of identity in each of the three towns on a complex relation of town elites to those forces against which they define themselves: materialism, the state, the law. The symbolic terms of this relationship differ in each locale, as shaped by different local histories (see Chapter 6). In each, however, specific institutions appear as symbols of local autonomy on the one hand, and of the absorption of local society by the state, the translocal market, and by "outside" forces that threaten local hierarchies and structures of power on the other. The court is one such institution; corporations (for example, the tap and die industry in Riverside) may also act as key signifiers in a world sustained by "outside" capital even as it is defined by independence from it. The tension between connection and separation is revealed in struggles around these institutions (or more generally, around the meanings of law and of money) in which the "external" is domesticated by the "community," even as the community (as represented by local hierarchies of inclusion and exclusion) is constructed by the state and the market.

We begin with Hopewell, where separation from the material world is central to local Southern Baptists' sense of identity, yet where material concerns reinsert themselves as stewardship and tithing. Some of these same tensions are felt by others in town, as shown in diffuse expressions of the competing demands of material success and personal happiness.

THE SACRALIZATION OF MONEY

Mature Spirituality in Hopewell

Of the three locales that are the focus of this book, Hopewell presents the most explicit paradigm of identity constructed through opposition. Although in Riverside there is an ambiguous relationship of separation from the law and definition through it, in Hopewell the Southern Baptists (hereafter, Baptists) as a "community of Christ" defined themselves in opposition to the unsaved, the secular community of conflict, law, the state, and the market, all of which, in their terms, constitute "the world" (Greenhouse, 1986:122). For Hopewell's Baptists:

> All conflict is said to flow from the self-interest of non-Baptists; thus the two important experiences associated with belief — absence of conflict and resistance to materialism — become linked. Since all conflict is said to come from non-Baptists, conflict is also equated with non-Baptists, and non-Baptists are said to be avoided partly because one can expect trouble from them. Furthermore, it is known that non-Baptists have none of the spiritual faith that would prevent them from going to great lengths in their own interest. Because non-Baptists do not belong to the community of God, Baptists believe them to be dangerous and corrupting. (Greenhouse, 1986:117–18)

Materialism is viewed by Hopewell's Baptists as the major sin of secular society, and it is the principal marker of difference from secular society. At the same time, Baptists themselves are active participants in the capitalist economy. This participation is sacralized, however, specifically through institutions such as stewardship and tithing, but more generally through a concept of "egalitarianism," in which all believers are equalized in Jesus. "Egalitarianism does not eliminate differences in material wealth or prestige among church members; it transforms their meaning" (1986:109). Egalitarianism also neutralizes secular power for Baptists: "No believer should judge another, since Jesus is the sole author of judgments" (109). Thus, pressing one's own interests as a claim or as an expression of anger is unnecessary, because Jesus "has everyone in mind" (109). In this ideology, law (as claims, as rights, as conflict resolution) is rejected, and market relationships are transformed through the salvation of its players into an arena "in which Jesus can play a part in their lives; a financially successful Christian can be (by his very success) a good witness" (101).

By sacralizing materialism in this way (in effect "domesticating" competitive relations in the market by making them elements of Christian faith), Baptists can be "in the world but not of it" (116). Indeed, Baptists

are indistinguishable from non-Baptists on every visible dimension: they include no disproportion of poor, unemployed, or disadvantaged. Their ranch houses and split levels are as well kept and well furnished as the non-Baptists', and their jobs are just as high paying. Baptist men participate in exactly the same business world as the non-Baptist men, and their economic constraints are identical. *The difference is in the way in which Baptists understand and value their material situation.* . . . Promotion, for example, is discussed not so much in terms of reward for merit as a God-given opportunity for greater service through personal responsibility. Education is seen in terms of training for service, not for personal satisfaction or for the instrumentalities of a higher degree in the job market. Wealth is seen as an opportunity for tithing and charity, not as an end in itself. . . . The spiritually mature are presumed able to resolve the inner conflict that derives from the conjunction of the sacred and the profane and to live lives of perfect witness in a world of stress and distraction. . . . *The idea of mature spirituality is a standard by which Baptists can measure the effect of their participation in the secular world on their own spirituality and assess their own spirituality in relation to that of others.* (1986:129–30, emphasis added)

For Hopewell's Baptists, the contemporary stance that defines identity in opposition to conflict and conflict as the mark of a "worldly" domain of material temptations, of hierarchy, and of secular authority is continuous with a position taken by Baptists in the first half of the nineteenth century, when local churches were involved in a series of struggles that culminated in the explicit exhortation (in 1840) that politics and religion should be separated. After this period, church minutes and letters reflect an increasing tone of "other-worldliness" (Greenhouse, 1986:190–91). This distinction between secular and "natural" orders is familiar from other aspects of American culture in the nineteenth century (Greenhouse, 1986: 183, citing Perry Miller) but is given an intense and a specific cast in the southern historical context in which Hopewell's Baptist community developed. In particular, the Civil War "cement[ed] the equation, then newly formed, between Christianity and silenced conflict" and formed "the conclusive bond of harmony, Christianity, and southernness" that is the central dimension of identity for Hopewell's Baptists today (Greenhouse, 1986:191–92).

We have argued, however, that although conflict is silenced in an ethic of harmony, it is also reinterpreted and, in effect, "tamed" in a form of antimaterialism that redefines basic concepts of the marketplace to express religious values of witnessing, tithing, and stewardship. "Success in the marketplace is interpreted by local Baptists as an individual's ability to actualize his or her own potential (by accepting Christ) in the public domain." As Weber noted, Baptists "accomplished the religious rationalization of the world in its most extreme form" (Weber, 1958:148, in Greenhouse, 1986:101). Indeed, Baptist identity was constructed over time in the dialogue that this rationalization and reinterpretation represented.

Selfless Neighbors in Riverside and Sander County

In our three studies, Hopewell's Baptists represent the most developed embodiment of an ethic that rejects the world (as market) as a way of defining a distinct community identity but that, in constructing that identity, recasts the world in sacralized form. Similar processes, however, appear in the communal ideologies of Riverside, Sander County, and elsewhere in Hopewell, where the relationship of local economic elites to a translocal capitalist economy is also complex. There, as for Hopewell's Baptists, local autonomy and a distinct local identity can be explained only in terms of connections to and reshapings of that which is seen as "outside." As in Hopewell, however, local transformations are not simply masks: stewardship and tithing, after all, are ideologically (and politically) powerful reinterpretations of the meaning of money, as evidenced in the emergence of these concepts (in a slightly different form) in the televangel-ist phenomenon and especially in the Jim and Tammy Bakker scandal (Fitzgerald, 1990).[1] Thus, what is defined as "local" (as mature spir-ituality, as witnessing, or as selfless neighbors) has both a specific histor-ical referent and a general cultural referent. Familiar economic themes are reinvented in the lives of Southern Baptists, of Yankee mechanics, and of midwestern farmers.

In Riverside, people sacralize commerce by recasting it in ideologically acceptable terms when they draw a contrast between "Yankee resource-fulness" or the "native wit" of local mechanics on the one hand, and the greed of capitalists, lawyers, and businessmen on the other.[2] "Greed," in this account, is associated with those who "make deals" with outside money and thus create an unpredictable local economy. Yet (as with tithing and stewardship), the line between "greed" and "resourcefulness" or between "deals" and "shop-wise spirit of adventure" is blurred, defin-able only in the context of local understandings of what constitutes "self-interest" rather than a public good. The New York industrialist whose investment in the cutlery industry became a mainstay of Riverside's econ-omy in the nineteenth century is seen as a beneficent employer, concerned for the welfare of the mechanics in his employ and a visionary whose foresight is still imprinted on the social landscape of the town (in the form of single-family versus tenement-style housing for workers).

By contrast, the Riverside banker who subsidized the move of a key in-dustry in 1860 to develop a mill on the site of a waterfall 3 miles to the east of the town is condemned today as "the one man who got more money out of *agua pura* than Moses did when he hit the trail and then the rock" (Jen-kins, 1982:129–30). Similarly, the "resourcefulness" of (northern Euro-pean) immigrant mechanics who founded the tap and die industry in small local shops following this move is praised in a recent history of Riverside as "wit" and "enterprise." The transformation of these shops into a large, multinational corporation with branches in present-day Riverside has not altered the symbolism of tap and die as a trope for "local," "small," and the family firm.

The crafts shops, alternative bookstores, video arcades, and other small businesses that have transformed the appearance of downtown Riverside in the past ten years are used to suggest the downfall of the town and its takeover by alien life-styles. "This is not Coney Island. This is not Hamp-ton Beach," the chairwoman of the Board of Selectmen stated in a recent interview, commenting on the potential licensing of a new arcade and an amusement center in the town. The imagery used to characterize these ventures (greed, gambling, and teenagers hanging out, versus family togetherness and money earned through hard work) is linked to commentary on "the other half of America," on "people like that," or on "the ghetto moving in." In this local paradigm of development, greed and urban decay become a metaphorical backdrop against which the significance of "native" projects by "resourceful" entrepreneurs is judged.

Just as local people characterize material success by Baptists as a moment for the actualization of spiritual potential (an opportunity for spiritual maturity, rather than spiritual damnation), so do they characterize business ventures as the actualization of "Yankee resourcefulness" (rather than self-interest as greed) for New England capitalists. Both spiritual maturity and Yankee resourcefulness suggest the independence of spirit that is a familiar part of the American myth of success, allowing progress (spiritual, technological) without greed, and making it possible to be "in the world" without falling prey to the temptations that destroy communal endeavors in favor of individual ones.

Today, the same communal ideal is held up in Riverside when neighbors and townspeople come to blows, literally and figuratively, over issues of economic development. The good neighbor, like the spiritually mature Baptist, is celebrated for his restraint, his willingness to curtail self-interest (for example, testing noisy motorcycles on the track behind his shop) in favor of a "way of life" in which other forms of noise (threshers operating at night) are deemed an economic essential rather than a social nuisance. Tales of good neighbors neutralize claims of individual rights (which are interpreted as private greed) in favor of the entitlements of established farmers or businesses. These entitlements are encoded, along with the economy that supports them, in the language of a customary "way of life." In this way, law is constructed in the vocabulary of community, and particular forms of self-interest are valorized over against others, which are cast as embodiments of greed.

In Sander County, similar themes emerge in tales of Cosmo, a large industrial plant owned by a well-known multinational corporation, as an example of outside capital moving in, as a foreign element that is "here today and gone tomorrow," transforming local society socially and economically, and undermining communal traditions of exchange and mutual support. Cosmo, like certain forms of industrial venture in Riverside, provides a context within which Sander County's identity as a small-scale, face-to-face, agricultural community is sketched. Specifically, it has become a paradigm for the arrival of "strange" versus "familiar" foreigners in Sander County.

Familiar foreigners — earlier immigrants from northern Europe — were the grandparents of today's "insiders" and symbolize the values of rugged self-reliance that were so important to many of the local elite. Even the small group of refugees from Southeast Asia were, when they first arrived, perceived as "patriotic soldiers" against Communism, and were linked in local narrative to traditional values of selfless sacrifice, courage, and hard work. Strangers, by contrast, are "here today and gone tomorrow," are "looking for the easy buck," and are guided by self-interest, rather than by an ethic of service shaped by family and community ties. Such strangers were associated primarily with Cosmo, which was brought relatively recently to Sander County by a faceless "outside" corporation rather than by local entrepreneurs.

Cosmo, as we have seen, was believed to have attracted racial and ethnic outsiders, union members, and other newcomers. These groups were lumped together and stereotyped collectively as grasping and intrusive, and their behavior and values were thought to bear no relation to those of the "familiar foreigners," Northern European parents and grandparents, who were part of the local heritage. The inclusion of industries such as Cosmo, immigrants from Southeast Asia, and migrant workers from Mexico within a single account of community juxtaposes greed and selflessness. "The strange" is subtly interwoven with the familiar, shaping a local tale of community from familiar themes of connection and separation. "The strange" is increasingly at the center of political life in Sander County, as key political and administrative positions are occupied by newcomers employed in externally based businesses.

THE DOMESTICATION OF LAW

Hopewell

Just as the different meanings of money signal the inherent ambiguities of a concept of the local conceived as separate from yet in complex relationship to an "outside" economy or state, so too do the different meanings of law encode the complex relationship between the local and the outside world. Among Hopewell's Baptists, law is excluded from an epistemology that defines rules as irrelevant to salvation. At the same time, law is "let in" to Baptist ideology through a back door, in that crime as defined by state courts is accepted as evidence of being "unsaved." Thus, law is constitutive of Baptist identity in subtle ways, even as its effects are neutralized by its subordination to Jesus.

For economically affluent non-Baptists in Hopewell (a group that symbolizes the secular world of the unsaved against which Baptist identity is cast), the world (as state, as law) also serves as a negative marker of identity. This group includes the judge and the clerk at the county court (established residents of Hopewell's non-Baptist elite) whose position at the court is inextricable from their social identity in the town. Yet, even for these men (who *are*, in effect, the law), "court" and "law" are signifiers of disorder, indicators of disintegration, and a standard against which disintegration is measured. In their view, people who appear at the court are "isolated individuals or nuclear families living without social resources and without trust." Isolated individuals who are "thrown together" need courts and law, but people like themselves who are embedded in ties of kinship and neighborhood and who have connections to place through time do not. "People with good neighbors don't need courts."

In Hopewell, as in other American towns, the courthouse is a complex and contradictory symbol for both "the high" and "the low" in local political, social, and economic hierarchies. The elites' definitions of order and disorder shape powerful rhetorics and practices. Still, their definitions may be and are contested, as shown in Chapter 4. Those contests, however, are themselves sometimes transformed through the "inherent dominative mode" (R. Williams, 1973) into spectacles that occasion a form of reverse "witnessing." Such spectacles (e.g., the courtroom dramas described in Part I) become opportunities for renewed stereotyping and rejection of "outsiders" and renewed refusals of their way of life or what is presumed to be their way of life. In Hopewell, police, court staff, and regular spectators "rolled their eyes in mock despair, laughing silently" at the lack of self-control and endless family troubles of those who sought assistance from the court in ordering their lives.

In Riverside and in Sander County, the court plays a particularly powerful role. Like the fair or the marketplace in seventeenth- and eighteenth-century European towns, the court in Sander County and in Riverside is "the epitome of local identity (often indeed it is what defined a place as more significant than surrounding communities)" (Stalleybrass and

White, 1986:27). At the same time, the court represents "the unsettling of that identity by the trade and traffic of goods from elsewhere" (ibid.). Just as for Baptists a complex relation to the market is central to the construction of an identity defined as separate from the market, so for citizens in Riverside and Sander County a complex relation to law allows the construction of an identity defined by absence of "litigiousness." Litigation is condemned as "self-interest" when it is framed in the discourse of rights by outsiders who are excluded from the local economy, but litigation is "sacralized" in the discourse of principle and morality when it supports existing market relations.

Riverside and Sander County

The understanding of law as moral rules is fundamental to traditional concepts of social order in New England and in areas of the Midwest of which Sander County is representative. (People from Hopewell might well agree with the equation of law and moral rules, although many Baptists drew a distinction between rules promulgated "by men" and the preferable social order based on the active understanding and acceptance of "the Lord's will.") From the earliest days of the Puritan colonies, religion, "the primary basis of private and public morality" (Haskins, 1960:85), was translated into action through political and legal institutions. In the belief that government existed to regulate man's corruption, the colonists set up an elaborate system of courts (the general court, the court of assistants, county courts, commissioners' courts, strangers' courts, justices of the peace), and the magistrates who meted out justice in these institutions were considered "the essence of lawfully and divinely constituted authority" (Haskins, 1960:44). Indeed Black (1980:241) argues that in seventeenth-century New England "there was no room for a communal ideal so constituted as not to include [the magistrates] and the justice they administered." Just as the courts enforced morality, so too did churches enforce the law. The covenant through which members constituted themselves as a church transformed them into a community of "visible saints," and these communities engaged in "holy watching" as well as in various forms of discipline to punish offenses that were simultaneously deemed immoral and illegal (a meaningless distinction at that time). Church and court supervised family life, business relationships, and other areas of personal conduct.

The close connection between communal and legal institutions and orders began to loosen fairly early, as magistrates were criticized and their powers curtailed. By the mid-eighteenth century the legal and governance roles of courts in New England were officially separated, and suspicion of law as a tool that could be used for the manipulation (and potential destruction) of community is a familiar theme in eighteenth-century documents. Lawyers came to be associated with business interests, with the promotion of litigiousness, and were said to "amass more wealth without labor than the most opulent farmer" (Crèvecoeur, 1926 [1782]:140). In Riverside, it was an alliance of lawyers and businessmen that shaped the town's economy during the nineteenth century, as agricultural land was gradually taken over for development in what was described by more conservative members of the town as "schemes developed in secret by lawyer-promoters and sustained by public land grants and tax revenue" (Jenkins, 1982:95). Although the significance of these "schemes" to the town's economy was acknowledged, legal activity was popularly associated with private greed and seen as potentially (and in practice) directed against collective interests. (The relocation of Riverside's major employer to Milltown in 1860 was staged by lawyers and bankers. The crisis that ensued was portrayed in the local press as inspired by private greed and as threatening the town's survival). In the 1930s and 1940s unionization was interpreted as destroying the "family" ties of owners and workers, and a strike of workers in the town's major industry in 1983 was described in the local paper as "tearing apart" the relationship of workers and management. In all of these situations, legal action was interpreted as coming from "outside" the community and as threatening established patterns of order. Concern about the separation of private ends from collective needs (and the legitimation of these in legal terms) is echoed today in the lament of the court clerk in Riverside (in 1981) that there are "all these people walking around with all these rights" but lacking what he calls "moral sense."

Even as litigiousness came to be separated from moral sense, and the place for litigiousness was located outside the community of meaning shared by established residents in places such as Riverside, Sander County, and Hopewell, law was preserved at the center of this community as the order represented by the courthouse. In Riverside, where today "litigiousness" refers both to "all these people wandering around with all these rights" and to the improper use of the court for "garbage" or nuisance complaints brought by people who lack self-control, "clerk's" or "show cause" hearings were officially separated from other criminal hearings in 1978 as the appropriate place for "interpersonal" matters. These hearings typically involve private parties as complainants and are predominantly complaints of assault, of threats, or of disturbing the peace. By contrast, the court proper is reserved for "serious cases," in which the police are complainants. Police become watchdogs for serious crime, in which the court becomes a monitor of community order, and court clerks act as watchdogs for interpersonal morality in private hearings that protect the law. Indeed, clerk's hearings are defined (at the Riverside courthouse) as taking place "out of court." The assistant clerk uses a religious metaphor in describing his approach to the hearings, in which he delivers "little sermons" rather than judgments. His sermons underscore the responsibilities of parents, the "way of life" of neighborhoods, and the shared consequences of action but rarely involve the formal issuance of a criminal complaint.

Clerks' hearings domesticate the unruly litigiousness of the people "with all these rights" who can't take responsibility for their actions and can't "put their hands in their pockets and walk away" from conflict. They transform litigation into an occasion for delivering sermons (that is, for witnessing) about traditional values to people who "don't belong." They valorize the watchfulness of the court clerk while implying that watchfulness by complaining neighbors is a nuisance created by people who lack self-restraint and must use the court to control their own lives. At the same time, the hearings encourage neighborly watchfulness, because they provide a space within the law in which response can be made and in which watchfulness can be transformed into legitimate vigilance by court officials.

In Sander County, the negative emphasis on litigiousness underscores greed ("looking for the easy buck") rather than garbage, but the distinction between appropriate use of law for the maintenance of public order and inappropriate or frivolous litigation for private ends is similar to that in Riverside. In an area that is still predominantly agricultural but where mechanization is rapidly transforming the pattern of relationships typical of farming communities in the past, "the law" is seen by established farmers and local businessmen as encoding core values about promises and obligation that were fundamental to the traditional way of life in the county. Today, these values and the law that encodes them symbolize the continuity of this way of life for established residents. The notion that "It's a law, it should be acted upon," is a way of affirming traditional values, which should also, in the view of local elites, be "acted upon." When they are not, "we should go out and arrest the man" (Engel, 1984:576).

Established county residents approve of efforts by the police to "try and enforce the laws that protect life and property" and support attempts by the schools "to teach students to obey the laws, all of them" (Engel, 1987:628); but they reject what are defined as uses of the law that undermine traditional patterns of respect and authority. In Sander County, as in Riverside, litigation affirming individual rights at the expense of established hierarchies of relationship is defined as "litigiousness" and is equated with selfishness and greed. Thus, in a lawsuit brought against the local school district by a woman whose son had been expelled from high school for smoking on school grounds, there was widespread condemnation of the plaintiff's argument that her son's rights had been violated. One letter to the local newspaper compared proper school discipline to "building a better nation" and implied that rights litigation undermined morality and order. The plaintiff's claim for damages was dismissed in the Sander County Court. Established residents were similarly opposed to a suit brought by a Mexican immigrant and his family against a tavernkeeper for injuries he had suffered as a bystander in a barroom fight. The plaintiffs sued to recover income that was lost by the man as a result of the injury. This suit was settled by the parties, but the more established defendant interpreted the plaintiffs' action as manipulation of the law by people who "are not too dumb," because they "know how to come here without papers and get a job or go on welfare" (Engel, 1984:569). Here again, litigation was interpreted as undermining collective values embodied in the law by "greedy" and "sue-happy" complainants who were "looking for the easy buck" and could turn law against the community to achieve this.

The invocation of materialism draws a line between Hopewell Baptists' sense of themselves and their image of those who are determinedly the "unsaved," and the invocation of greed, of "garbage" cases, and of litigiousness delimits the community of "insiders" in Riverside and in Sander County from "strangers." "Strangers" include Mexican and Hmong immigrants, Puerto Ricans, African-Americans, and more generally any newcomers whose ethnicity or class marks them as "different" and whose reliance on the state to secure food, housing, medical care, and other basic needs marks them as "dependent" (and thus as lacking in the fundamental attributes of mature personhood.) In Sander County, these strangers are described as people "who would rather collect unemployment than work, so that they can 'lay around, go fishing, and set in a tavern and everything all day' " or who " 'would raise babies illegitimately, because they get $13 to $17 a month more on their ADC check' " (Engel, 1987:623).

The stigma of dependence on the state is juxtaposed to the spirit of hard work and self-reliance that forms the core of local myth celebrating self-sufficiency in an agricultural community. Tales of Hmong and Latino dependence explain their nature as lazy, and tales of self-reliance by local businessmen explain their nature as tough. One businessman who lost thousands of dollars in a snowstorm that destroyed his lumber storage shed described how he "thought the whole world had come to an end" but then realized that "the same thing happened to other people. They could feel the same as I. So get off of it, don't feel sorry for yourself, get out there and go to work. . . . If you die in your tracks at least you know that you have tried. So I'm still trying, and I'm putting in eighteen hours a day. But I'll make her because I've got the guts and the willpower" (Engel, 1987:633). This narrative affirms a concept of mature personhood, in which autonomy and independence (even in the face of great need) are central characteristics.

Particularly offensive (from the perspective of the social and economic elite of the county) is the appropriation of law by "outsiders" in a way that undermines this notion of self-sufficiency. Personal injury litigation, because it uses the legal system to gain compensation from others, works against the concept that people should strive to be autonomous and able to survive by "getting out there and going to work." This attitude confirms notions of particular litigants as greedy and of the law as undermining traditional values of self-sufficiency.

By contrast, litigation to recover unpaid debts for sales, services, and loans was interpreted by established residents as a matter of collective values, rather than self-interest. Because contract breaches were "morally offensive" (Engel, 1984:577), it was appropriate to enforce them in court. A small businessman who sued to collect in the county court explained that "it wasn't the money, because it would cost me more to collect it than it'd be worth, but because of the principle of it that I would definitely go to whatever means necessary, moneywise or whatever, to get it collected" (Engel, 1984:577).

By defining debt collection through the courts as moral action, litigiousness was domesticated in Sander County. Similarly, wealth was sacralized in Hopewell by interpreting capital accumulation as an opportunity for tithing and stewardship. Through such processes of domestication, the meanings of law and money are refashioned around particular forms of moral and religious action that are connected to the ways of life of specific social groups. These are considered "legal" in a positive sense and are valorized as legitimate ways of acquiring material wealth. Domestication is thus crucial to understanding how law use and wealth can be signs of both social success and failure.

In Riverside, law was also constructed through the association of particular forms of court action with particular understandings of morality and of personhood. Specifically, Hispanic and white ethnic litigants from nearby Milltown who appeared at the courthouse with complaints of assault or of threats were described as "brainless," as people from "unstable" families who lacked fundamental capacities of self-mastery and "needed" the court to supply this. Repeated complaints by the same parties simply confirmed the perception of Riverside's middle class that fighting was a "way of life" for these people and that it was part of their "psychology." When these fights appeared at the courthouse, they were described in the language of nuisance, as "lovers' quarrels," "family disturbances," or "kidstuff," rather than in the language of crime. Parties to the complaints were positioned as "brainless" through their excessive use of the law and were further marginalized at the courthouse by their exclusion from "real" legal arenas on grounds that their problems were "trivial" (read, everyday quarrels that rational people could solve without going to the law).

In Riverside fighting as a "way of life" was measured against the ideal of the self-restrained citizen who could "walk away from conflict." Restraint was associated with proper parenting and with a life-style in which industry did not spill over into greed and people went "where they belonged" and stayed "in their place." The antithesis of restraint was neighboring Milltown, where the absence of clearly defined boundaries between one family and another ("they are in each other's homes, they know what's going on," in the words of one social worker familiar with the area) and the intermingling of racial and ethnic groups in the "downstreet" area of the town were interpreted as undesirable forms of connection, as a lack of autonomy, and as "chaos."

Court use by Milltown litigants was denounced as garbage but la-

mented as necessary for social control. Criminal complaints were reinterpreted as restraint, however, as an effort to "solve little problems before
they get to be big ones," when more socially embedded parties appeared at
the courthouse. Thus, a series of cases that was widely commented on in
Riverside, both in popular conversation and in the newsmedia, involved
two middle-class parties who appeared numerous times in front of the
clerk and in hearings at the criminal and superior court levels. In this series
of cases each of the parties made use of the law (and of other official
forums in town, such as the planning board) to fight a neighborhood
battle about values and life-style that was related in turn to social and
economic tensions surrounding the place of "alternative" industries in the
town. Most of the appearances in court dealt with a tree that was growing
in a right-of-way separating the parties' land, but it was clear to everyone
that the case was not "about a tree" but about efforts to find "a legal way"
to get rid of the other side in the dispute. Unlike cases from Milltown, in
which complaints of "assaults" and "threats" were also used to "get rid of
someone" but were termed "brainless," in the case of the expanding tree
judges at all levels of the court commended the parties for coming to the
law. Indeed, in mobilizing "the law" in this series of cases, the parties (and
particularly one of the families in the case) in practice mobilized a network
of familiar relationships: the cop "who used to bust me when I was a
teenager" and who was now the court clerk; a friend who was the court
librarian and helped them research their case; and a judge whom they
knew socially. Although this network did not help the family to "win" the
neighborhood battle, it did transform the meaning of litigation from
brainlessness to virtue. It also transformed the court from an arena where
chaos was played out in a morality play with "the other half of America"
as central players to a forum in which town politics could be reframed in
the technical language of injunction and restraint. In either case (as morality play or as familiar relationships) the centrality of state legal institutions
to the management of local affairs was reaffirmed.

The ambiguous placement of the law as emblematic of core values and
simultaneously as signifier of difference in both Riverside and Sander
County makes the courthouse a particularly powerful site of struggle for
those who would transform community. It is equally crucial for those who
seek to maintain particular relations of power and the systems of knowledge through which these relations are explained and justified. Critics in
Riverside and in Sander County note the laxity of courts, which are seen as

severely restricted in their capacity to maintain order because of due process requirements. A Sander County resident argued that "the court system stinks . . . I think the court has really caused a lot of problems, and it's caused problems, I think, in all areas and even in the small communities. . . . Now everybody sues. There's a lot of suits through the courts once you get there. . . . A cop don't dare lay a finger on somebody because they've done something wrong" (Engel, 1987:631). In Riverside, the court is referred to as "a wet noodle," although even complainants who use it to protest established hierarchies perceive their treatment as unjust (see the Bad Neighborhood case, Chapter 2). At the same time efforts to shift control of the court away from the localities in which it has been a central institution since the earliest days of the colonial period generate a heated response in towns such as Riverside. The 1978 Massachusetts Court Reorganization Act, which placed administrative and budgetary control of local courts in a centralized office under a chief administrative justice, led to calls for a sit-in at the courthouse and claims in the local newspaper of "rape" by the Commonwealth. At issue in this struggle, as in more local ones, was the capacity to claim the courthouse as an emblem of local values or of "outside" interests — a "symbol of county government" (in the words of county officials in Riverside) or a signifier of state power at the very center of community life.

What is important, of course, is not whether the court is "state" or "local" but the fact that it is both. The struggle between these contrasting representations also links them, embedding the state ever more deeply in local institutions and practices.

CHAPTER SIX

History and Place

It is this backward motion toward the source, against the stream,
that most we see ourselves in . . .

ROBERT FROST, "West-running Brook"

In this chapter we explore concepts of history and place in our three
locales and suggest that these concepts play a crucial role in local contests
over the nature of community and the indices of belonging. Here we
continue to develop the paradox of community, focusing particularly on
the ways in which the very notions of time and space are drawn into local
sociologies.[1] In this chapter, we make primary and explicit what has been
more or less secondary and implicit throughout the volume, and that is the
ways in which "community" involves potent meanings of history and
place.

In all three towns, the systems of meaning we have been exploring are,
in a sense, communicated by certain conventional narratives of local
change. Yet, as the previous chapter showed, the concept of "the local" is
not only about geography for the people we are primarily concerned with
in this book but also about control. From this perspective the link between
"community" and "place" is similar to the link between "community" and
"history." Local constructions of the past heighten the contrast between
the former community and the transformations that brought it into contact with the national and transnational movements of capital and people

that are a feature of modern times. Particularly in relation to various idealizations of that past, the modern redemptive dimension of community is now in flux. In other words, local people are uncertain as to whether their communities continue to comprise the collective goods that they believe they once did. Their uncertainties take many forms. These are some of the issues involved in the public (and local) meanings of time and space in Hopewell, Riverside, and Sander County. Here, by asking directly what time and space mean to people, we reenter the paradox of community where history and place converge, in the pervasive local sense of the present as turning point.

First, we explore the temporal dimension of community. In all three towns, local invocations of community values stipulate a point in time when these values actually "worked," a sort of local golden age. But they also—and this is the second theme of this chapter—talk about their communities' journeys from the past to the present as successive departures from this golden age. Thus, "community" not only conceptually distinguishes the past from the present but also authentic members of the community (insiders, locals, and so on) from a host of "others" whose presence is perceived to be undermining in any number of ways. The local view that the charter of community was forged by history and that the critical transition from the past to the present has been the expansion of socioeconomic diversity (and its alienations) represent separate but related lines of analysis.

FOUNDATIONAL MYTHS AND THE
MEANING OF CONFLICT

People around the world express their concerns with the origins of their own societies in a variety of ways; American national narratives of origins focus on the first European encounters with "Indians," the Revolution and the Founding Fathers, or "the melting pot," and so on, depending on the context and period. In general, U.S. narratives of national origin build on the theme of "e pluribus unum," the creation of a single national society out of the "raw material" of myriad self-interests and personal origins. Such formulations are by no means universal. For example, the theater state of nineteenth-century Bali offered the inverse story: From a unified society founded in a mythic conquest, diversity was said by the Balinese to expand at an accelerating rate (Geertz, 1980). In New Guinea, the Kaluli conceptualize their social history as a tree: unified long ago (at the trunk) but now divided into many branches (Schieffelin, 1976). The general point is that such narratives can be read as myths, that is, carefully sculpted systems of explanation that provide codes of interpretation in the present. The local conceptions of community that we have been exploring are mythic in this sense.

All myths are multidimensional. They draw intensely complex systems of connections among ideas. In this respect, myths cannot be said to be "about" any one thing, because they are about many things and their interrelatedness. At the same time, it is worth noting that origin myths differ in their interpretation of conflict as normal or not. A myth that situates the forces of disunity in the present establishes a link (even a corollary) between conflict and society. A myth that defines disunity in the past, on the other hand, legitimates the claim that a society can exist without conflict; in that context, conflict is either regressive or pathological.[2] The conventional U.S. national myths of origin, as well as the community myths we are about to explore, are of this latter sort. American myths of origin emphasize the convergence of separate peoples in the American space; their *becoming* a nation is mythically the same as their *being* a nation.[3] We encountered local versions of this myth in Sander County, Riverside, and Hopewell.

MYTHS OF COMMUNITY IN SANDER COUNTY, RIVERSIDE, AND HOPEWELL

In all three towns, people talk about how things used to be. In Sander County, the preference for the past focuses on old technologies and the social relations with which they were associated. In Riverside, the connection to the past is thought of as a link to a traditional moral community. In Hopewell, people express both elements, social technology and moral community; however, they do not regret the passing of the old way of life as such so much as they do the quality of social life. They lament a loss of common understandings, durable values, a certain predictability. Perhaps these different forms of nostalgia (if that is what they are) amount to the same thing.

In Sander County, the agrarian past is the context for representations of community. One man sketches the contours of his community myth with a few deft strokes: "[Our] roots are in agriculture. Now the agricultural roots are very close roots where people work together. They help each other. They do all the things that we admire about America" (Engel,

1987:612). These remarks are offered in the context of an observation that Sander County is no longer rural, as if explanations of community require a "digging" into the past. Engel (1987:615–16) recorded a conversation between two very elderly farmers that elaborates on this mythic code and its temporal structure:

> *Farmer A:* I can remember back years when I was younger. . . . We got together for everything. We had an old thresh machine, and the whole gang would come and thresh, you know, pitch bundles and do that. And heck, the Arnesons down there would either be up here or we'd be down there playing cards in the evenings. And all of a sudden, it seemed to disappear. . . . The combines [came] and you started doing your own work, where you didn't have to depend upon the neighbors to do something, and it seemed like everything kind of fell apart.
> *Farmer B:* I can remember the folks bringing the shocks or the bundles in from the field, putting them in a stack. Then when they got through with this big threshing run, we used to call it, they'd come to your farm and then you'd pitch it into the machine yourself. . . .
> *Farmer A:* I can remember, everyplace we'd go, the cook would try to outdo the other one. Sometimes you'd have three or four different kinds of cakes. And oh, my God, you'd eat so much you'd have a bellyache for the rest of the day. . . . [laughs] Very few people help each other [now]. You and I work back and forth a little. We get stuck. You see, he lost his wife and he had [three] young boys he was bringing up . . . and I had five kids, and mine were going to school, and we got so, well, heck, what could one guy do alone on units like that? So, well, we just go over there and work a while and come over here and work a while, the two of us. Like filling a silo. What could one of us done alone? We'd get no place.

In this testimony, the men present the ideal form of society (neighbor helping neighbor) as dependent on a scale of technology that made reciprocal exchanges of labor necessary. These forms of exchange remained desirable when "the combines came," but they were no longer necessary or efficient. But circling in and out of the memories of old farming technologies are also memories of domesticity and abundance, of the ritual feasts served up among neighbors at the end of a workday during which they had helped each other. The death of one man's wife, the death of an era, these merge in the narrative Engel recorded. The men's conversation links farming, family, and community together; significantly, the locus of these social meanings is in the past.

The implicit and explicit contrast to community in this sense is the modern town — specifically, new industry and its consequences. The individual quoted follows his comment on farming being "all the things that we admire about America" this way: "The industry roots basically are just the opposite. Here today and gone tomorrow. Lose a job or business, you get transferred maybe from one place to another. And I think the community [in Sander County] has changed that way. I think it's not as close a community as it used to be. On the other hand, I think our horizons get broadened in a way; I think we see some things that we didn't see before. We see how the other half lives" (Engel, 1987:612). Such representations of a rural communal past and an industrial present systematically understate the extent to which complex processes of change were long under way in Sander County.

In Riverside, the past community is not presented as a work community, as in Sander County, but as a moral community in which the courts played a role that was both powerful and symbolically significant: "The connection of local courts to local identity and their use as arenas where images of community are contested and forged have deep roots in colonial legal culture" (Yngvesson, 1989:1695). Town selectmen in the colonial period played a central role in the transformation of interpersonal complaints into moral issues; lay judges were equally important "in transforming private claims into a vision of moral order" (Yngvesson, 1989:1696). The centrality of court personnel in the social processes by which interpersonal conflicts are translated into moral terms continues today; in Riverside, conflict is "read" as an important sign of social status, such that the courthouse — and particularly the clerk's office — is the "arena" where people come together to "structure the political and moral contours of their families and neighborhoods" (Yngvesson, 1988:410). The moral vocabulary that surrounds legal activity at the clerk's office is a link with the past; *how* that link is forged and maintained is a subject for subsequent discussion.

In the contemporary towns Yngvesson studies, the myth of the moral community endures and is evident in local people's comments on the quality of public life today. For example, Yngvesson describes the local understanding of an extended legal case over a right of way as being "a case about protection from 'these kind of people,' about the erosion of the community by alien life-styles, and the dangers this posed to families who have 'lived in the same spot for almost seventy years'" (Yngvesson, 1988:431). In another set of cases from a town that neighboring locals consider to be a "bad neighborhood," court personnel "described the complainants as 'brainless,' as having 'no moral sense,' and as acting 'like children'" (Yngvesson, 1988:434).

Such derogatory references are not obviously references to the past; however, court staff and others in Riverside frequently express the view that conflict itself is a new, negative development in Riverside:

> Court staff share concerns expressed by others in Riverside and articulated on a daily basis in the county paper regarding the changing face of the town in the past decade or two as represented by loitering youth, runaway teen-age women, and more serious juvenile crime; vacant buildings left as the major employers moved to other regions; and neighborhoods where there is "nothing that pulls people together." An imagined community of people who "go where they belong," avoiding the need to confront different life ways, is perceived as being threatened by "scum" moving in from nearby cities. In the downtown area, transients and other "undesirable" roam the streets, a reminder of the proximity of nearby Milltown, whose "downstreet" neighborhood epitomizes the disintegration of community and defines chaos for the working-class residents of Riverside. (Yngvesson, 1988:413)

In this passage, the connections between community, conflict, and change are made both implicitly and explicitly — implicitly in the assumption that disputes arise from conflict of life-styles, and explicitly in the association of new life-styles with specific events in Riverside's recent past. As in Sander County, these events are primarily the social consequences of local economic activity. In Riverside, capital is moving out of town; in Sander County, the expanded industrialization draws on external sources of capital. Local people's sensitivity to the locus of control of the capital that funds their towns' "progress" suggests the extent to which progress is a highly qualified good, one whose status is very much bound up with the local critiques of law that are the subject of this volume.

In Hopewell, too, recent change provides the context within which references to community take on a temporal cast. As in Sander County, although on a somewhat more expanded scale and accelerated rate, Hopewell County has been the beneficiary of major regional expansion over the past thirty or more years. In the years since World War II, Hopewell has been drawn into the perimeter of the nearby city economically and socially. Not only does most of the local work force commute daily to the city, but the newcomers increasingly consider themselves to be "from" the city — they do not participate in Hopewell at all beyond shopping, renting, and paying taxes. Some of Hopewell's locals consider such newcomers to be isolated outsiders who in distressingly large numbers use Hopewell but do not fit in there. Others see the newcomers as potential sources of revitalization for Hopewell.

When people who remember the old Hopewell invoke the past, they tend to focus their "memories" around two periods: the period of full recovery and social revival after reconstruction (the late 1880s and 1890s) and the period just before World War II, in the 1930s. For adults interviewed in the 1970s, these were the periods of their own youth and that of their parents' or grandparents'. To the extent that Hopewell's present social landscape was defined in the past, it is in the earlier of these periods. Some locals might claim with some justification that the more formative period was in the 1840s, when Hopewell itself was new; however, too few modern families can "claim" that earlier time, because the original group of families who were the first white settlers in Hopewell was small.

When local people invoke community, then, they illustrate their references with images from the late nineteenth century and the early part of this century. In contrast to Sander County, where the focus is on an agrarian past, and Riverside, where the motif of the past is of pastoral commerce, Hopewell's historical images are urban. These urban images are interesting, because they explicitly link the present to specific points in the past. The favorite (if local reference is any guide) local historical images date from the period when most institutions of today's town were already in place — churches, courthouse, schools, and other large public and domestic structures; however, the actual buildings that housed these ancestral institutions are now gone. The Baptist Church burned and was rebuilt on new ground, the school was torn down, the courthouse has been largely replaced, and the "big houses" were, with one exception (a project of the local historical society), torn down to make room for new housing developments. Even the railway depot, once the vital node in a rail network that made Hopewell an important place in the past, now functions as a sort of ground-level attic for the Historical Society.

Thus, to invoke the community of Hopewell is to claim a visual memory of a vanished urban landscape. Such memories can be inherited in the form of narrative; indeed, relatively few of today's adults would have seen the actual sites in their former guises. Such legacies are highly prized. They can also be donated to others who have no personal connection to Hopewell's past. The modern town is thus a palimpsest for people whose visual memories qualify them to consider themselves to be "from" Hopewell or who have been bestowed with the social knowledge that substitutes for such memories.[4]

In all three towns, even when "community" is presented as a living and modern thing—a synonym for "place" or "town," for example, in ordinary conversation—we interpret it to be a reference to the mythic past. Specifically, during our respective field research "community" found its opposite in change or at least in the kind of change that all three towns had experienced since mid-century: a shift to sources of capital outside the local community, with consequent industrialization or deindustrialization. All three witnessed changes in the region and world that led to the arrival of new populations into "their" locales, although they prefer to think of themselves as homogeneous. The towns also experienced the transformation of the meanings of difference on the national scene, where cultural identity, partisanship, and politics have become difficult to distinguish in national political discourses. "Community" is a code word in all of these contexts (as well as others), referring indirectly to movements and trends whose origins, controls, and ultimate significance are perceived to be elsewhere.

As the foregoing comment suggests, "community" need not necessarily invoke the past, although it appears to be used in this way in the three towns involved in our work. It *might* represent local interests against others (in important respects it does this; see Chapter 5). It *might* define a future program aimed at increasing local participation and civic identity for a host of purposes bearing on social welfare and reform. It is against this array of hypothetical alternatives that the temporal referents, cast as varieties of nostalgia and critique, are so strikingly employed in Sander County, Riverside, and Hopewell.

THE PRESENT IN THE PAST

The question that emerges directly from the foregoing discussion is: Why do "insiders" in the three towns cast their definitions of community in terms of local social history and personal memory? A second question follows: To the extent that "community" involves both positive and negative assessments of processes of change, what is the content of its affirmations and critique? Neither question can be settled with any finality; either can only return us to the problems of order and diversity with which we began. In the abstract, these questions pertain to all three towns, although the towns involve somewhat different problems of change and, hence, somewhat different temporal codes and charters. We begin with Sander County.

Time and Change in Sander County

Social changes in Sander County were perceived quite differently by various members of the community, and these different perceptions were related to the ways in which people and groups oriented themselves to the past.[5] Residents invoked both iterative and linear models of time when they attempted to define their community and explain the recent changes it had undergone.[6] Both iterative and linear time are to some extent available in any context, but in Sander County the two models represent conflicting interpretations, logics, and visions of social reality. Emphasis on the iterative view in Sander County tends to stress the relationship between social change and sociocultural disintegration as a failure of basic values to reemerge in traditional patterns. Emphasis on the linear model in Sander County tends to stress a positive view of change, relating change to the actualization of basic values in social life.

Such conflict proved significant in Sander County during the late 1970s. In the struggle between contending social factions, iterative representations of time were associated with traditional groups, and linear representations with those who advocated social and economic change. Conflicting conceptions of time were therefore closely related to the social conflicts that marked Sander County's recent history; indeed, models of time became conflict discourses in themselves. The relationship between time consciousness and social conflict was dialectical. That is, different perceptions of time helped to determine who came into conflict with whom, but the intensification of conflict also transformed the imagery of time and caused residents to invoke it with greater passion.

In Sander County, the relationship between time concepts and conflicting social visions was further complicated by the subjectivity of historical memory. The nature and extent of social change in this community was subtle and complex. Some changes that were often cited by residents in the most dramatic terms turned out to have had historical antecedents that were ignored or suppressed in the local folklore. There was a selectivity and (to an outsider) a distortion in local accounts of change that were best understood in terms of how time was conceptualized.

The event most Sander County residents considered a turning point for their community was the establishment in the mid-1960s of a large manufacturing plant by the Cosmo Corporation, a well-known multinational organization. The opening of this plant, which employed as many as 6,000 people, was viewed as a watershed in the county's transformation from a small-scale, face-to-face society based on agriculture and small business to a more anonymous, impersonal community with a highly mobile and ethnically diverse population. It was this event that people had in mind when they described recent changes:

> We're in very much of a changing community, yet our roots are in agriculture. Now the agricultural roots are very close roots where people work together. They help each other. They do all the things that we admire about America. The industry roots basically are just the opposite. Here today and gone tomorrow. Lose a job or business, you get transferred maybe from one place to another. And I think the community has changed that way. I think it's not as close a community as it used to be. On the other hand, I think our horizons get broadened in a way; I think we see some things that we didn't see before. We see how the other half lives.

Such characterizations of the changes wrought by Cosmo, although very common, turned out to be problematic. First, the opening of the plant was not unprecedented in Sander County: For many years, the Agro Corporation had been operating a large canning factory in the county and employed many residents as tenant farmers and factory workers. Other industrial plants had also existed there from time to time. Thus, Cosmo was by no means the first corporate employer in the community, and even residents who had been farmers often knew what it was to be an employee in a large industrial operation:

> It used to be called Sander Canning Company, and then later on Agro bought it, and now I think Amalgamated owns it. They've been here for years and years, as long as I can remember. When I was like 4 and 5 years old, my folks picked corn with wagons and mules. And I can remember, they made a wooden box, and they took me with them, and I rode along in that wooden box, up at the front of the wagon. . . . [My father] got rheumatism just terribly, and of course our family all blamed it on picking corn. And you have to realize when they picked this corn, it was early in the morning, and it was wet. You know how wet grass is, and they didn't provide, the canning factory never provided them with rubber, nowadays they'd probably be forced to provide them with those rubber trousers that at least come up to the waist. And you would be just soaking wet and you'd be wet all day. And he had rheumatism until the day he died, just terrible. And when we left the farm, he was so bad that he was in bed for like two years. And have you heard about this gold injections they give now sometimes for arthritics and rheumatics? Well, he had all, they have so much that the doctors felt was safe to give you, and he had all that you could take. And he did finally get so he could get up and walk, but his legs were very deformed, and his one knee was stiff. But he did get well enough to take a job in this [screw] factory as a, not really a janitor, but he washed screws in this oily mixture and then they drained them and put them in wooden boxes.

Agro had also accounted for a certain degree of mobility and ethnic diversity before Cosmo arrived. Latino workers had long been associated with Agro's operations, typically as migrant laborers but in some cases as permanent residents of Sander County. Thus, the demographic changes that were usually ascribed to Cosmo's presence had actually been under way for many years, although perhaps at a much slower pace.

Another rather different event in Sander County's recent history may have transformed its socioeconomic life far more profoundly than the arrival of Cosmo. In the late 1950s, nearly a decade before the opening of the Cosmo plant, a large expressway was built linking Sander County to several major urban centers, including Chicago. The expressway, in the words of one local observer, "created a lot of problems, because it split up some of the farmers' area, and that generated a lot of animosity among the rural type. . . . I think that really started the whole thing, and then as industry started to move in, that just increased the animosity among the rural people." In addition to splitting local farmland and generating conflict between farmers and townspeople, the expressway provided easy access to urban centers for a community that had been relatively isolated and self-contained. The impact was thus cultural as well as economic. Yet, the construction of the expressway was seldom cited as the pivotal event for the community. That honor was reserved for the arrival of Cosmo.

Finally, there were some indications that Cosmo's impact had been much less dramatic than had been anticipated and far more subtle and indirect than was subsequently believed. Many of its employees commuted on the expressway from other cities and thus had little contact with residents of Sander County, despite the common perception that Cosmo had brought a major influx of newcomers. Although the plant employed African Americans as part of its affirmative action program, almost none settled in the county, whose population remained white with a small (but growing) Latino minority. The anticipated economic "ripple effects" on local businesses and the relocation of other businesses into Sander County in connection with Cosmo were, in the view of at least one city planner, almost imperceptible: "And so we might not be ready to conclude that nothing happened there, but I think not as much as it was anticipated in terms of a business boost. . . . [And] the increase in housing demand or the increase in subdivisions and sites didn't really come about after Cosmo announced their location here."

If the tangible effects of the opening of Cosmo's new plant were relatively modest, why did Cosmo's arrival carry such significance and, more than any other recent event, come to mark the boundary between "then" and "now" for most people in the community? Perhaps one reason was that Cosmo came to Sander County after an explicit debate about the community and its past and future, in which conflicting ideas about time and change were openly expressed. On the one hand, a faction invoking linear and progressive imagery argued that the community was stagnating socially and economically. This alliance of future-oriented businesspeople and political liberals maintained that the failure to bring in Cosmo would mire the community in "sameness," which to some implied a failure of vision and will and hence a cultural deterioration. On the other hand, another faction, drawing on iterative imagery, argued that change implied the erosion and loss of their traditional culture and values and that if Cosmo were brought in, the community would never again be the same. This group of farmers, "antidevelopment" businesspeople, and other conservatives feared that old patterns of interdependence and local autonomy would be lost.

In the debate over Cosmo, the linear, progressive vision prevailed. Although the consequences of Cosmo's arrival may ultimately have been far less dramatic than anticipated, it was perhaps the debate itself that made the plant such a potent symbol of change. Changes were occurring in Sander County even as the debate took place. In part, they were attributable to causes just as significant as Cosmo, such as the expressway and the long-term impact of Agro and other local industries. In part, too, they were attributable to more diffuse factors, such as nationwide transformations in farming and retailing. Fundamental social changes might well have occurred in Sander County even if the Cosmo plant had never opened. Yet, the plant came to symbolize the social and economic transformation of the community not only because of its size and conspicuousness but also because discussions preceding its arrival had led to a direct, public confrontation between two contradictory ways of "reading" time and social change. These two perspectives and the event that precipitated their articulation were to dominate local perceptions for years to come.

History and Change in Hopewell

In Hopewell, as in Sander County, overt conflict played a crucial role in defining certain events as pivotal in the formation of "the community."[7] The situation in Hopewell differs from that of Sander County in at least two respects. First, the crucial events that "made" the present took place at intervals over the period of nearly a century in Hopewell's case. Second, in Hopewell, the local response to conflict ultimately redefined these events as nonevents, that is, as generic human situations rather than specific local developments.

One result of this transformation is that local history is effectively detemporalized in favor of larger local notions of community. In other words, "history" becomes a collection of stories about human situations, rather than a chronology of stories whose temporal sequence matters. This transformation — the detemporalization of history — is itself significant, because it implies that the embrace of community and the world of events are more or less mutually exclusive from the local point of view.

Indeed, people in Sander County, Riverside, and Hopewell talk about the past as if their community were the source of its own times, the source of the events that became its stories. Now, the community is prey to time, the object of events. The detemporalization of historical narrative — the conversion of chronology into a collection of near-fables — is a gesture of accommodation to the present. The present is tacitly acknowledged in the invocations of the "timeless" community, the narrative version of the imagined visual palimpsest within the modern landscape.

Hopewell has always been diverse, although it is not clear at what point its diversity came to be locally associated with conflict. Certainly, Hopewell's past involved crucial contests: at the national level, between Cherokee and settlers, and at the local level, between populists and aristocrats. Indeed, the very founding of Hopewell County appears to have been a strategic move by populists to swell their ranks in the Georgia legislature in 1858. The area had been settled by whites since the 1820s, but Hopewell was incorporated as a town only when it became the new county's seat in 1858. The establishment of the county was proposed in the legislature by one J. T. Smithson (a pseudonym, as are all place names here), of neighboring Lynette County to the west. His bill passed by a comfortable margin, but the nay votes clustered together in the wide swath of aristocratic counties to the east. That group included Harold County, which forms Hopewell County's eastern border (Lynette County forms the western border).

In sculpting the boundaries of the new county out of territories formerly under Lynette's and Harold's jurisdictions, Smithson was careful to include several of his own political allies within Hopewell's territory and even successfully proposed an amendment to the legislation establishing the county to revise its boundaries to include several individuals with whom he had political association. The net result appears to have been in effect to double Lynette County's voting strength in the legislature by creating its clone in the new county.

At stake in these maneuvers were a number of issues that had already proved to be profoundly divisive locally, regionally, and nationally. The populists applauded Cherokee removal (indeed, the county was named for the Federal District Judge who stood with President Jackson against Chief Justice Marshall and against the Cherokee); the aristocrats lamented it. The populists took up the southern causes of antiabolitionism and states' rights; the aristocrats supported states' rights only.

Hopewell County itself was divided over these issues, though the populists were consistently the stronger faction in terms of dominance over the political institutions that ran the town and county. The Southern Baptists, who had migrated into the area that became Hopewell from the north and east, had ties of kinship and sentiment in Harold County; indeed, their history in Hopewell County is one of successive (and eventually successful) efforts to manage the costs of their anomalous political status in relation to the rest of Hopewell (see Greenhouse, 1986). In general, Hopewell's political history almost until the present day was one of constant push and pull between rival forces. The contest between populists and Democrats slackened only in the 1930s and 1940s, when the state's Populist Party had collapsed and the rural vote lost force in the face of rising suburbanization.

The local version of Hopewell's history reads very differently. The political origins of the county are entirely submerged (and forgotten) in another story, of a group of families arriving by wagon train from north Georgia and the western Carolina hills. They established farms and churches, witnessed Indian life, and founded the community that became Hopewell in the hope of securing a modest subsistence for their families. The weathered gray skeletons of their farmhouses remain to give testimony to the fact that these families were, for the most part, too poor to own slaves; modern locals interested in the past are careful to point out that Hopewell did not participate in the slave culture, at least not in any direct way.[8]

Churches and graveyards, a jail, and the old farms are considered historic landmarks of the antebellum period and are venerated as such. Most of what is now "old" in Hopewell dates from the period of recovery and capitalization in the 1880s: the courthouse facade, most of the downtown commercial district, and many residences within the borders of the town of Hopewell date from this period. In-between was devastation during the Civil War, as Hopewell was the site of major and decisive battle late in the war — a critical loss for the Confederacy, in fact.

Locals preserve a sense of duration and continuity in spite of the circumstances of radical wartime disruption and destruction, intense local political conflicts that preceded the war, and processes of recovery, agricultural collapse and second recovery in the century between the war and the modern town. Local historical narrative in conversation and in print accomplishes this for them by referring to "Hopewell" as if it were somehow an entity whose existence and essential character was long ago fixed, but whose context gives it a series of new guises—as if Hopewell were a person, perhaps, continually changing garb and household furnishings.

This essential reification transforms the character of events. Since the "community" is believed to exist apart from events, events themselves are effectively canceled as forces of fundamental change. Thus, events in local, southern, or national history provide a temporal grid against which the changing landscape can be presented: Its buildings rise and fall and rise again, its social life takes this form or that, its institutions were founded or not yet founded. At the same time, it is not events that explain Hopewell to itself but individuals, their mettle, and their enterprising efforts that are, instead, what one needs to "understand" the "community" in the local view of the town's social reality. Communities in this sense might be made *in* time, but they are not made *by* time; the iterative and the linear models of time are thus deftly interwoven.

In practice, the distinction between locals and newcomers captures the temporalities we discussed. Locals literally represent the past; newcomers by definition cannot. Indeed, it is in their *having* a past that locals are the "community." From the insiders' point of view, the "community" keeps alive the encoded past, valued because it has been encoded for its own sake. It is not just a question of knowing about the past. Local identity is vested as much in the etiquette of knowing how to talk about the past— *not* talking about certain aspects of the antebellum period, the war, and the more recent past, for example—as in knowing other things.

One indication of the importance of the temporal charter of Hopewell's "community" is in the extent to which newcomers seek to participate in it. Newcomers were most active in instituting a historical society in Hopewell, and their attempts to mobilize local support involved (initially, at least) tangles of controversy over priorities, financing, and other matters (the publication of a town history was a major project). The society, now energized and managed by those who consider themselves insiders, has been highly successful in restoring historically significant properties, managing a small museum and archive, publishing local history, and so on. The past is a scarce and exclusive resource: In theory, its list of participants brooks no additions, yet "insiders" readily acknowledge the generosity of newcomers who have mobilized and capitalized the collective local historical memory. Thus, the very value placed on the past by "insiders" provides the point of entry to external forces in the present.

Time and Change in Riverside

Like Sander County, Jefferson County (and Riverside, the county seat) also lays claim to an agricultural past.[9] Riverside was settled by second, third, and fourth sons of families in nearby Deerfield, where land pressures forced younger siblings out of the parent community. Its early history as a small and relatively homogeneous settlement of subsistence farmers (it was incorporated in 1753) was transformed within forty years into what a recent history of Riverside (commissioned by the town) represents as "a complex society of farmers, merchants, and mechanics" (Jenkins, 1982:46). Riverside's first two lawyers arrived in 1790 and are described as "colleagues of speculator-businessmen . . . writing their contracts and deeds and collecting debts due" (Jenkins, 1982:51).

Today, agriculture serves to ground the pastoral character of a town and a county that are portrayed in their official history as "full of contradictions" and in which "community" (even in the eighteenth century) is characterized as made of a "thin fabric" (Jenkins, 1982:39). Tensions between "gentlemen farmers" on the one hand and the "native wit" of skilled mechanics whose inventions shaped Riverside's economic growth on the other are key themes in this history. The gentlemen farmers (whose numbers had dwindled to insignificance in Riverside by the early nineteenth century) stand for "stagnation" or at best "quiet" and are perhaps evocative of the iterative view of time that emerges so prominently among traditionalists in Sander County. It is their image that comes to mind in contemporary descriptions by residents of Riverside that speak of its homogeneity, its distance from urban problems, or its identity as "the ideal place to live and raise a family" (Jefferson County Chamber of Commerce, 1982). Traces of the linear view are perhaps evident in the acclaim given to such local heroes as John Grant or the Wells brothers, sons of British immigrants whose "Yankee resourcefulness" led to the invention and refinement of a machine for cutting threads on bolts. This machine was a forerunner for the die, and it subsequently led to the development of the tap and die industry, for which Riverside is internationally known.

Like Hopewell, however, the past in Riverside is constructed within a frame in which iterative and linear views of time are interwoven. A key theme in the myth of "Riverside present" is that the pastoral and industrial dimensions of its past are both constitutive of the town: It is "peaceful" *and* progressive, it is a place where there are "the luxuries of . . . the metropolis, with scarcely none of its miseries" (Selectmen's Annual Report 1895, quoted in Jenkins, 1982:6). Unlike Hopewell, the tensions that produced Riverside are not effaced in local accounts but are seen as crucial ingredients of what is unique about a town in which the pastoral has been retained in spite of industrialization. Yet, this portrayal of the town, recognizing the salience of divergent interests, is nonetheless a highly selective one. Key points of tension, although acknowledged, become vehicles for depicting a place in which conflict produces "the good life." In this portrayal, the working class emerges in idealized form as the "resourceful, civic-minded citizen" (male), who through his own ambition and "native wit" constructs the good life. For example, the economic crisis that ensued in 1870 when local industrialists and bankers decided to move Riverside's principal industry and main employer 3 miles to the east, creating the new village of Milltown, is a central event that punctuates the story of how and why Riverside differs from other, less desirable, industrial towns. Milltown, depicted in contemporary accounts as a "desolate, barren waste," a "wilderness," was the vision of a man who "mixed law, real estate, and restrictions . . . in all sorts of deals" (Jenkins, 1982:129–30, citing the obituary of Wendell Davis in a Riverside newspaper, 1876). Born of what was then (and is now) represented as a lack of commitment to the home town of its founders, Milltown stands today as testimony to the dangers of private greed: tenement houses, drugs, a place where "fighting is a way of life," and where "the psychology of the people" condemns them to poverty and a hopeless future. Riverside, by contrast, is depicted as "quiet" and "clean" (Jenkins, 1982:5), a town where the "post–[Civil] war spirit of maverick, every-man-for-himself enterprise" (Jenkins, 1982:141) transformed the economy after the exodus of capital in 1870 and gave Riverside its place in history.

In this account, greed is attached to "deals," to lawyers and capitalists, and to industrial development elsewhere, but local investment and business are termed "Yankee resourcefulness" and a "shop-wise spirit of adventure" (Jenkins, 1982:185). Immigrant-mechanics who founded the tap and die industry become central to the myth of local self-sufficiency, whereas the suppliers of outside capital become beneficent employers, driven by concern for the town and those whose labor sustains it. Thus Henry Clapp, who retired to Riverside from New York in 1835, financed

Riverside's major industry, and was the town's single largest property owner by 1860, is praised today for his pursuit of a vision of Riverside as a "homogeneous community of well-spaced individual houses" (Jenkins, 1982:108). Class and structural conflict are eclipsed in this account in favor of tensions that are dissipated in a model of paternalistic care or in the exit of greedy industrialists.

But just as Clapp is idealized, blurring the class structure of Riverside, so is the presentation of the tap and die industry as a symbol of local autonomy and of community identity problematic. Owned since the 1920s by a multinational corporation, and its local base seriously jeopardized by strikes and plant closings in the 1970s and 1980s, Riverside Tap and Die is an increasingly fragile symbol of locality and of the importance of place, of shared geography, as a code for shared history. Indeed, a strike in the early 1980s brought into sudden focus the discrepant experiences of community by machinists, managers, town police, and the editorial staff of the local newspaper (Yngvesson, 1993:32–34).

These differences, always implicit, but represented as healthy, as part of the "progressive" spirit of the town, emerge over time at particular moments of crisis or in stories about "outsiders" who are more easily caricatured: "scum" from Springfield, "undesirables" hanging around local business establishments, and most of all, the threat represented by Milltown, which over a century after its founding continues to embody for Riverside's middle- and working-class citizens "the other half of America," ruled by irrational passions and lacking in the "common sense" that is attributed to the town fathers. It is in these imageries and their regular articulation in court, in the newsmedia, in meetings of the Board of Selectmen, and in everyday conversations that the vulnerability of locality in a translocal economy is given voice.

In Hopewell, time is frozen to constitute a timeless "community" that is embodied in a sense of place; in Sander County, "community" can be constituted only by time repeating itself, bringing an imagined past into the present; in Riverside, "community" repeats itself over time in a familiar process of reinterpretation in which the boundaries of the outside and the inside are continually renegotiated.

TIME, HISTORY, AND THE POLITICS OF LOCAL IDENTITY

Although the contours of change and the ways in which local people represent change to themselves and others differ in the three towns we studied, they are similar in the following respect. In each town, "community" is frequently and positively invoked as a reference to the social space in which local ways of life have meaning. Yet, in each case we question the spatial aspects of such references and see instead the extent to which spatial references tacitly symbolize temporal ones. In other words, locals talk about "community" as if it were simply a matter of being "from" someplace; however, the shared geography seems to stand in for a deeper and more important set of claims to a shared relationship over time. The temporality at issue here is quite problematic, because, as we have seen, people refer to the past in relation to the present in ways that are categorical rather than chronological. In any case, "time" does not end the matter either, as references to the past are structured by people's perceptions of contests in the present.

As the ethnographic discussion about Hopewell, Riverside, and Sander County demonstrates, local people define community contrastively, that is, against the predations of new technologies and new "groups" that make up the modern scene. Such contrasts are not merely symbolic. They are not just convenient semiotics in the ongoing narrative of everyday life (although they are also that). Rather, as we have already seen in the words of local people themselves, the salient contrasts are framed by conflicts that center on the locus and demographics of local control. In both Sander County and Hopewell, the loss of control of the towns' power elite (both political and economic) has shifted from insiders to outsiders, and this shift is likely to broaden and accelerate; at least, such was the local perception.

Such a definition of community — one locked in, or constituted in, both specific and general perceptions of conflict — involves a fundamental contradiction: To the extent that "community" is predefined as harmonious, conflict must be located outside of the community. Community, or at least the sense of community born in the contexts of change that we have sketched here, is culturally committed to locating the sources of conflict outside itself. To the extent that history is the history of the present moment, and, even more so, to the extent that history is the story of the transformation of controversy and dispute over time, history and community become mutually exclusive.[10] Any recognition of the salience of the temporal dimensions of community would, in effect, blur the very distinction that is so important to local people, the one that divides them from the newcomers and others who make the present so unlike the past they prefer to remember.

The romantic historical narratives popular in Sander County, Riverside, and Hopewell serve this distinction well; it is what they are in a sense designed to do. In the guise of valorizing the past, these stories, told in the present, also tacitly critique the modern alienating forms of social life in general and capitalism in particular. In different ways, they accomplish this critique by depicting a past in which diversity and money were not only fully domesticated but circulated freely in a community of mutual engagement and concern. In Sander County, narratives of the agrarian past reproduce key cultural icons: the good farmer, the good neighbor, the good wife. In the stories people like to tell (and that we have considered in this chapter), each of these figures — consummately skilled — freely donated his or her labor to others for the sake of a collectively flourishing community. In Riverside, the narratives of the pastoral community of the past provide a cherished template of Yankee character, Yankee resourcefulness. In Hopewell, narratives of the urban past dwell on the spontaneous and happy harmony of the town's founding agricultural and commercial entrepreneurs, a collective social life that modern locals place under the rubric of "southern" life.

Although their stories are different, Sander County, Riverside, and Hopewell tell one another's story to some extent. They share a certain moral and historical geography, that is, a sense of community defined as the reservoir of meaning that conserves the past and faces uncertain renewal — or even depletion. Each of the towns apotheosizes its founding pioneers; yet in each of them, locals have contempt for new settlers, newcomers. Each of the towns was once a center in its own right, agricultural or commercial; now they are virtual "nonplaces," ancillary to the metropolitan centers that outstripped them, who knows precisely when? Each town celebrates its original self-sufficiency, yet regrets the diversity and infusions of capital "from the outside" that now animate their growth. Each town has stories about the events that revealed the communities of the past, yet insiders in all three towns now narrate current events as if they conceal the community, even to itself.

We return to the notion of paradox. In each of these examples, the paradox is that the very forces that made the community in the past (in the local view of things) (geographic and social mobility, risking and redeeming capital, a commitment to "progress") are seen as destroying the community in the present. It is in this paradox that time and space merge, in the very notion of community, and borrow from each other's lexicon. To

[handwritten marginalia: paradox of community & the forces that forge it defined.]

emphasize paradox, however, is to miss how those paradoxes came and continue to come into being, that is, in contests, sometimes fiercely embattled ones, in the arenas of politics and the marketplace. These are placeless arenas, of course (see Agnew, 1986), merely geographized metaphors for particular instrumental social relationships and the transactions for whose sake those relationships are forged.

As we have seen in all three towns, local meanings of community envision an irreducible, indivisible entity that, at least in the past, has always been itself, though in different garb. We have already noted the extent to which these meanings of the past in their particular local detail offer well-focused critiques of modern social forms. Now we can go a step further to observe that the juxtaposition of the past and the present (for such narratives are both rhetorically and actually in the present) — nostalgia — masks the issue of how the present came into being. By stripping history of its chronology, for example, narratives of the present preclude the possibility of another kind of critique of the people whose alliances and partnerships (for the sake of progress? for the sake of survival?) made the modern towns. Whatever else they are, these are inevitably stories of winners and losers.

The historical narratives, translated into narratives of character, are ostensibly directed outward, as commentaries on newcomers, big business, and all the other forms of trouble that this volume reports. Yet, their subtext is inevitably directed inward. Indeed, in all three towns, former elites made alliances that subsequently made them inconsequential: They sold the properties that now support other buildings; they sold the banks that now belong to companies based in New York, Boston, and Chicago, and so on. Of course, the scenario is infinitely more complex. In Hopewell, for example, neighbors went hungry to keep each other's farms from the auctioneer's block during the Depression; forty years later, virtually no farms remained; it is all subdivisions, apartment complexes, and neon "miracle mile." Who are the winners and the losers?

It is the former elites who provide the core meanings and historical images of the modern "insiders." The children and grandchildren of those elites are not elites themselves in today's instrumental terms. They are in a sense bystanders; at least, this is how they sometimes describe themselves (or are described that way by the new elites). In this sense, some newcomers have become "insiders." That is the central irony in the narratives of community we have been discussing.

The republican democracy of the United States is based on property and towns, aggregate places that stand as the ready symbol of the civic relationship. The relevance of the symbol of place (civic space) is not only semiotic. It is, as Tocqueville knew, fundamental to whatever reality the concept of national identity has for Americans. Certainly, there are high stakes in it. The refrain of the narratives depicts the community as a locus of responsibility. Inevitably, the narratives' subtext is also a depiction of the institutions within which that responsibility was discharged: in courts, churches, on the ledger books of households, stores, farms, and banks, at the ballot box, and so on. Here, perhaps, is the point where the idioms of history and place converge: in the forms of social participation that constitute American democracy and capitalism.

In invoking their communities as moral bulwarks against the negative eventualities of the present and future, the local perspectives we have explored in this volume emphasize both the solidarity of civic life and the forms of contest and resistance that make that solidarity recognizable as an experience. In situating themselves in their communities, local people assiduously disentangle what they see as the positive and negative aspects of democracy and capitalism. Invoking the past is to them a way of insisting on the distinctions between community and interest, order and authority, harmony and compromise, and, as we have seen in this chapter, "them" and "us," "here" and "there," "then" and "now."

The past does not so much explain the present as it allows people in the present to keep two sets of norms in the foreground simultaneously: the ones that the world seems likely to live by, and the ones that they imagine to have governed their local worlds in some lost era. Thus, the relevance of the past as the "code" for place would appear to be in the access it provides to norms (both explicit and implicit) that answer the forces of the change. In this sense, the historical myths of Hopewell, Riverside, and Sander County make available a normative repertoire that is very much a part of the present, although how and where it is negotiated — or even what its bearing on particular interests might be — is unclear. Even so, the repertoire's responsiveness to specific vectors of local change is clear. The form and content of that response are matters for the next chapter.

Conclusion

The Paradox of Community

In realising the new fact of the city, we must be careful not to idealise the old and new facts of the country. For what is knowable is not only a function of objects — of what is there to be known. It is also a function of subjects, of observers — of what is desired and what needs to be known.

— RAYMOND WILLIAMS, *The Country and the City*

Powerful American myths have been built around the self-reliant, but righteous, individual whose social base is the life of the small farmer or independent craftsman and whose spirit is the idealized ethos of the township. . . . Myths often tell important truths about the tensions people experience and their hopes for resolving those tensions or somehow turning them to constructive use.

— ROBERT BELLAH et al., *Habits of the Heart*

COUNTRY, CITY, AND COMMUNITY

In this book we focus on one of the most powerful American myths, that of a "fundamentally egalitarian ethic of community responsibility" (Bellah et al., 1986 [1985]:38). The myth is typically represented as existing in tension or balance with an equally powerful ethic of individualism.[1] For those people in Hopewell, Riverside, and Sander County whose voices prevail in our respective ethnographic records, this tension is a complicated one. In some contexts, as we have seen, the tension produces narratives of achievement and success, as in people's stories of "good men and women" who became "pillars" of church and community. In other contexts, as we have also seen, the tension produces stigmatization and denunciation. Either way, the perception that an individual sometimes faces a choice between self-interest and community interests makes the distinction between "insiders" and "outsiders" a moral one, as well as one of personal residential history. Part of our effort in this volume has been to understand the local concerns and rhetorics that drive these distinctions and define their use in everyday talk.

The myth of community, on the one hand, emphasizes harmony, or "getting along" and a distinctive "way of life" that links people in a collective endeavor with other like-minded individuals. The ethic of individualism, on the other hand, emphasizes self-reliance, toughness, and autonomy—qualities that are posed as being central to progress and "getting along" in a market economy. The ambiguity of "getting along" (either as harmony or progress) captures the tension to which we refer. Here we see the inherent contradictions of an ideology of community in which harmony is extolled but where only the tough (spiritually, economically) can belong.

A further contradiction is that viable human associations, in this worldview, are the outcomes of individuals *choosing* community (compare Varenne, 1977:156–57) (whether all individuals are qualified to make this choice is another question to which this worldview gives rise). According to the myth, communities shaped in this way produce both economic progress *and* authentic human connections.

What of the voices that are not heard in this book? This concluding chapter also acknowledges the significance of those silences. The worldview we have described in the previous chapters defines "persons" as autonomous individuals who are strong, self-reliant, and capable of "free" (rational) choice.[2] We can also try to imagine, in an ethnographically grounded way, the perspectives of those whom these criteria exclude, people whose life-styles and practices are seen as emblematic of their inability to "get along" (without the state, the court). In the dominant myth of individualism, dependent persons such as women and children are "outside" community, or at least in an ambiguous or subordinate relation to those persons who in our narrative are fully entitled (culturally speaking) to participate (see Minow, 1990). Here, we would add that the same loss of status extends to those persons in our analysis who are incapable of obtaining redress through their own efforts or their neighbors' promises and must venture instead into lawyers' offices and courts. In this sense, as we noted in Chapter 4, the egalitarianism implicit in the concepts of community we encountered in the field also paradoxically implies a hierarchy of those who are worthy and those who are not.

The paradoxical aspects of community in the United States are masked but not resolved by what we have termed the renunciatory dimension of community. The value of selflessness and restraint are expressed in everyday references to good neighbors, civic-minded businessmen, and self-sacrificing wives, for example. The hierarchical and self-interested ethics that inform the practice of community and of getting along are for the most part silenced or displaced into other idioms, as we have seen. One of these idioms involves conflict itself as a *cultural category*, that is, as a meaningful symbol. Conflict may be interpreted negatively as a discordant element, as deviant and grasping behavior by those incapable of selflessness, or neutrally as a regrettable but unavoidable by-product of playing by the rules. Sometimes, according to the latter interpretation, even the best of citizens must see to it that rules are enforced. Indeed, such rule enforcement may seem such a natural part of everyday life that it is not even viewed as conflict at all. The paradox of community thus extends to the varying interpretations of conflict itself.

This book has explored the links between cultural ideas of community and individualism, focusing particularly on the place of law and the court in the cultural construction of community and hierarchy in three locales in the United States. We began with separate studies of the experience of community in the eastern, southern, and midwestern regions of the United States. The book then developed as a collaborative account of local experiences of community as a particular "way of life" and of the law's role as both central to and disruptive of this lifeway. In the preceding chapters of Part II we examined local orientations toward courts and law use more generally from the point of view of "locals" who have multiple means for interpreting their personal experience as "social." We also emphasized variations in local interpretations of diversity. Drawing selectively on the variety of meanings embedded in the concept of the individual (and individualism), people who claim memories of the towns' pasts interpret the new demographic diversity of their "communities" with ambivalence (at best) or negatively. We tried to show how issues of demographic diversity are "translated" into collective moral concerns. via courts.

A pair of key terms — the polarity of "the community" and "the state" — are particularly important in the process of "translation." When people decry what they perceive to be excessive recourse to litigation, they emphasize the impropriety of involving the state in affairs that they consider to be essentially private or local. Thus, litigation becomes a negative "sign" of difference. Those who ask the state to intervene into "local" affairs are defined as "different," as not belonging. At the same time, though, people who think of themselves as insiders will defend their communities — even by recourse to litigation — through opposition to the behavior of those who are "different" (in terms of race, ethnicity, union membership, religion, and social class). Thus, litigation — the invocation of state legal authority — is a sign of difference and anticommunitarianism, but difference is also a justification of litigation by "insiders" in defense of their community. Once again, one can see that insiders are caught in the paradox of community: The same cultural vocabulary that undermines community is simultaneously that community's idiom of self-affirmation.

The paradoxical meanings of community play on the contradictory possibilities of democracy, which sometimes empowers the individual, but sometimes overpowers the individual's voice (see Varenne, 1977). In terms central to this volume, sometimes the link between the individual and the state is forged positively, as when individuals call on the courts to validate their interpretation of events or relationships, or to add to their personal supply of authority in their own out-of-court negotiations. Sometimes the link is forged negatively, devaluing the role of law in ordering interpersonal relationships. Either way, the notion of "community" stands symbolically as the fulcrum between these possibilities, in that through "community," the individual might achieve his or her fullest expression or be suppressed and excluded from participation in civic life.

Focusing on the relationship between law and local concepts of community, we were able to explore the connections between egalitarianism and hierarchy, between inside and outside, and between local autonomy and state power. We were also able to probe the distinction some people draw between "insiders" and "outsiders" and examine some of its referents. Our major theme has been an ideology of community in which local autonomy, self-reliance, and harmony (or "getting along") are central issues. Yet these issues are deceptively complex, despite their usual expression in a "euphemized" form, "under the veil of enchanted relationships"

(Bourdieu, 1977:191) that obscure the inextricability of the "local" from the translocal, of "autonomous" insider from powerful outsider, or of "getting along" from greed. An earlier "take" on such enchantments was Weber's (1958), who also saw the spiritual and pragmatic dimensions of capitalism fused in the concept of social duty. In our field sites, linkages between local and translocal were embedded in the meanings of work, which, as Weber suggested, involved practical and spiritual values simultaneously. We saw these hidden linkages in the "enterprise" of the resourceful Yankee capitalist, the mature Southern Baptist who "actualizes his potential" through stewardship, the southern philanthropist who underwrites local preservation, and the midwestern businessman who brings debtors to court "as a matter of principle," and so on. To express the full complexity of "local autonomy," "self-reliance" and "harmony" in everyday speech would be impossible, but to present them in euphemized form allows progress without greed, sacralizes entitlement in the name of a shared code of honor, and permits engagement *in* the world without being *of* it.

At the same time, through these same "enchanted relationships," the single-minded quest for wealth is transformed into resourcefulness, and rights become honor. In this way, power is both reproduced and neutralized in the locales we studied. "Yankee resourcefulness" and "spiritual maturity" are terms that seem to speak of self-reliance while masking the connections (to a transnational economy, "outside" capital, the secular world) on which a particular "way of life" depends (see also Errington, 1990: 641). Yet, local power is maintained through the same connections, thereby shaping local hierarchies of inclusion and exclusion that constitute a particular "way of life."[3] The legitimacy of this way of life is contingent on muting the disparities of power and social class upon which it is founded and on locating connections to the world of money and self-interest *outside* the community. Thus, the recurrent oppositions of "insiders" versus "outsiders," and a local "way of life" versus external disruptions and influences animate the narratives of law and community on which our book has focused.

OPPOSITIONS AND ADVERSARIES

We argue that the oppositional distinctions mentioned in the preceding section lie at the heart of both the rhetoric and the experience of community for those people privileged to speak *for* "the community" in each of our three settings. The key opposition that concerns us here is the one that posits the "greed" of lazy "outsiders" (who rely on the state and the courts for support) against the foil of "enterprising" natives (whose independence is revealed in their economic success in the marketplace). As noted, we view such classifications as cultural categories. They emerge from and reproduce two related forms of hierarchy: a hierarchy of values that people reaffirm in their use of public symbols *and* a hierarchy of interests, or scale of priorities, that prevails in public life.

In this sense, the classifications themselves have a subtle but important political dimension. They both obscure and neutralize the potentially negative implications of complex relationships between local elites and the state, the market, and the law. Context is key here, because it is only in the context of the particular types of change affecting these three settings at the time of our respective fieldwork that one can make such a statement. *In these contexts*, to be "enterprising" means to forge new kinds of alliances with external sources of capital and successfully managing ever-expanding local, state, and federal laws and regulations that govern the sorts of development that all three locales experienced. In effect, the image of the "lazy outsiders" brightens the line between insiders and outsiders, but the image of the "enterprising" person in these circumstances blurs it.

At the same time that these categorical oppositions address the boundaries of "community," they also characterize the "local way of life" within the community by celebrating self-sacrifice over entitlement and collective welfare over self-indulgence, for example. In conversation, corporate employers in Riverside are cast as paternalistic visionaries, and striking workers are disruptive troublemakers. Among Hopewell's Southern Baptists, wealthy Christians (i.e., Baptists) are seen as especially appealing "witnesses for Christ," and some Baptists view "non-Christians" who are wealthy as icons of self-interest. Insiders view outsiders' wealth as nourishing Hopewell's identity when it involves local investment and giving; however, they see it as potentially undermining local traditions in other contexts. In Sander County, small businessmen are "pillars of the community" through their affiliations with the Kiwanis and Rotary clubs, but Hmong refugees eventually came to be seen by some as greedy welfare recipients.

In each of these symbolic oppositions, the *self*-interest of "outsiders" as individuals is imagined to be set against *collective* interests of "insiders" as a group. Thus, in situations of conflict or in other circumstances, insiders operate within a worldview that symbolically reinforces their legitimacy as acting on "the community's" behalf. (No doubt, this is a contested view.) It is important to note that these dichotomous oppositions fail to acknowledge the existence of those former "insiders" who were displaced from power by the emergence of new local elites. As we have seen, this submerged real-world opposition resurfaces in the historical myths that make "the community" a legacy of the past.

Recently, other anthropologists working in the United States of the early 1980s have also reached the conclusion that local struggles over the presence and activities of "outsiders" involve an implicit critique of these individuals by persons whose experience puts them "inside" local and translocal arenas of power and influence (Nash, 1988; Dorst, 1989; Ginsburg, 1989). Ginsburg's ethnographic context is Fargo, North Dakota, where controversy over the opening of an abortion clinic involved both local and national activists. The presence of the national activists was intensely divisive; until they arrived, local "insiders" had more or less successfully managed to live with their differences. In Nash's case, the ethnographic domain is Pittsfield, Massachusetts, where the transition from heavy to "high-tech" industry involved complex negotiations between insiders and outsiders, insiders — the workers, at least — eventually losing control of the process. Dorst's work was in Chadd's Ford, Pennsylvania, where the process of suburbanization (in his description, at least, reminiscent of that in Hopewell) eventually culminated in the commoditization of "small-town life," now designed to appeal to the executives who commute to national and multinational corporate jobs up the line.

In Riverside, Sander County, and Hopewell, as in these other settings (in yet different ways), the insiders' critique is addressed to transformations in two domains: market relationships intrinsic to late-twentieth-century capitalism in the United States and the social relationships involved in the "melting pot" notion of American society. These critiques are expressed most explicitly and fully in the context of specific local contests, such as consolidating a rural school district or enlarging a school building, opening a new factory, resolving a strike, settling a personal injury suit, opening an abortion clinic. They are also embedded in the very terms and categories with which people describe their milieus. Thus, symbolic oppositions and partisan contests over local issues are in constant dialogue. In our field experience, the symbolic and the partisan divisions tended to reinforce each other. It is possible to imagine, however, that in other circumstances, symbolic categories of opposition and "real-world" partisan factions would be less congruent and, through their lack of "fit," challenge and reshape each other.

Local partisan conflicts (as we encountered them) are interpreted symbolically in terms of a relatively constant framework and reproduce a shared set of structural themes: restraint versus self-indulgence, virtue versus money, community versus state, self-control versus law, commitment (responsibility, nurturance) versus self-interest. Within this framework, as we have noted, the content of the conflicts might vary considerably. In this way, partisan oppositions are reproduced as dichotomies, in which people are virtuous or materialistic, are "inside" or "outside" in terms of their opposition to or support for school, strike, factory, suit, or clinic. Sometimes the link to specific contests is direct (as in Sander County and Riverside); sometimes it is much more diffuse (as in Hopewell). In either case, local struggles framed in the rhetoric of "community" preservation inevitably assert "community" as a positive force with renunciatory dimensions (family life, virtue, nurturance, and other arenas of fulfillment through self-denial). As Raymond Williams (1983:76) has noted, ' "*Community*" can be the warmly persuasive word to describe an existing set of relationships, or the warmly persuasive word to describe an alternative set of relationships. What is the most important, perhaps, is that unlike all other terms of social organization (state, nation, society, etc.) it seems never to be used unfavourably, and never to be given a positive opposing or distinguishing term." The paradox associated with the concept of community — the internal contradiction resonant in this passage as well as in our own fieldwork — is the major theme linking our separate accounts of Hopewell, Riverside, and Sander County.

One aspect of this paradox is people's use of the term "community" to refer to whatever it is that they deem particularly valuable about their own locale, though, at the same time, "community" has a generic quality that is distinctively translocal. Almost certainly, while people in our three field sites might (often) use the phrase "in this community" to introduce its distinctiveness, that sense of distinctiveness is strikingly shared across these settings. By this we mean not only that local people feel their home places to be special, but also that people in the three towns define their special character in more or less the same way. It is as if "community" is national, yet accessible only through some particular home ground. Again, we return to the double metonymy of community and country (as rural and as nation) (see Williams, 1973).

We have stressed that our informants construct community in opposition to a host of local and more generalized pressures. As the ethnographic chapters show, some people in Riverside, Sander County, and Hopewell think of their communities as bases to defend; however, the threats they perceive are of many different kinds. Some, as we have said, are close to home. The names and details of these would be intensely local. Other threats are more abstract and generic. These also have names: "big government," "big industry," "suburbia," "outsiders." It is important to be clear about what such oppositions entail. In what follows, we recapitulate some of the most important of these oppositions: in this section, local versus extralocal, and in the next egalitarian versus hierarchical and narrative versus silence.

One striking feature of the discourse of community we explore in this book is the extent to which local developments can be (and are) so easily renamed by local people in more abstract and generic terms. Instead of talking directly about the controversies (or the absence of controversy) associated with each locale's recent development, people talk in generic terms about the encroachments of the city, unions, the multinationals, "blacks," and so forth. This translation from the local and particular to the national (or multinational) and general displaces the locus of such developments from local arenas of conflict to arenas outside the "community." In so doing, local people manage to preserve their communities — at least rhetorically — against forces that, in their discourse, originate outside them and are deemed irrelevant to their essential character.[4]

We have shown this rhetorical strategy, by which "community" is asserted against diverse "outside" interventions, to be a potent one in at least three respects. First, Part I shows several ways in which the rhetoric of community is deployed against "troublemakers" and "outsiders" of various kinds. The rhetorical displacement of the locus of change to sources outside the community preserves the distinction between insiders and outsiders and its relevance as a moral boundary; the construction of this boundary is the theme of Chapter 4. Second, by shifting from the particular to the generic, local people can sometimes defuse local disputes by moving them, by definition, outside the community, transforming them into some much more highly generalized (and unresolvable) conflict intrinsic to modernization; this is the theme of Chapter 5. Third, this rhetoric involves a tangled temporality in that it depicts the community itself as defended ground, but not contested ground. More important, the salient contests are always represented as being against the community, not within it. Local people might attribute their communities' solidarity to its survival from the past, but the expressions of solidarity that we encountered are relevant primarily in relation to the pressures of today (this latter point is the theme of Chapter 6). One of our main findings is that solidarity cast in these terms is first and foremost rhetorical; in the ethnographic contexts we studied, "community" was neither a basis for collective action nor the definition of a social field.

EQUALITY AND OTHER HIERARCHIES

Local assertions of civic identity, framed and instantiated in the ways we have just described, are shaped by particular silences, especially about the past. These silences obscure the adversarial and alliance relationships that "modernized" the communities and the local people who won and lost in the process. The meanings of community that we explore in this book express rich idioms of experience and yearning, but they are not everyone's. Some of the silences are those of people who are, in practice, excluded from the loose collaboration by which local identity is designed and revised. Others are encoded in the terms and concepts that are part of everyday language, such as "community" (as we have discussed throughout). In this section, we consider the ways in which silences shape three other concepts that are related to and clarify local notions of community: equality, domesticity, and the sacred.

In different ways, people we knew in the three settings implicitly defined equality in the ways they used categorical and hierarchical distinctions in practice. In Riverside, we infer that equals are considered to be alike in their virtue; in drawing the line between "good people" and "bad people," they draw a line around a community of equals and exclude those others who are beyond the community. In Sander County, equality seems to mean "good neighbors"; it means never displaying or expressing interest in personal wealth. In Hopewell, equality appears to imply a constant circulation of wealth, and equality in this sense is not undone if, at a particular moment in time, some people have more money than others. Another sort of social tie figures beyond equality, among the people who hoard wealth, or would if they could—the people "with dollar signs in their eyes," categorically deemed outsiders.

Those people, it is thought, view wealth and social class not merely as arbitrary distinctions within a community of equals but as natural distinctions, as entitlements based on inherent differences between individuals.

This characterization of "their" views becomes part of the general process of disparagement that negatively defines the category of outsiders. People who think of themselves as insiders thus view hierarchy as provisional and equality as enduring, but they imagine that, for outsiders, the opposite is true: For *them* equality is provisional and hierarchy ultimately enduring.

The contrast between these two visions of equality and hierarchy is highly suggestive. First of all, it implies one subject that is silenced in the discourse of community, the relational aspects of class. In Riverside, people's narratives displaced "class" to Milltown but more or less suppressed any reference to class relationships in Riverside itself. This displacement also made Milltown the perceived locus of self-interest, corruption, and greed. Riverside, on the other hand, was represented as the creation of virtuous, public-spirited, and resourceful middle-class citizens and neighbors. People in Riverside also located corporate power outside of their own community; the community is in this sense a community of virtue and equality by definition, all exceptions being by definition alien.

Similarly, in Sander County, people tell stories about factory workers and ethnic outsiders who challenge local values. The stories put them in another class — an "underclass" — from the insiders' point of view. By contrast, social "outsiders" who are politically and economically powerful actors in the town are absent from local narratives of community identity, although they now occupy many key positions in local government. This was also true in Hopewell, where the collaborative processes by which coalitions of residents and capitalists from outside Hopewell transformed the town were never retold as part of the "community's" history. It is as if the suburbanization of Hopewell came entirely from the outside, as something that "happened" *to* Hopewell. In all three cases, the specific events and transactions that changed the face of the towns are merged, and then recast as generic and largely anonymous processes of change.

So far, we have discussed people's idioms and concerns in the most public aspects of their civic life. In all three locales, the domestic sphere is rhetorically framed by precisely the same range of considerations that isolate "outsiders" beyond the "community." Indeed, in many ways, idealizations of home life that we encountered in Hopewell, Sander County, and Riverside symbolically reiterate local representations of outsiders versus insiders: Outsiders are alien and alienating; the home is an extension of the self. Outsiders are greedy; family members sacrifice for each other. Outsiders are motivated and connected by money; families are motivated and connected by love. The outsiders' economy involves amassing capital and distributing it as narrowly as possible; the economy within the home is predicated on the gift. Outsiders do things only for money; at home, labor is free, and so forth. We take these contrastive terms from the conversations reported in the ethnographic chapters; however, echoes and parallels can be found in other contemporary ethnographies of American life (see, for example, Varenne, 1977, 1986; Perin, 1977, 1988; Nash, 1989; Newman, 1988; Ginsburg, 1989).

Local ideas of family, home, and domesticity constitute yet another element in the local commentaries on modernity that we analyze. Against the foil of the threats to community, domesticity is demanded—or yearned for—as a sanctuary. In Hopewell, Riverside, and Sander County, people's idealizations of domesticity can be summed up in the idea of renunciation. These idealizations offer emblems of an imagined refuge where there can be an authentic economy of community: the gift (with husband-father as its provider), the donation of labor (by the wife-mother), and sharing (with the household as a unit of consumption.) The idealizations of home life that we encountered in the field are strikingly parallel to Rousseauist formulations of the family as a model for society; in our fieldwork, we found that people did indeed extrapolate from their models of family life at home to paradigms of social integration on much larger scales.

Domesticity in this sense is easily figured in a woman, but it is also recognized as an attribute among men. Indeed, "domesticity" as a trait is not attached to the notion of gender per se but to particular forms of social tie. For example, it is not women who are said to be domestic in the sense we described but "good wives." Among men, "good neighbors" are animated by these qualities (women can also be good neighbors). The old farmers recalling Sander County's past evoked both of these images. For both men and women, "good Christians" are also domestic in this way; in Hopewell, a more or less constant refrain of church sermons and prayer was for a strengthening of one's personal capacity for renunciation of anger, self-interest, and material things.

The qualities of domesticity—indeed, the very distinction between the "domestic" and "the public"[5]—readily return us to the same questions of virtue and the moral order of equals discussed in this section. Here, we would add the further observation that the contrast between the domestic and public spheres is in itself a distinction between the sacred and the profane, as locally understood. From the local points of view we are describing, sacredness is inherent in the renunciations that distinguish the domestic from the public. The strongest link between renunciation and the sacred is made by Hopewell Baptists, who ascribe the possibility for individuals to renounce desire (for material and other things) as the fruit of their faith in Jesus. For others in Hopewell, as well as in Sander County and Riverside, our interpretation is more inferential.

In the Baptists' idiom of faith in Hopewell, renunciation is the inverse of consumption; this opposition, although not expressed so directly by others, appears to hold in other domains in all three locales. The positive value accorded renunciation is evident in a wide array of contexts, from the church, to some people's idealizations of proper gender roles, models of neighborly exchange, and so forth. We interpret local valorizations of renunciation as the very emblem of refusal to be existentially involved in the modernization that daily brings the world to the doorsteps of these formerly rural Americans. Naturally, such refusals are not practicable on a daily basis; hence (we believe) the special value placed on the full-time (unpaid) homemaker and community volunteer, the ritual occasions of sharing labor or food, the pageant ceremonies of the grange and collective church worship. These icons represent a broader stance against generalized alienating forms of capitalism and labor, symbolically distancing the forces of change even further from local arenas of experience.[6]

One conclusion is that the community discourse we have been exploring involves implicit criteria prerequisite to what are perceived to be authentic forms of economy and society. The authentic economy, in this worldview, constantly circulates wealth among local hands; an artificial economy distorts and disrupts the local social order by amassing capital and managing its distribution. The former is locally viewed as engaging, motivating and rewarding. The terms people in Hopewell and Riverside use to define themselves (farmers and small businesspeople, not rich but satisfied, and so on) are rhetorically powerful in this regard, even though they might fail to describe people's actual situations today. The rural past is more proximate in Sander County. In all three towns, the people whose points of view concern us see the new large-scale factories, franchises, and agricultural corporations as alien, alienating and seductive, but ultimately not rewarding.

Many of the people we knew in these three locales imagine an authentic society as one that would obviate the social conflicts they associate with modern life. The oppositions that we (and our informants) read in local discourses of community ultimately come to rest in the silences that local narrators weave into their accounts of local life and lore. We have tried to interpret some of those silences here. In this chapter, we have argued that the silences ultimately insist on a boundary between insiders and outsiders, the "self-sufficient" and those on welfare, "good wives" and "women's libbers," "family" and "families today," the middle and upper classes and the "other half of America," who are said to exist "outside" the community. In these terms and distinctions — so familiar on the American scene generally — people asserted both a theory of history and a model of the good life. The silences keep the negotiation of basic values off-stage, leaving the stage itself as a clear rhetorical ground on which local people can conceptualize themselves as "the same" and leave their notion of equality untroubled by difference, dependence, and disparities of fortune among their neighbors and other fellow citizens.

When some of the silences we have explored here are broken, certainly the first casualty is the bright line between insiders and outsiders. As statements by striking workers in Riverside made clear, "outsiders" were at the heart of local industry, and they were there because "insiders" sold their land and their businesses (by choice or necessity) to people who were not local. In Sander County, some people were prepared to acknowledge this fact. In Hopewell, some people speculated that others might feel this way. In Riverside and in Sander County, the official town histories and local narratives make it clear that the local economy has long been dependent on its connection to a translocal market.

Keeping the silences means obviating commentary and canceling the social memory of what were inevitably cooperative ties (at best) or cooptive ties (at worst) between locals and nonlocals in the course of the transformations whose results we observed. Keeping the silences means that "community" can be represented as a site of equality, not — as has typically been the case in our three locales — a site divided by profoundly different and rival interests. Avoiding reference to this possibility means that "the community" can represent itself as a classless society in a highly stratified world. Breaking silences would sooner or later mean acknowledging the extent to which local societies, too, were stratified in ways that shaped individual destinies. We feel, but cannot prove, that the silences protect the cultural machinery by which local class interests were transformed into values questions and values in turn inserted as distinctions between insiders and outsiders. Sometimes these distinctions were actualized as exclusions; sometimes they were not. This ambiguity would account for some of the ease with which the partisan and symbolic dimensions of opposition share the same terms.

COMMUNITY, LAW, AND RIGHTS

We have focused primarily on the role of law and of the court in maintaining and contesting community boundaries, examining how the law is both used and discussed. Unlike "community," which is invoked exclusively as a positive force in the rhetoric of everyday people in our three locales and elsewhere, the invocation of law has more bivalent connotations. Law is both a force for order and a conduit for disorder; it is a symbol of local morality *and* the penetration of the local by the state, by the "outside," and all that is locally interpreted as undermining "community." By using law, "insiders" may succeed in enforcing norms central to their way of life; by talking disparagingly about law and about "all these people walking around with all these rights," the same insiders define their community as a domain of mutual engagement in which the concept of "rights" (and, in some sense, of law itself) is out of place. At the same time, in the hands of outsiders, law and rights are vehicles for asserting other meanings of "community" and for contesting the silences in insiders' articulations of a "way of life."

To complicate things further, the "insider" discourse we have been tracing here is used not only by actual "insiders" in the sense of power elites (Mills, 1956) but also by numerous others, who identify with some or all of its communitarian elements. Given the meanings — even sacred meanings — that link gender roles, family and household, and broader spheres of action it is not difficult to see how the positive, renunciatory values of "community" might appeal to people who enjoy no particular elite privilege. Adopting the style of civic talk we have explored in this volume provides newcomers (and others) with a means of actively identifying themselves with, and participating in, a particular semantic field associated with insiders. Thus, we return to the conundrum mentioned in the introduction, that terms such as *insiders* and *outsiders* are first semantic categories with local meanings and, much more doubtfully, terms of analysis applicable to actual groups.

We have been primarily concerned with the elements and logics of these classifications as they emerge from our respective ethnographic studies;

however, the fact remains that one does not have to be from Hopewell, Riverside, or Sander County to be familiar with the myth of community or fluent in its discourse. In one style or another, it is broadly available in the United States, if only through the public speeches of the nation's highest government officials. For example, aspects of the worldview we have been exploring also surface in the arguments of advocates of market-based and other deregulatory approaches to the administration of commerce, worker health and safety, the environment, and so forth. Other aspects are voiced by advocates of voluntarism in lieu of public spending for social services or the arts. Yet others, particularly at the time of our respective fieldwork, were voiced by those who were concerned with what they claimed was excessive litigation clogging the court dockets; then-Chief Justice Warren Burger was a leading spokesman for this view. Our point is not to cast the locales that feature in this book as somehow typical but to connect the local meanings of community to the social forces involved in these larger-scale positions and developments in the contemporary United States.

In Hopewell, Riverside, and Sander County local talk about law encodes a critique of specific forms of modern social life, particularly national and multinational corporate capitalism on the one hand and the melting pot on the other. Now we would add that the myth of community, by virtue of displacing values questions to the boundaries that are constructed around and between groups, subsumes questions of rights into these same constructions. The local talk we heard, particularly in Riverside and Sander County, locates rights *outside* the community. In this talk, rights assertion is interpreted as a narcissistic claim for the self at the expense of community, and the "selves" who claim rights are condemned as irresponsible and dependent. Still, people who talk this way tacitly acknowledge another form of right, a more or less natural right to participate in community life — if one qualifies. Among "insiders," this right is unquestioned, and, for the most part, unarticulated. From the perspective of this natural right of a qualified individual to his or her community life, the demands of "outsiders" are *by definition* excessive, a surplus.

In Riverside and Sander County particularly, the right to community, as locally conceived and rhetorically preserved for insiders, entitles some but not others to speak for it, to sketch its landscape, and to define the terms for relating its present to its past. This (unarticulated) right "is the magic wand of visibility and invisibility, of inclusions and exclusion, of power and no-power" (P. Williams, 1987:431). It is a form of right that trumps the efforts of outsiders to claim power and status in the community through litigation. As we have seen, it sometimes blurs the distinctions between insiders and outsiders and sometimes insists on them. It is a form of right that takes its most palpable forms against the real or hypothetical demands of individuals and groups subordinate by virtue of gender, class, ethnicity, or race.

One of our central projects has been to suggest how the law, the courts, and claims of right define the boundaries of community. To a more limited extent, we have been able to show how these boundaries are contested by subordinate groups and how "insiders" respond to these contests. We have described, for example, how insiders denounced claims of entitlement or constitutional right when such claims raised questions about the previously unchallenged authority of school officials to punish students, of parents to discipline children, or of employers to protect their money from greedy people who use the law, not the market, to benefit at the expense of others. When the more established local groups respond to rights claims by less powerful residents, the insiders' unarticulated but taken-for-granted "rights" become clearly visible. As we have also seen, the distinction between insiders and outsiders and between legitimate uses of the law and illegitimate ones is apparent in the very terminology local people bring to their descriptions of their town and their neighbors.

In deploying their own "rights," insiders rhetorically deny any legitimacy to contrary claims of entitlement in local courts. We are not referring to judicial outcomes here but to a motif of local conversation. Insiders invoke imagery that connects the claimants to a materialistic ethic that places them, "by their nature," beyond the boundaries of the community that insiders define as their own. This is a process that tends to protect and reproduce the hierarchies, in spite of a language of "rights" that would seem to preclude hierarchies. For insiders, the myth of community is self-reinforcing. It is ironic, then, that the definitions of community we encountered are constituted in a cumulative experience of conflict, yet that they require that conflict be symbolically and rhetorically externalized for community to "exist."

A critical commentary on this vision of community is implicit in the struggles and rights claims of outsiders in Riverside and Sander County. For these local people, rights imply "a respect which places one within the referential range of self and others, which elevates one's status from human body to social being" (P. Williams, 1987:416). For outsiders, in other words, legal rights can bestow dignity and personhood. For insiders, a claim of rights is a claim to forms of recognition they (insiders) presume as an unquestioned given, in no need of explicit or formal definition. For them, the negative meanings of rights, as expressions of materialism or untempered self-interest and intrusions of "the state" into local values, culture, and communities, are negative by default. The positive meanings of rights are not absent but, rather, taken for granted.

In this sense, the claims by outsiders in Sander County and Riverside, like those of outsiders in other settings, represent an alternative vision of civic life pointing to the places where the insiders' myth of community does not reach.[7] At the same time, insiders' resistance to their claims encodes a critique of what insiders perceive to be modern alienating forms of social life. Yesterday's "insiders" in our three locales were men who had "sufficient *rights* to manipulate commerce" (P. Williams, 1987:408) and who used them to construct the communities that are celebrated in local histories and defended against incursions from "outside." Increasingly, such persons are today's bystanders. Experiencing themselves now as the objects of commerce, they resist their exclusion from an expanding capitalist economy they helped to shape. They do so, in part, by denouncing rights, even as those they define as "outsiders" (a category that collapses key differences between groups as diverse as Hmong and Hispanic immigrants and the management personnel of powerful new business organizations) may assert rights in court and elsewhere in order to participate in communities where only others have been "free" to engage.

Our account in these chapters has focused more on the tensions and contradictions in the position of these insider-bystanders than on the different ways that "outsiders" relate to community ideologies. At the same time, in attempting to decode the meanings of community for "insiders" and their fears about its demise, we found that the enemies and adversaries, "real and imagined" (Ginsburg, 1989:196), were a vital part of the story. Indeed, we found that the boundaries between "inside" and "outside" shifted over time and in space, so that, as Raymond Williams suggests in his essay on "Knowable Communities" with which we began this chapter, "any assumption of a knowable community — a whole community, wholly knowable — [becomes] harder and harder to sustain" (R. Williams, 1973:165).

The shift from one knowing subject to another brings into focus different "communities" and different perceptions about the place of law, rights, and the court in community ideologies. The perception of local elites in Hopewell, Sander County, and Riverside that traditional lifeways are disintegrating is as much a consequence of a gradual shift in their position away from the locus of power (from insider to bystander) as of any sudden disintegration in a rural order. The rural order, we have argued, was never quite as self-sustaining nor as independent of external influences and connections as the insiders' myth of community might suggest.

Bender (1978:149) notes in an overview of literature on community and social change that "for American elites . . . power and community often overlap," whereas for the poor and less powerful, "the experience of community seldom has any significant connections with the levers of power." Our analysis supports this observation, at least in part. Laments by elites about the disintegration of community and their perceptions of the role of law in this process may speak as eloquently about loss of power and the ability to influence local political and economic life as they do about the demise of "community." To find and understand "community" we must look closely at local contests where different people and groups struggle for voice and control. Here we may differ from Bender in that we sometimes see that the poor and less powerful attempt to gain access to the levers of power through law (and by other means) in order to pursue their struggle for inclusion in the "rights" that are "naturally" given to others. We have suggested that one can understand "community" by studying these local contests rather than by searching for some core of "local" tradition and values or for a romanticized "way of life" set apart from the larger, "law-ridden" society.

Our principal conclusion is that "community"—at least for elites and former elites in these three towns—is a term that expresses a modern retrenchment against new forms of pluralism in the United States. This finding suggests that significant difficulties may confront social scientists and others who propose to invoke the concept of community as a vehicle for new approaches to governance in the hopes of expanding democracy for a diverse nation (see various manifestations of this aspiration, e.g., in Unger, 1976, or Etzioni, 1991). Certainly, the word *community* does stand for important local values, but they are values that we heard voiced primarily by individuals who were searching for a term with which to name the price they feared the future might demand from them.

Local claims notwithstanding, we found no evidence that linked evocations of community to any particular form of collective or inclusive endeavor, although individuals might be moved to act by what they identified as a community spirit. "<u>Community</u>," for the local elites with *defined.* which this book has been principally concerned, appears to be less about the pluralist possibilities of collective action (as communitarian advocates claim) than it is about the rhetorical management of change as local *the critical* settings face new challenges beyond their design and control. If this book *process* tells a single story, it is that whatever the past traditions of these local settings might be, their sense of community is only superficially a direct legacy of the past and, even less so, a sure promise of an autonomous and inclusive social life in the future.

security of local elite status over time is alluded to here & not taken on in full. Also, the nature of what elite means seems to be very flexible & at a loss in the rural context via the urban definition. This is a different question about power & class.

9/10/94.
RML.

Notes

1. We use the word *hierarchy* deliberately here, and perhaps controversially. In general, anthropologists follow Dumont (1970) in distinguishing between *hierarchy* (as a system of ascribed *moral* statuses) and *rank* (as a system of ascribed *social roles*). Simply put, this means that they distinguish between societies that make some people *better* than others and societies that make some people *more powerful* than others. In his essay on the United States, Dumont (1970) argues that American racism is an example of the latter, not the former, as African Americans (with whom he is primarily concerned) might have restricted upward mobility but are not viewed by whites as categorically inferior *as persons*.

Although we have not explored the status of African Americans directly, our findings with respect to the significance of Americans' social distinctions lead us to disagree with Dumont on this point. We conclude that Americans *do* draw hierarchical distinctions in precisely the sense of attributing more positive moral qualities to some social categories and denying the moral qualities of others. This is, in our view, part of the meanings of race and class as they are locally lived and discussed.

Our comparative project brought out the ways in which differences in wealth might obviate the need to make other distinctions explicit in the course of everyday life, but those other distinctions, which ascribe the intrinsic superiority and inferiority of social categories, are nonetheless evident. Furthermore, hierarchy is not just a matter of talk or semiotics; it also structures personal interactions in a variety of institutional settings. (Yngvesson's ethnography is particularly clear on the lived aspects of moral hierarchy in Milltown and Riverside; see Greenhouse, 1992, for an analysis of moral hierarchy in Hopewell and other U.S. contexts.)

2. The idea that the legalistic quality of British legal anthropology in Africa emerged from its encounters with African ideas of legality would once have roused virulent controversy and might still today. For different positions, see Bohannan (1969 and 1989 [1957]), Gluckman (1967), and the synoptic reviews cited in the text.

3. Our informants tended to view their own communities (on the whole) as exceptions to this national trend, citing their own capacity for local harmony as one proof of the superior quality of their traditional way of life over that of other, unspecified locales. Indeed, although they are correct in identifying themselves as people who are not particularly litigious, they are incorrect in assuming that they are exceptional in this regard; most Americans use the courts only as an extreme last resort, if at all.

CHAPTER ONE

1. I am deeply grateful to the residents of "Sander County" for their generous participation in this study. I also thank the following friends and colleagues who read and commented on this article at one stage or another in its development: Richard L. Abel, James B. Atleson, Guyora Binder, Donald Black, Marc Galanter, Fred Konefsky, Virginia Leary, Richard O. Lempert, Felice J. Levine, John Henry Schlegel, Eric H. Steele, Robert J. Steinfeld, and Barbara Yngvesson. I am also grateful to Linda Kelly for her skill and patience in typing and retyping the manuscript.

The research on which this article is based was supported by the National Science Foundation under Grant No. SOC 77-11654 and by the American Bar Foundation. Opinions, findings, and conclusions are those of the author and not of the supporting organizations.

2. By litigation I simply mean the filing of a formal complaint in the civil trial court, even if no further adversarial processes occur. The annual litigation rate for personal injuries was 1.45 cases filed per 1,000 population as compared with 13.7 contract cases (mostly collection matters), 3.62 property-related cases (mostly landlord-tenant matters), and 11.74 family-related cases (mostly divorces). All litigation rates are based on the combined civil filings for 1975 and 1976 in the Sander County Court. Population figures are based on the 1970 census and are therefore somewhat understated. That is, the actual litigation rates for 1975–76 are probably lower than those given here.

3. McIntosh reports a rate of approximately six tort actions per 1,000 population in the St. Louis Circuit Court in 1970. He does not state what proportion of these involved personal injuries (McIntosh, 1980–81:832). Friedman and Percival (1976: 281–81) report 2.80 and 1.87 cases filed per 1,000 population in the Alameda and San Benito Superior Courts (respectively) in 1970 under the combined categories of "auto accidents" and "other personal injuries." The two California courts had original jurisdiction only for claims of $5,000 or more, but the Sander county figures include personal injury claims of all amounts. Friedman and Percival do not indicate what proportion of the auto accident cases involved personal injuries as opposed to property damage only. Statewide data for California and New York, compiled by the National Center for State Courts (1979:49, 51) for tort cases filed in 1975, also tend to indicate litigation rates higher than Sander County's. These aggregate litigation rates, however, are understated in that they exclude filings from smaller courts of limited jurisdiction in both states and are overstated in that they fail to separate personal injury cases from other tort actions. Litigation rates for tort cases filed per 1,000 population in 1975 were 3.55 for California and 2.21 for New York (but in 1977, when additional lower court dockets were included in the survey of tort cases filed, the rate reported for New York more than doubled to 4.47; see National Center for State Courts, 1982:61). In comparing the Sander County litigation rates with those in other cities or states, it should also be remembered that, because Sander County was quite small, the *absolute number* of

personal injury actions filed in the county court was also very small compared with more urban areas.

4. I use the term *community* somewhat loosely in this discussion to mean the county seat of Sander County and the surrounding farmlands. Since Sander County is rather small, this takes in most of the county. There are a handful of very small towns elsewhere in the county. Although they are not far from the county seat and are linked to it in many ways, it is probably stretching things to consider them part of a single "community." I should add that the problem of defining the term *community* as a subject of empirical study has vexed social scientists for many years, and I aspired to no conceptual breakthrough in this regard. My interest was in finding a research site where the jurisdiction of the court was roughly congruent with a social unit comprising a set of meaningful interactions and relationships.

5. Hostility toward personal injury litigation as a form of "hyperlexis" may also have been influenced in Sander County by mass media treatment of this form of legal claim. Yet, the attitudes and antagonisms I describe had deep roots in the culture of Sander County itself and in the popular culture of the country as a whole. A critical appraisal of the hyperlexis literature, which parallels this discussion in some respects, is found in Galanter, 1983.

6. The sense of social change and disintegration in Sander County helped to crystallize a set of values opposed to personal injury litigation. These values were almost certainly rooted in long-established norms, but the targets of their expression and the intensity with which they were asserted may have been new. This chapter focuses on how and why such values came to be expressed and acutely felt in the late 1970s by many Sander County residents. See note 19.

7. A 20% sample was taken for the years 1975–76 within each of twelve civil categories mandated by the Administrative Office of the Illinois Courts: (1) law (claims over $15,000); (2) law (claims $15,000 or less); (3) chancery; (4) miscellaneous remedies; (5) eminent domain; (6) estates; (7) tax; (8) municipal corporations; (9) mental health; (10) divorce; (11) family; and (12) small claims. After the sample was drawn, the cases were reclassified into the substantive categories referred to throughout this chapter.

8. I interviewed parties in sixty-six cases. Wherever possible, I included all parties to each case. Particular attention was given to the individuals themselves, the relationship between them, and to the origin, development, and outcome of each case.

9. Among the seventy-one community observers were judges, lawyers, teachers, ministers, farmers, a beautician, a barber, city and county officials, a funeral parlor operator, youth workers, social service workers, various "ordinary citizens" from different segments of the community, a union steward, a management representative, agricultural extension workers, doctors, a newspaper reporter, the members of a rescue squad, and others.

10. The other three substantive areas were injuries to reputation, contracts, and marital problems.

11. This distinction between the two types of individualism emerged from an ongoing dialogue with Fred Konefsky, whose contribution to this conceptualization I gratefully acknowledge.

12. I heard of only a few cases where injured persons negotiated compensatory payments from the liability insurance of the party responsible for their harm. In these cases expectations (or demands) appeared to be modest. One involved a woman who lived on a farm. When visiting a neighbor's house, she fell down the basement stairs

because of a negligently installed door, fractured her skull, was unconscious for three days, and was in intensive care for five days. As a result of the accident she suffered a permanent loss of her sense of smell and a substantial (almost total) impairment of her sense of taste. Her husband, a successful young farmer, told me that their own insurance did not cover the injury. Their neighbor had liability insurance, which paid only $1,000 (the hospital bills alone were approximately $2,500). Nevertheless, they never considered seeking greater compensation from their neighbor or the neighbor's insurance company: "We were thankful that she recovered as well as she did. . . . We never considered a lawsuit there at all. I don't know what other people would have done in the case. Possibly that insurance company would have paid the total medical if we would have just, well, I have a brother who is an attorney, could have just wrote them a letter maybe. But, I don't know, we just didn't do it, that's all."

13. In Sander County as a whole, the litigation rate for automobile-related personal injury cases in 1975–76 was 0.88 cases each year per 1,000 population. For all automobile-related tort actions, including those where there was no personal injury claim, the litigation rate was 1.87 cases per 1,000 population. In the absence of reliable or meaningful comparative data, it is difficult to say how low or high these countywide rates are; but my hunch is that these are rather low for a jurisdiction in which no-fault approaches were not used for motor vehicle cases.

14. This is particularly striking, as Laurence Ross's observation of insurance company settlement practices in automobile accident cases suggests that general damages are a standard part of the settlement package and are rather routinely calculated "for the most part . . . [by] multiplying the medical bills by a tacitly but generally accepted arbitrary constant" (Ross, 1970:239).

15. These figures are from a sample of cases for the years 1975–76. See note 6. From these data alone one cannot conclude that Sander County attorneys were less often approached by potential personal injury plaintiffs, because the data consist only of cases that were filed and tell us nothing about cases brought to an attorney but not filed. We know that Sander County attorneys were sometimes reluctant to bring such actions even when approached by prospective plaintiffs. Attorneys elsewhere, particularly those who were tort specialists, may not have shared this reluctance and may have filed a higher proportion of the Sander County claims that were brought to them.

16. In this discussion of geographic and social distance and their impact on patterns of legal behavior, I draw on a body of theory that has been developed in several earlier studies. See Black, 1976; Perin, 1977; Engel, 1978; Todd, 1978; and Greenhouse, 1982b.

17. The disproportionate number of cases involving geographically distant adversaries is especially striking when one considers the relative infrequency of interaction between persons living in separate counties and states as compared to persons living in the same county or town. In absolute terms, injurious interactions must have occurred far more frequently between neighbors than between distant strangers, yet injurious interactions between distant strangers ended up in the Sander County Court about as often as those involving local residents (compare Engel, 1978:142–44).

18. Four percent of my case sample were personal injury cases, and 37.5% were contract cases.

19. On many occasions, of course, courts import external standards into contracts and impose them on the parties regardless of their agreement or disagreement with such terms.

20. Were personal injury lawsuits in the late 1970s, although relatively infrequent,

more common than they had been before the recent influx of social "outsiders" in Sander County? Because of the unavailability of reliable historical data, it is impossible to say, nor is the answer central to the analysis presented here. It is true that recent social changes in Sander County had brought striking juxtapositions of insiders and outsiders, and some increase in the frequency of tort claims may have resulted; but in earlier periods there may have been other kinds of outsiders as well, and some of them may have brought personal injury actions. In this chapter, I am interested in the past primarily as it existed in the minds of Sander County's citizens at the time of my study. It is clear that current perceptions of Sander County's history and traditions, whether accurate or not, played a crucial role in constructing and justifying responses to the problems that now faced the community, and such perceptions were often invoked to support the assertion of "traditional values" in opposition to behavior that provoked long-time residents.

21. Frequent plaintiffs in collection cases were doctors, hospitals, merchants, collection agencies, and the telephone company. Cases of this type constituted 76.5% of all contract actions. The remaining 23.5% of contract cases involved actions based on construction contracts, promissory notes, wholesale transactions, and other less frequent kinds of contractual transactions.

22. Sander County tort and contract cases are not unique, of course, in these basic structural differences. In other localities one might also expect to find that the majority of tort plaintiffs are individuals asserting claims against "deep pocket" defendants, but the majority of contract plaintiffs are business organizations attempting to collect debts from individuals. See, for example, Galanter, 1974, and Yngvesson and Hennessey, 1975. It is possible that outside of Sander County perceptions of the legitimacy and illegitimacy of contract and tort actions are also influenced by these basic structural differences. In Sander County, however, this set of distinctions between the parties to tort and contract actions combined with local reactions to recent societal changes to produce a powerful symbolism of insiders and outsiders and of injuries and individualism. The extent to which a similar symbolism may be found in other localities is a subject for further investigation.

CHAPTER TWO

1. The research on which this chapter is based was supported by the National Science Foundation Grant SES 81-22066. Research assistance was provided by Randi Silnutzer, whose skill and dedication in helping with the fieldwork were invaluable. I also thank David Engel, Robert Gordon, Christine Harrington, Maureen Mahoney, Lynn Mather, Lester Mazor, and Frank Munger for their comments on earlier versions of this paper. Conversations with David Engel and Carol Greenhouse on a related project have also contributed to the shaping of this one; and discussions of the paper at a meeting of the Amherst Seminar on Law and Ideology in September 1987 were helpful in sharpening and clarifying certain parts of my argument.

2. The district court is the entry point to the court system for virtually all criminal offenses tried in Massachusetts. District courts have original jurisdiction over all misdemeanors except libel, over local ordinances and bylaws, and over felonies punishable by up to two and a half years in a house of correction (*Mass. Gen. Laws Ann.*, 1977, ch. 218, §26, 30, 35A; 55).

3. Skocpol's definition borrows from W. B. Taylor's (1985) work. I came on both

through a paper by Monkkonen (1987:7) that points to the relevance of this approach for an understanding of the place of local trial courts in state theory. Monkkonen (1987:18) argues that the activities of trial courts *are* the state.

4. Lukes (1974:31) notes that "the central interest of studying power relations [is] . . . an interest in the (attempted or successful) securing of people's compliance by overcoming or averting their opposition." This may involve persuading in the face of obvious conflict, or it may involve silencing potential issues, or underscoring others through particular institutional practices or by invoking shared cultural assumptions. These ways of structuring bias may be the intended consequence of individual choice but are as likely to result from tacit and unquestioned cultural understandings and social practices (Lukes, 1974:21–22).

5. Bourdieu (1987:239) defines symbolic power as power that is exercised "through the complicity of those who are dominated by it." Similarly, in explaining the reproduction of dominance and subordination, Ignatieff (1983:202–6) and Ortner (1984:157) discuss the importance of "diffuse, enduring solidarity" and of other ties experienced as reciprocal and uncoercive. See also Hunt's (1982) discussion of the consent/coercion dichotomy in liberal and Marxist analyses of law. He argues for a conception of law "not reducible to a choice between opposites or a fluctuation between them" (1982:95).

6. This chapter is based on the quantitative analysis of 617 cases filed with the clerk of the Jefferson County District Court in Riverside, Massachusetts, between June 1 and December 31, 1982, and on seven months of observations and interviews at the court and in the two communities that used the court most heavily. Quotations were taken from these interviews. At the court, I observed over 200 complaint hearings and followed complaints that were issued through other stages of the court process. In addition, I observed filing procedures and informal exchanges about complaints; interviewed judges, attorneys, clerks, and probation staff; and spoke with the parties to complaints when possible. In the community ethnography, I followed forty-three cases back into the neighborhoods where they began, speaking with participants and other residents. I also interviewed police, local attorneys, a schoolteacher, two newspaper reporters, social workers, a housing bureau official, a landlord, a community organizer, housewives, blue-collar workers, and businessmen. I regularly read the county newspaper, *The Riverside Record*, and attended meetings of the Board of Selectmen, where many local problems are debated.

7. The courts' local roots give them their traditional identity as "people's courts" (McDermott, 1983:23). At the same time, district courts constitute one department of the Massachusetts trial court system, centrally regulated and funded and under the administration of a chief administrative justice in Boston. Tension between the court's role as both a state institution and a local forum is basic to its identity (Bing and Rosenfeld, 1970; Robertson, 1974:xvii–xxix; Hartog, 1976; Auerbach, 1983; McDermott, 1983).

8. Both judges are Riverside natives; and the assistant clerk, the clerical staff in the clerk's office, and all but one of the five staff in the probation office are either long-time residents or natives.

9. Analysis of hearing data indicated that complaints brought to the courthouse are also dealt with in other forums, although typically in different forms: at town meetings, in appeals to the Board of Selectmen, or in complaints to other town committees (such as the Planning Board); in calls about child abuse to the Department of Social Services or the Massachusetts Society for Prevention of Cruelty to Children; in complaints to the

Board of Health, the Housing Department, or the Fire Department; and in letters to the Jefferson County newspaper.

10. This statement is based on information from 95 family and neighbor complaints brought by private citizens to the district court clerk between June 1 and December 1, 1982. Of these, 81 had involved at least one (and in some up to ten) call to the police before they were brought by a citizen to the clerk.

11. The 617 complaints filed by both citizens and police constitute all complaints filed with the clerk between June 1 and December 31, 1982, except for fifty nonsupport complaints filed by the Department of Public Welfare and sixty-seven fuel tax complaints filed by the police. I excluded these from my analysis, because they typically involve routine decisions by the clerk and because the issues of complaint definition on which my project focused were minimal. The total non–motor-vehicle criminal caseload of the court was 1,500 complaints for fiscal 1982. Of these, 341 were entered through an application filed with the clerk.

12. See Harrington (1985:144–49) for a discussion of the handling of "garbage" in other misdemeanor courts.

13. Police and citizen complaints differ in other significant ways. Unlike the latter, which typically involve intimates, friends, and acquaintances, those brought by the police are more likely to involve conflict between strangers (85% of those brought by individuals involved intimates, and 15% involved strangers; 75% of those brought by police involved strangers, and 25% involved intimates). Police complaints are more likely to involve property offense (63% were property offenses, 18% were offenses against the person, 19% were victimless); the citizen complaints, by contrast, typically involve an assault on a friend or intimate (35% were property offenses, 61% were offenses against the person, 4% were victimless).

14. Of citizen complaints, 96 (33%) were allowed, 92 (31%) were denied, and 71 (24%) were withdrawn; 34 (12%) were classified as "other." Withdrawal by a complainant and denial by the clerk are sometimes hard to distinguish. Almost half of the 71 withdrawals (48%) occurred during or after the hearing; of the hearings I observed, many of these resulted from efforts by the clerk to mediate a conflict. Of police complaints, 265 (82%) were allowed, 26 (8%) were denied, and 16 (5%) were withdrawn; 17 (5%) were classified as "other."

15. During fifteen months of research on this and a similar project at an eastern Massachusetts court, I observed five different clerks. My observations suggested that the style of the court significantly affects the leeway of clerks in conducting hearings (Yngvesson, 1985a).

16. Although the style of the clerks differs, there is no significant difference between them in patterns of issuance. Of 507 hearings in which the identity of the clerk could be established, 271 were conducted by the assistant clerk and 234 by the head clerk. The assistant clerk allowed 60% (165) and denied 23% (62) of the complaints he handled; 17% (44) were withdrawn or unknown. Corresponding figures for the head clerk are 68% (159) allowed, 18% (43) denied, and 14% (32) withdrawn or unknown. For complaints filed by private citizens only, figures for the assistant clerk are 37% (46) allowed, 37% (47) denied, and 26% (33) withdrawn or unknown. The head clerk allowed 37% (37), denied 33% (33), and 29% (29) were withdrawn or unknown.

17. Foucault (1990 [1968]:100) argues that "we must not imagine a world of discourse divided between accepted discourse and excluded discourse, or between the dominant discourse and the dominated one; but as a multiplicity of discursive elements that can come into play in various strategies" (see also p. 27). Schattschneider (1960:71)

describes this as the "mobilization of bias" by organizing some issues "into" politics "while others are organized out." See also Lukes (1974:24) and Mather and Yngvesson (1980–81).

18. Of the 51 neighbor complaints and 44 family complaints that were brought to the clerk between June 1 and December 31, 1982, I observed hearings on 31 neighbor complaints and 16 family complaints.

19. Of the 44 family complaints taken to the clerk, 19 (43%) were issued; only 10 (20%) of the 51 neighbor complaints were issued. The overall issuance rate for citizen complaints was 33% (96) of 293 complaints. In a multiple regression analysis designed to predict outcomes from a list of variables that included charge, agent (police or individual), and relationship, the most significant predictor was agent ($b = 0.499695; p < 0.0001$); the second best predictor was relationship ($b = 0.145433; p < 0.01$). Specifically, cases were more likely to be issued if they were brought by the police or if the parties were family or strangers rather than acquaintances, lovers, or neighbors.

20. In twenty-six of the thirty-one hearings on neighborhood conflicts I observed, the clerks sought a compromise as a basis for withdrawal or for denying the complaint.

21. The complainants with the least "capacity" (in terms of experience and connections) in my sample were working-class parties such as those in the next case. Of the neighbor hearings I observed, thirteen involved working-class parties, and in only two of these (both involving the same participants) were the parties experienced court users. Class of participants was determined by matching addresses with information from the 1980 census and from observational and interview data. The tentative relationship between class and experience that I suggest is supported in other work (Merry and Silbey, 1984).

22. Quantitative data on the effect of representation by an attorney on outcome suggest that this is a more general pattern. In 57 cases brought by private citizens that involved attorneys, the pattern of issuances was significantly lower when an attorney represented either the complainant or the defendant (but not both) than if neither or both were represented. Of 170 complaints in which no attorney was present, 37% (63) were allowed, 54% (92) were denied or withdrawn, and 9% (15) were unknown. Of 23 complaints in which both were represented, 39% (9) were allowed, 57% (13) were denied or withdrawn, and 4% (1) was unknown. Of 22 complaints in which the defendant alone was represented, 27% (6) were allowed and 73% (16) were denied or withdrawn. Of 12 complaints in which the complainant alone was represented, 25% (3) were allowed and 75% (9) were denied or withdrawn. Although these figures are too small to be conclusive, the results suggest an alliance between clerk and attorney when only one party is represented, as in the case that follows.

23. Atkinson and Drew (1979:61–62) describe courtroom examination as involving fixed "turn order" and an organization of turns into question-and-answer pairs.

24. I draw explicitly here on Gilligan's (1986:242–43) analysis of 4-year-olds working out a solution to a conflict over whether they should play a game of pirates or next-door neighbors. The solution incorporated both into a game about the pirate who lived next door.

25. Discussion of these issues in a politicized rhetoric that spoke of "anti-reform forces" and of opposition to "constructive change" dominated editorials and other articles in *The Riverside Record*, during my research (February 8, 1983:8, col. 1; April 5, 1983:1, cols. 2–4; November 22, 1983:10, col. 1).

26. The land in question was small, involving a triangle 18 inches at its widest and 6 feet long.

27. I consider both families to be middle-class in occupation and demeanor. Census data on the neighborhood presents extremes of income and considerable diversity of occupation, reflecting its transitional character. Middle-class complainants were unusual in the neighbor and family cases I observed (there were only two), but this case suggests some of the ways that middle-class status (which here is combined with modest political and economic prominence) may affect the handling of a complaint.

28. Perin (1977: 105–6) discusses the use of spite fences in neighbor conflicts. In this case, the Smiths bought used plaster casts made by plastic surgeons for facial reconstructions, painted them, and hung them on a fence erected between their land and the Busonis'.

29. This discussion is based on information in *The Riverside Record* (July 9, 1983:1, col. 1; July 29, 1983:12, col. 2; August 15, 1983:10, col. 1; October 13, 1983:12, col. 1).

30. Between June 1 and December 31, 1982, twenty-six neighborhood cases were brought to the clerk from Milltown, and I observed sixteen of the complaint hearings on these. The "downstreet" area from which the cases came is characterized by low incomes (mean income $14,549); multiple-family, renter-occupied housing (62% of the housing occupied by renters, 43% of the population in units of three or more), and a high percentage of households on public assistance (22% of 747 households) (Census of Population and Housing, 1980). This area also makes heavy use of police and the court. The number of complaints filed with the clerk per capita from Milltown during the research period was 2.8% (130 complaints from a Milltown population of 4,711); the corresponding number from Riverside was 1.4% (262 complaints from a Riverside population of 18,436).

31. "C & P" (Care and Protection) or "CHINS" (Child in Need of Supervision) are terms used by social service and court personnel to describe court orders through which families are placed under the supervision of the Department of Social Services, so that social workers can monitor the children. "C & P" suggests that the principal problem lies with the family, whereas a "CHINS" order is brought to control a rebellious or otherwise hard-to-control child. Both result in family supervision by a state agency.

32. One social worker noted, "You go to one home, and there is another person we are also dealing with. They know what's going on; they are in each other's homes."

33. This complaint was subsequently issued when the complainant returned after two weeks to say that the agreement to pay for the damaged clothing had not been complied with.

34. This form of disposition was used in 20% of the complaints filed by citizens; it almost always led to dismissal. Of 1,984 denials in citizen complaints, 37 were "held at the 'show cause' level," "issued technically," or "continued for a few months to see if there is any more trouble." Continuances of this kind lasted from three months to a year. Of the continuances I observed, only one (see note 32) was later issued.

35. Eco (1976:79) discusses the coexistence of superimposed semantic fields in contexts of cultural pluralism and the diverse possibilities open to a language user in these situations for coupling a particular "sign vehicle" with a particular meaning. He notes the rapidity with which a semantic field can disintegrate and restructure itself into a new field in these situations. See also Bourdieu's (1977:40, 170–71) discussion of the political significance of official, "authorized meanings and the objectification (legitimation) of particular versions of reality through the imposition of these.

36. There were twelve African-American and no Hispanic residents out of a population of 1,648 in this part of Milltown in 1980. Dominant ethnic groups in this area are

Polish (17%), French (14%), English (10%), and Irish (6%) (Census of Population and Housing, 1980).

37. Perin (1977:114, 120) notes that children "are a dangerous category par excellence" and like other transitional social categories "should be collected together, for spreading such anomalies in space (and in social time) will be disturbing to social safety."

38. In my sample, twelve complaints were related to runaway teenagers. All but one (brought by a runaway against her foster parents) were issued by the clerk.

39. Emerson (1969:89) discusses the handling of teenage runaways at another Massachusetts court and notes the assumption by court staff that running away is an indication of more serious "trouble," particularly in the form of sexual activity: "The severity of the probable 'trouble' in the judge's mind is indicated by his handling of the case, i.e., holding the girls in detention and ordering psychiatric study. (Girls, except state wards, are very rarely held in detention.)"

40. The social worker who attended this hearing had said to the clerk beforehand that "it's hard. We've told them [the foster parents] that they may not touch the kids."

41. The role of lower-court officials and especially of the clerk is reminiscent of that described by Gordon (1985:15–16) for nineteenth-century American lawyers, who as a "practical intelligentsia" sought to provide the "moral glue" holding an increasingly commercial society together. Similarly, the lay clerks in today's criminal court infuse the business of law (its everyday practice) with a moral dimension, structuring cases to conform with their own notion of the "good moral order" and tempering what they view as the self-interested pursuit of "rights" by the parties appearing before them.

42. This is reminiscent of Hay's (1975:49) discussion of the relationship of eighteenth-century English gentry to those they ruled. Hay notes the importance of the personification of authority and of the use of mercy by paternalistic justices of the peace to create a "spirit of consent and submission" among the governed.

43. *American Heritage Dictionary*, 1978, under "know." See also Keller's (1985: 115) discussion of knowledge as being both about power and "being in touch" and Benjamin's (1988) discussion of relationships of "mutual influence," where each partner is both mover and moved. Benjamin in particular, who grounds her analysis in Hegel's understanding of recognition as the core of relationships of domination, is attentive to the fragile balance in relationships of mutual influence and the ease with which they are transformed into relationships of domination.

CHAPTER THREE

1. In thinking about this chapter, I benefited from a number of conversations. First, it is a pleasure to acknowledge David Engel and Barbara Yngvesson, with whom I enjoyed extensive conversations comparing analytical problems and findings in our three independent ethnographic studies of court use in American towns. Their contributions are cited as Engel, 1987 and Yngvesson, 1988. The earliest version of this chapter was the basis for my contribution to a series of presentations that we gave jointly at the Law & Society Association annual meeting, the Cornell Law School, and the American Anthropological Association annual meeting, all in 1987. A second debt is to organizers and participants in the American Bar Association's workshop on "Teaching America: Pluralism and Community in a Republic of Laws" who provided an occasion for developing some of the implications of the ethnographic material I

present here. I am grateful to the College of Arts and Sciences, Cornell University, for the study leave during which I wrote the first draft. I am also indebted to P. Steven Sangren, Austin Sarat, and anonymous readers for their comments.

2. For discussion of interpretive approaches in law and society disciplines, see Hunt, 1985; Silbey and Sarat, 1987; Silbey, 1985; and Starr and Collier, 1989.

3. My research in Hopewell extended from 1973 to 1975, with a brief return in 1980. The initial period was funded by a training grant from the National Institute of Mental Health to the Department of Anthropology, Harvard University. The second period was funded by a Faculty Research Grant from the College of Arts and Sciences, Cornell University. The principal aims of my study in Hopewell centered on local Southern Baptists' conceptions of conflict and conflict resolution as intrinsic elements of their religious faith. I was interested in accounting both for the negative valuation they accord conflict and the terms in which conflict is devalued (Greenhouse, 1986). This chapter emerges in part out of my efforts to relate local Baptists' views to other local commentaries on conflict in Hopewell. Although there are many parallels (Baptists draw on a distinctly local set of symbolic referents), there are also differences. Essentially, where Baptists in Hopewell insist that restraining conflict is a sign of spiritual maturity and an index of one's faith in personal salvation, the view I outline here holds that restraint is an index of social acceptability, that is, of one's capacity to form "community" ties. These may be two sides of the same sociocultural coin; indeed, the boundaries between the Baptist congregation and "the world" are flexible and permeable both in theory (evangelicalism) and practice (conversion or loss of faith).

4. I should add, *when* legal systems are meaningful (I have set aside questions of legitimacy for the moment).

5. It is not only in Hopewell that the temporal dimension is experienced as competing sociologies. Engel (1987) describes the multiple visions people in Sander County have of their own "community"; these are expressed in terms of different images of time. Engel shows that temporal discourse offers speakers potentially different rhetorical strategies in discussions of social change.

6. This ambivalence is deeply rooted in Western thought (Unger, 1975, 1976), American political philosophy (Pocock, 1975), and contemporary debates about the meaning of litigiousness (Galanter, 1983; Engel, 1984).

7. The purpose of this section has been to sketch generally where the court sits in the multiple contingencies that define the social system of Hopewell to people who live there. Beyond this, the perspective I present is clearly a particular one, that of people who consider themselves insiders. I hasten to add that in practice, insiders and outsiders are utterly flexible and permeable categories that shift according to the same sorts of criteria I discuss later in this chapter.

8. Because Hopewell is a county seat, its citizens have ready access to the courts and its services. The county constitutes its own circuit, unlike smaller counties that must share a court and a judge with neighboring towns. Hopewell's Superior Court has two full-time judges, one of whom hears almost exclusively domestic relations cases. Two retired judges sit regularly on a part-time basis to ease the burdens of the docket on the bench. The size of the bench remained stable for the ten years prior to the research, that is, during the period of Hopewell's most intense growth and change. The facilities of the courthouse itself did increase: An annex was added to the old Victorian building that more than doubled the courtroom and office space of the building. The resident lawyer population also doubled in size, to twenty-seven. In contrast to this physical and professional expansion of legal activity in the town, the actual business of the court-

room itself has contracted. The number of suits filed has increased, but the number of cases brought to a verdict has declined. The role of the judge as third party has expanded somewhat beyond adjudication. See note 10 for a discussion of the Superior Court's dockets.

9. I do not discuss Baptist perspectives here; see Greenhouse, 1986.

10. I spent a brief period observing court sessions in Hopewell's Inferior Court, officially called the State Court (the term Inferior Court is a popular archaism dating back to the early days of the county's government), at the invitation of its clerk, who was instrumental in arranging access to other local institutions of law enforcement as well (the police, the jail, the county ordinary's, or probate judge, office, as well as his own, and the Superior Court clerk's offices). The interviews discussed in the previous section were with the judge and clerk of the Superior Court. Both men were widely known (in local opinion as well as in the local press) as astute observers of social change. Although I was interested in the activities of the courthouse, the central questions of my research were elsewhere, as I explained in note 3. For this reason, unfortunately, I did not interview the judge of the Inferior Court.

Observing in the Inferior Court was a frustrating business, because most cases were dispatched in a minute or two of conversation among attorneys and other personnel clustered at the judge's bench and were inaudible to me. The cases I report on here were the business of a single morning. They are presented here in the order in which they were heard.

This state has a supreme court, a court of appeals, and superior court circuits (Hopewell County constitutes its own circuit). The Inferior Court, or State Court, is a county-level court; its appeals are heard in the Court of Appeals. Justices of the peace are also state judicial officials. They serve militia districts, a subcounty designation. Hopewell has no small claims court and no city court, although some counties in this state have both as well as others. Every court in this state below the superior court level was established by a separate legislative act; there is no uniform procedure mandated by law, although most state courts follow the procedure of the superior courts.

11. In addition to brief periods of observation in the county courts, I compared the dockets of 1973 and 1962–63, tabulating frequencies of suits by type, both for criminal and civil courts. I summarize these data here, for readers who are interested in the activity of the jurisdiction. My purpose in making these data available is to enrich the context of my ethnographic presentation, not to validate (or invalidate) specific aspects of the judge's, clerk's, or other participants' sense of things. Indeed, as cultural propositions, their statements obviate empirical challenge.

Although divorce, drugs, and damage suits contribute important segments of the court calendar, the dockets largely reflect the activities of a commercial jurisdiction. The impact of the city, if it is shown in these data, is seen in the growth of commerce. In general, most cases on the dockets have no alternative forum for resolution, that is, they are problems of administration that require some action by the court. Indeed, a relative minority of cases consist of suits filed by individuals (see Galanter, 1983; Engel, 1984). In 1962 and 1963, as now, the principal litigants were businesses and individuals for whom the law itself leaves no alternative but the court.

12. In general, the use of restraint in potential conflict situations to measure maturity and, in a larger sense, the worth of a person, is an essential dimension of local Baptist views of the importance of salvation. Salvation is, to an important extent, measured (in that it is tested) by an individual's ability to avoid disputes. One meaning of salvation is said to be a person's faith that Jesus is the omnipresent and only appropriate proactive agent of one's own cause, which thereby ceases to be one's own.

13. This is precisely what norms are (Greenhouse, 1982a).

14. In their ethnographic studies of court use in a midwestern and a New England town, respectively, Engel (1984, 1987) and Yngvesson (1988) note the extent to which people stigmatize litigants in symbolic terms constituted in issues of local identity. Their analyses develop the symbolic importance of litigation in community contexts, as well as the importance of the concept of community in the towns' current urbanizing contexts. Although the court plays somewhat different symbolic roles in the three towns, the significant parallels are in the symbolic distinctions locals draw between litigiousness and status in the community.

CHAPTER FIVE

1. Many Hopewell Baptists expressed distaste for televangelism as too entrepreneurial and impersonal; however, Billy Graham was not in this category.

2. The following discussion draws on material presented in Yngvesson, 1993:32–39.

CHAPTER SIX

1. When we refer to these concepts as analytic terms, we use *time* and *space*. When we refer to local views, we use *history* and *place*.

2. Neither myth is intrinsically more effective than the other in explaining or limiting conflict. The fact that the Balinese, for example, celebrate a myth of expanding social conflict does not mean that there is "more" conflict there than in the United States, which celebrates a myth of harmony. Each offers different propositions as to the meaning of conflict and different responses to the hypothetical question, "What is a society?"

3. See Varenne (1977) on the way in which the image of the melting pot reinforces an understanding of the nation as encompassing—and hence symbolically neutralizing—diversity.

4. Knowing such stories and how to tell them to some extent distinguishes insiders from outsiders, locals from newcomers. Indeed, in some ways this knowledge forms a rival mode of "belonging"; no one who knows these stories and seems to value them could be called a "newcomer." Literal newcomers who have been instrumental in the suburbanization of Hopewell (bankers, businessmen, and so on) demonstrate their solidarity with locals by learning the stories and reproducing them. By 1980 the local Historical Society—founded by newcomers in part to preserve valued sites (some of them vacant lots), together with a tour agency, had organized a regular commercial bus tour of the locations, featuring a guide's narration of the same cherished local stories.

5. This subsection is a slightly modified version of Engel (1987:610–15).

6. The iterative model has often been associated with nonindustrial societies, in which activities such as farming are organized in seasonal cycles. When time is perceived primarily in iterative terms, it provides the culture with a space or field in which fundamental patterns, relationships, and values can repeat from year to year and from generation to generation. Comparisons of past with present are culturally significant, because they establish recurring images of sameness that reaffirm and reinforce essential enduring qualities of a culture. When the passage of time is represented primarily in linear terms, on the other hand, it enhances the awareness of incremental change over

the years. Comparisons of past with present are culturally significant, because they establish difference rather than sameness. This second view of time has been associated with a variety of social and cultural factors, most importantly the advent of industrialization. Linear time emphasizes change and development; the iterative model emphasizes stability and closure.

7. This section is adapted from Greenhouse (1989:258–63).

8. It is more accurate to say "in any large-scale way," as there were over 1,000 enslaved people in the county when the Civil War began. One man owned several hundred slaves, and the others were held by the many farmers who owned one or more slaves.

9. This section is adapted from Yngvesson (1993:36–39).

10. For an extended discussion of the relationship among the sense of community, avoidance of overt dispute, and ahistoricism, see Greenhouse, 1986.

CONCLUSION

1. For a discussion of the contradictions of an ethic in which people must be both "tough" and "neighborly" (Errington, 1990:630), see Bellah et al., 1986 [1985]:39–41. Lynd and Lynd, 1929, 1937; Tocqueville, 1945, vol. 2; Vidich and Bensman, 1958; Warner, 1962 (1953); Varenne, 1977.

2. For example, F. Errington, in a recent article about the "Rock Creek" rodeo in Montana (1990:630), describes the concerns of "community-minded" men responsible for staging the rodeo as involving what they term "the American way of life." This way is characterized by and virtually synonymous with the "free enterprise system." This system provides the freedom necessary for the exercise of choice as well as the competition that both motivates choice and requires careful control in making choice. Through this system of competition, individuals struggle to achieve a success that will mark them as having worth, as having a valued individuality. These views, widely shared in Rock Creek, often take the form of freely volunteered and consensually validated negative evaluations of those, such as Native Americans and others, especially in Eastern cities, who rely on welfare or other "handouts" without trying to "better" themselves.

3. Natalie Zemon Davis makes a similar point in a discussion of the emergence of "selves" in sixteenth-century France, where, she notes, the self was defined "in conscious relation to the groups to which people belonged. . . . Virtually all the occasions for talking or writing about the self involved a relationship: with God or God and one's confessor, with a patron, with a friend or lover, or especially with one's family and lineage" (Davis, 1986:53).

4. Thus, the meanings of "community" in the settings we studied are close to those of "country" in R. Williams's (1973) study of the emergence of "country" and "city" as tropes in English literature. In general, he argues that the distinction between these images was less a reflection of differences between rural and urban England than it was (and is) an expression of the irreconcilability of the moral orders that shared the same social space:

> The English landowning class, which had changed itself in changing its world, was idealised and displaced into an historical contrast with its own real activities. In its actual inhumanity, it could be recognised only with difficulty by men linked to and dependent on it, and the great majority of the poor and oppressed were

without a connecting voice to make clear the recognition which was their daily experience. . . . The real ruling class could not be put in question, so they were seen as temporarily absent, or as the good old people succeeded by the bad new people—themselves succeeding themselves. We have heard this sad song for many centuries now: a seductive song, turning protest into retrospect, until we die of time. (Williams, 1973:83)

Although some version of this statement might apply to Riverside, Sander County, and Hopewell, it would have to include the recognition that it is the new elites who sing the "seductive song" along with the descendants of the old.

5. This distinction, which dominated feminist arguments by anthropologists in the 1970s (Rosaldo and Lamphere, 1974, especially the opening essay by M. Rosaldo), was subsequently criticized by 1980s feminists (Rosaldo, 1980) on grounds that it assumed domestic/public as an explanatory frame, rather than illuminating the dynamics of power that relegated women's lives to the domestic sphere. Olsen (1983) critiques that dichotomy. The point (for feminists) is to question what "domestic" assumes, that is, a rationalization of women's subordination. Our discussion (like that of Ginsburg, 1989) points to the embedded critique implied in local "domestic" ideologies.

6. For Hopewell's Baptists, at least, the master icon that contained these others was Jesus, represented as the great teacher of renunciation. In the Baptist Church, the connection between renunciation and the money economy was made directly in the encomium to tithe. Tithing is a complex proof of faith, but one element is the demonstration to oneself and others that wealth is not the objective of a person's work but only its artifact. Renunciation is not limited to tithing, but is relevant in every domain, as we indicated. In this generalized sense, people in all three locales connect domesticity with the sacred. For example, one of the first points of contact among the three sites to emerge in our early comparative discussions was the common value they place on restraint in conflict situations; Part I reflects this emphasis. The proximity of renunciation and the sacred also accounts for the relative ease with which people conflate good neighbors with good Christians or identify themselves as "good Christian" women (as in Chapter 3) or men. The public relevance of such claims to private faith appears to be shaped by the concerns we outlined.

7. See Mari Matsuda (1989:2322): "The places where the law does not go to redress harm have tended to be the places where women, children, people of color, and poor people live."

References

Abel, Richard L. (1973). "A Comparative Theory of Dispute Institutions in Society." *Law & Society Review* 8:217.

Agnew, Jean-Christophe. (1986). *Worlds Apart: The Market and the Theater in Anglo-American Thought, 1550–1750*. Cambridge: Cambridge University Press.

Atkinson, J. Maxwell, and Paul Drew. (1979). *Order in Court: The Organization of Verbal Interaction in Judicial Settings*. Atlantic Highlands, N.J.: Humanities Press.

Auerbach, Jerold S. (1983). *Justice without Law?* New York: Oxford University Press.

Austin, John. (1965). *The Province of Jurisprudence Determined and the Uses of the Study of Jurisprudence*. Atlantic Highlands, N.J.: Humanities Press.

Barton, Roy Franklin. (1919). *Ifugao Law*. Berkeley: University of California Press.

Baumgartner, M. P. (1984). "Social Control in Suburbia." In D. Black, ed., *Toward a General Theory of Social Control*, Vol. 2. New York: Academic Press.

——. (1988). *The Moral Order of a Suburb*. New York: Oxford University Press.

Bellah, Robert Neelly, Richard Madsen, William N. Sullivan, Ann Swidler and Steven M. Tipton. (1986 [1985]). *Habits of the Heart: Individualism and Commitment in American Life*. New York: Harper & Row.

Bender, Thomas. (1978). *Community and Social Change in America*. New Brunswick, N.J.: Rutgers University Press.

Benjamin, Jessica. (1988). *The Bonds of Love: Psychoanalysis, Feminism, and the Problem of Domination*. New York: Pantheon.

Bing, Stephen R., and S. Steven Rosenfeld. (1970). *The Quality of Justice in the Lower Criminal Courts of Metropolitan Boston.* A Report by the L.C.F.C.R.U.L. to the Governer's Committee on Law Enforcement and the Administration of Justice. Boston: Lawyers Committee on Civil Rights.

Bittner, Egon. (1969). "The Police on Skid-Row: A Study of Peace Keeping." In R. Quinney, ed., *Crime and Justice in Society.* Boston: Little, Brown.

——. (1974). "Florence Nightingale in Pursuit of Willie Sutton: A Theory of the Police." In H. Jacob, ed., *The Potential for Reform of Criminal Justice.* Beverly Hills, Calif.: Sage Publications.

Black, Donald. (1976). *The Behavior of Law.* New York: Academic Press.

——. (1980). *The Manners and Customs of the Police.* New York: Academic Press.

Black, Donald, and M. P. Baumgartner. (1983). "Toward a Theory of the Third Party." In K. Boyum and L. Mather, eds., *Empirical Theories about Courts.* White Plains, N.Y.: Longman.

Bohannan, Paul. (1969). "Ethnography and Comparison in Legal Anthropology." In L. Nader, ed., *Law in Culture and Society.* Chicago: Aldine.

——. (1989 [1957]). *Justice and Judgment among the Tiv.* Prospect Heights, Ill.: Waveland Press.

Boon, James A. (1982). *Other Tribes, Other Scribes: Symbolic Anthropology in the Comparative Style of Cultures, Histories, Religions, and Texts.* Cambridge: Cambridge University Press.

Bourdieu, Pierre. (1977). *Outline of a Theory of Practice.* Cambridge: Cambridge University Press.

——. (1987). "The Force of Law: Toward a Sociology of the Juridical Field." *Hastings Law Journal* 38:805.

Cain, Maureen, and Alan Hunt. (1979). *Marx and Engels on Law.* London: Academic Press.

Cain, Maureen, and Kalman Kulcsar. (1981–82). "Thinking Disputes: An Essay on the Origins of the Dispute Industry." *Law & Society Review* 16:375.

Census of Population and Housing. (1980). Summary Tape File 3. Boston: State Data Center.

Chatman, Seymour Benjamin. (1978). *Story and Discourse: Narrative Structure n Fiction and Film.* Ithaca, N.Y.: Cornell University Press.

Clifford, James. (1988). *The Predicament of Culture: Twentieth-Century Ethnography, Literature, and Art.* Cambridge, Mass.: Harvard University Press.

Collier, Jane Fishburne. (1975). "Legal Processes." *Annual Review of Anthropology* 4:121.

Comaroff, John L., and Simon Roberts. (1981). *Rules and Processes: The Cultural Logic of Dispute in an African Context.* Chicago: University of Chicago Press.

Committee on Juries of Six. (1984). Report. Boston: District Court Department.

Committee on Standards. (1975). Standards of Complaint Procedure. Boston: District Court Department.

Crèvecoeur, J. Hector, St. John de. (1926 [1782]). *Letters from an American Farmer*. London: Dutton.

Daniels, Stephen. (1985). "Continuity and Change in Patterns of Case Handling: A Case Study of Two Rural Counties." *Law & Society Review* 19:381.

Davis, Natalie Zemon. (1986). "Boundaries of the Sense of Self in Sixteenth-Century France." In T. C. Heller, M. Sosna, and D. E. Wellerby, eds., *Reconstructing Individualism: Autonomy, Individuality, and the Self in Western Thought*. Stanford: Stanford University Press.

Dollard, John. (1957). *Caste and Class in a Southern Town*, 3d ed. Garden City, N.Y.: Doubleday Anchor.

Donzelot, Jacques. (1979). *The Policing of Families*. New York: Pantheon.

Dorst, John Darwin. (1989). *The Written Suburb: An American Site, an Ethnographic Dilemma*. Philadelphia: University of Pennsylvania Press.

Douglas, Mary. (1966). *Purity and Danger: An Analysis of Concepts of Pollution and Taboo*. London: Routledge and Kegan Paul.

Dumont, Louis. (1970). *Homo Hierarchicus: The Caste System and Its Implications*. Trans. M. Sainsburg. Chicago: University of Chicago Press.

Eco, Umberto. (1976). *A Theory of Semiotics*. Bloomington: Indiana University Press.

Eidson, John R. (1990). "German Club-Life as a Local Cultural System." *Comparative Studies in Society and History* 32:357.

Eisenstein, James, and Herbert Jacob. (1977). *Felony Justice: An Organizational Analysis of Criminal Courts*. Boston: Little, Brown.

Emerson, Robert M. (1969). *Judging Delinquents: Context and Process in Juvenile Court*. Chicago: Aldine.

Engel, David M. (1978). *Code and Custom in a Thai Provincial Court*. Tucson: University of Arizona Press.

———. (1980). "Legal Pluralism in an American Community: Perspectives on a Civil Trial Court." *American Bar Foundation Research Journal* 1980:425.

———. (1984). "The Oven Bird's Song: Insiders, Outsiders, and Personal Injuries in an American Community." *Law & Society Review* 18:101. [Reprinted in this volume.]

———. (1987). "Law, Time, and Community." *Law & Society Review* 21:605.

Erikson, Kai T. (1966). *Wayward Puritans: A Study in the Sociology of Deviance*. New York: Wiley.

Errington, Frederick. (1987). "Reflexivity Deflected: The Festival of Nations as an American Cultural Performance." *American Ethnologist* 14:654.

———. (1990). "The Rock Creek Rodeo: Excess and Constraint in Men's Lives." *American Ethnologist* 17:628.

Etzioni, Amitai. (1991). *A Responsive Society: Collected Essays on Guiding Deliberate Social Change*. San Francisco: Jossey-Bass.

Feeley, Malcolm. (1979). *The Process Is the Punishment: Handling Cases in a Lower Criminal Court*. New York: Russell Sage Foundation.

Felstiner, William L. F. (1974). "Influences of Social Organization on Dispute Processing." *Law & Society Review* 9:63.

——. (1975). "Avoidance as Dispute Processing: An Elaboration." *Law & Society Review* 9:695.

Fitzgerald, Frances. (1990). "Jim and Tammy." *The New Yorker* 66:45.

Foucault, Michel. (1990 [1968]). *The History of Sexuality*, Vol. 1. New York: Vintage.

Friedman, Lawrence M., and Robert V. Percival. (1976). "A Tale of Two Courts: Litigation in Alameda and San Benito Counties." *Law & Society Review* 10:267.

Fuller, Lon L. (1969). "Human Interaction and the Law." *American Journal of Jurisprudence* 14:1.

Galanter, Marc. (1974). "Why the 'Haves' Come out Ahead: Speculations on the Limits of Legal Change." *Law & Society Review* 9:95.

——. (1975). "Afterword: Explaining Litigation." *Law & Society Review* 9:347.

——. (1983). "Reading the Landscape of Disputes: What We Know and Don't Know (and Think We Know) about Our Allegedly Contentious and Litigious Society." *UCLA Law Review* 31:4.

Geertz, Clifford. (1973). "Ideology as a Cultural System." In C. Geertz, ed., *The Interpretation of Cultures: Selected Essays*. New York: Basic Books.

——. (1980). *Negara: The Theater State in Nineteenth-Century Bali*. Princeton, N.J.: Princeton University Press.

——. (1983). *Local Knowledge: Further Essays in Interpretive Anthropology*. New York: Basic Books.

Gest, Ted, Lucia Solorzano, Joseph P. Shapiro, and Michael Doan. (1982). "See You in Court." *U.S. News & World Report* 93:58.

Gilligan, Carol. (1986). "Re-Mapping the Moral Domain: New Images of the Self in Relationship." In T. C. Heller et al., eds., *Reconstructing Individualism: Autonomy, Individuality, and the Self in Western Thought*. Stanford, Calif.: Stanford University Press.

Ginsburg, Faye D. (1989). *Contested Lives: The Abortion Debate in an American Community*. Berkeley: University of California Press.

Gluckman, Max. (1967). *The Judicial Processes among the Barotse of Northern Rhodesia*, 2nd ed. Manchester: Manchester University Press.

Gordon, Robert W. (1984). "Critical Legal Histories." *Stanford Law Review* 36:57.

——. (1985). "Lawyers as the American Aristocracy." Unpublished. Oliver Wendell Holmes Lectures, delivered at Harvard Law School, February 21.

Greene, Richard. (1983). "Caught in the Better Mousetrap." *Forbes* 132:66.

Greenhouse, Carol. (1982a). "Looking at Culture, Looking for Rules." *Man* 17:58.

———. (1982b). "Nature Is to Culture as Praying Is to Suing: Legal Pluralism in an American Suburb." *Journal of Legal Pluralism* 20:17.

———. (1985). "Anthropology at Home: Whose Home?" *Human Organization* 44:261.

———. (1986). *Praying for Justice: Faith, Order, and Community in an American Town.* Ithaca, N.Y.: Cornell University Press.

———. (1988). "Courting Difference: Issues of Interpretation and Comparison in the Study of Legal Ideologies." *Law & Society Review* 22:687. [Reprinted in this volume.]

———. (1989). "Interpreting American Litigiousness." In J. Starr and J. F. Collier, eds., *History and Power in the Study of Law: New Directions in Legal Anthropology.* Ithaca, N.Y.: Cornell University Press.

———. (1992). "Signs of Quality." *American Ethnologist* 19:39.

Greenwood, Davydd J. (1989). "Culture by the Pound: An Anthropological Perspective on Tourism as Cultural Commoditization." In V. L. Smith, ed., *Hosts and Guests: The Anthropology of Tourism*, 2nd ed. Philadelphia: University of Pennsylvania Press.

Handler, Richard. (1984). "On Sociocultural Discontinuity: Nationalism and Cultural Objectification in Quebec." *Current Anthropology* 25:55.

———. (1988). *Nationalism and the Politics of Culture in Quebec.* Madison: University of Wisconsin Press.

Harrington, Christine B. (1985). *Shadow Justice: The Ideology and Institutionalization of Alternatives to Court.* Westport, Conn.: Greenwood.

Hartog, Hendrik. (1976). "The Public Law of a County Court: Judicial Government in Eighteenth-Century Massachusetts." *American Journal of Legal History* 20:282.

Haskins, George Lee. (1960). *Law and Authority in Early Massachusetts: A Study in Tradition and Design.* New York: Macmillan.

Hay, Douglas. (1975). "Property, Authority, and the Criminal Law." In D. Hay et al., eds., *Albion's Fatal Tree: Crime and Society in Eighteenth-Century England.* New York: Pantheon.

Herzfeld, Michael. (1990). "Pride and Perjury: Time and the Oath in the Mountain Villages of Crete." *Man* 25:305.

Hollingshead, August. (1949). *Elmtown's Youth: The Impact of Social Classes on Adolescents.* New York: J. Wiley.

Hunt, Alan. (1982). "Dichotomy and Contradiction in the Sociology of Law." In P. Beirne and R. Quinney, eds., *Marxism and Law.* New York: Wiley.

———. (1985). "The Ideology of Law: Advances and Problems in Recent Applications of the Concept of Ideology to the Analysis of Law." *Law & Society Review* 19:11.

Ignatieff, Michael. (1983). "State, Civil Society, and Total Institution: A Critique of Recent Social Histories of Punishment." In D. Sugarman, ed., *Legality, Ideology, and the State*. London: Academic Press.

Jefferson County Chamber of Commerce. (1982). *Riverside and Jefferson County, Massachusetts*. Greenfield, Mass.: H. A. Manning Co.

Jenkins, P. (1982). *The Conservative Rebel: A Social History of Greenfield, Massachusetts*. Greenfield, Mass.: Town of Greenfield.

Keller, Evelyn Fox. (1985). *Reflections on Gender and Science*. New Haven, Conn.: Yale University Press.

Kelly, William W. (1986). "Rationalization and Nostalgia: Cultural Dynamics of New Middle-Class Japan." *American Ethnologist* 13:603.

Kidder, Robert L. (1980–81). "The End of the Road? Problems in the Analysis of Disputes." *Law & Society Review* 15:717.

Lévi-Strauss, Claude. (1983). *The Raw and the Cooked*. Trans. J. and D. Weightman. Chicago: University of Chicago Press.

Llewellyn, Karl N., and E. Adamson Hoebel. (1941). *The Cheyenne Way: Conflict and Case Law in Primitive Jurisprudence*. Norman: University of Oklahoma Press.

Lukes, Steven. (1974). *Power: A Radical View*. London: Macmillan.

Lynd, Robert S., and Helen Merrell Lynd. (1929). *Middletown: A Study in American Culture*. New York: Harcourt Brace.

———. (1937). *Middletown in Transition: A Study in Cultural Conflicts*. New York: Harcourt Brace.

McBarnet, Doreen. (1981). "Magistrates' Courts and the Ideology of Justice." *British Journal of Law and Society* 8:181.

McDermott, K. (1983). "The Development of the District Courts of the Commonwealth of Massachusetts, 1821–1920." Unpublished.

McIntosh, Wayne. (1980–81). "150 Years of Litigation and Dispute Settlement: A Court Tale." *Law & Society Review* 15:823.

Malinowski, Bronislaw. (1989 [1926]). *Crime and Custom in Savage Society*. Totowa, N.J.: Rowman & Littlefield.

Mass. Gen. Laws Ann. (1979). ch. 218, §26, 30, 35A: 55; ch. 276, §22. St. Paul, Minn.: West.

Mather, Lynn. (1979). *Plea Bargaining or Trial? The Process of Criminal Case Disposition*. Lexington, Mass.: Lexington Books.

Mather, L., and Barbara Yngvesson. (1980–81). "Language, Audience, and the Transformation of Disputes." *Law & Society Review* 15:775.

Matsuda, Mari. (1989). "Public Response to Racist Speech: Considering the Victim's Story." *Michigan Law Review* 87:2320.

Mensch, Elizabeth. (1982). "The History of Mainstream Legal Thought." In D. Kairys, ed., *The Politics of Law: A Progressive Critique*. New York: Pantheon.

Merry, Sally Engle. (1985). "Concepts of Law and Justice among Working-Class Americans: Ideology as Culture." *The Legal Studies Forum* 9:59.

——. (1990). *Getting Justice and Getting Even: Legal Consciousness among Working-Class Americans*. Chicago: University of Chicago Press.

Merry, Sally Engle, and Susan S. Silbey. (1984). "What Do Plaintiffs Want? Reexamining the Concept of Dispute." *The Justice System Journal* 9:151.

Messerschmidt, Donald A. (1981). *Anthropologists at Home in North America: Methods and Issues in the Study of One's Own Society*. Cambridge: Cambridge University Press.

Mills, C. Wright. (1956). *The Power Elite*. New York: Oxford University Press.

Miner, Horace. (1956). "Body Ritual among the Nacirema." *American Anthropologist* 58:503.

Minow, Martha. (1990). *Making All the Difference: Inclusion, Exclusion, and American Law*. Ithaca, N.Y.: Cornell University Press.

Monkkonen, Eric H. (1987). "Criminals, Voters, Courts, and Constitutions: The American State from the Bottom Up." Paper presented at The Conference on Longitudinal Studies of Trial Courts, Buffalo, N.Y. (August 21).

Moore, Sally Falk. (1973). "Law and Social Change: The Semi-Autonomous Social Field as an Appropriate Subject of Study." *Law & Society Review* 7:719.

——. (1977). "Individual Interests and Organizational Structures: Dispute Settlements as Events of Articulation." In Ian Hamnett, ed., *Social Anthropology and Law*. New York: Academic Press.

Nader, Laura, ed. (1980). *No Access to Law: Alternatives to the American Judicial System*. New York: Academic Press.

Nader, Laura, and Harry F. Todd, Jr. (1978). "Introduction." In L. Nader and H. F. Todd, Jr., eds., *The Disputing Process: Law in Ten Societies*. New York: Columbia University Press.

Nash, June C. (1989). *From Tank Town to High Tech: The Clash of Community and Industrial Cycles*. Albany: State University of New York Press.

National Center for State Courts. (1979). *State Court Caseload Statistics: Annual Report, 1975*. Williamsburg, Va.: The National Center for State Courts.

——. (1982). *State Court Caseload Statistics: Annual Report, 1977*. Williamsburg, Va.: The National Center for State Courts.

Newman, Catherine S. (1988). *Falling from Grace: The Experience of Downward Mobility in the American Middle Class*. New York: Free Press.

Olsen, Frances E. (1983). "The Family and the Market: A Study of Ideology and Legal Reform." *Harvard Law Review* 96:1497.

Ortner, Sherry B. (1984). "Theory in Anthropology since the Sixties." *Comparative Studies in Society and History* 26:126.

Peacock, James L., and Ruel W. Tyson, Jr. (1989). *Pilgrims of Paradox: Calvinism and Experience among the Primitive Baptists of the Blue Ridge*. Washington, D.C.: Smithsonian Institution Press.

Perham, John. (1977). "The Dilemma in Product Liability." *Dun's Review* 109:48.

Perin, Constance. (1977). *Everything in Its Place: Social Order and Land Use in America*. Princeton, N.J.: Princeton University Press.

——. (1988). *Belonging in America: Reading between the Lines*. Madison: University of Wisconsin Press.

Pocock, J. G. A. (1975). *The Machiavellian Moment: Florentine Political Thought and the Atlantic Republican Tradition*. Princeton, N.J.: Princeton University Press.

Robertson, John A., ed. (1974). *Rough Justice: Perspectives on Lower Criminal Courts*. Boston: Little, Brown.

Rosaldo, Michelle Zimbalist. (1980). "The Use and Abuse of Anthropology: Reflections on Feminism and Cross-Cultural Understanding." *Signs* 5:389.

Rosaldo, Michelle Zimbalist, and Louise Lamphere, eds. (1974). *Woman, Culture, and Society*. Stanford, Calif.: Stanford University Press.

Rosen, Lawrence. (1984). *Bargaining for Reality: The Construction of Social Relations in a Muslim Community*. Chicago: University of Chicago Press.

Rosenberg, Maurice. (1977). "Contemporary Litigation in the United States." In H. W. Jones, ed., *Legal Institutions Today: English and American Approaches Compared*. Chicago: American Bar Association.

Ross, H. Laurence. (1970). *Settled out of Court: The Social Process of Insurance Claims Adjustments*. Chicago: Aldine.

Santos, Boaventura De Sousa. (1977). "The Law of the Oppressed: The Construction and Reproduction of Legality in Pasargada." *Law & Society Review* 12:5.

Schattschneider, Elmer Eric. (1960). *The Semi Sovereign People: A Realist's View of Democracy in America*. New York: Holt, Rinehart, and Winston.

Schieffelin, Edward L. (1976). *The Sorrow of the Lonely and the Burning of the Dancers*. St. Lucia: University of Queensland Press.

Schneider, David Murray. (1968). *American Kinship: A Cultural Account*. Englewood Cliffs, N.J.: Prentice-Hall.

Schorske, Carl E. (1981). *Fin-de-Siècle Vienna: Politics and Culture*. New York: Vintage.

Seymour, Whitney North, Jr. (1973). *Why Justice Fails*. New York: Morrow.

Silbey, Susan S. (1985). "Ideals and Practices in the Study of Law." *The Legal Studies Forum* 9:7.

Silbey, Susan S., and Austin Sarat. (1987). "Critical Traditions in Law and Society Research." *Law & Society Review* 21:165.

Simmel, George. (1908 [1971]). "The Stranger." In D. Levine, ed., *On Individuality and Social Forms: Selected Writings*. Chicago: University of Chicago Press.

Skinner, Quentin, ed. (1985). *The Return of Grand Theory in Human Sciences.* Cambridge: Cambridge University Press.

Skocpol, Theda. (1987). "Social History and Historical Sociology: Contrasts and Complementarities." *Social Science History* 11:17.

Stallybrass, Peter, and Allan White. (1986). *The Politics and Poetics of Transgression.* Ithaca, N.Y.: Cornell University Press.

Starr, June, and Jane F. Collier, eds. (1989). *History and Power in the Study of Law: New Directions in Legal Anthropology.* Ithaca, N.Y.: Cornell University Press.

Steele, Eric H. (1975). "Fraud, Dispute, and the Consumer: Responding to Consumer Complaints." *University of Pennsylvania Law Review* 123:1107.

Sugarman, David. (1983). "Introduction and Overview." In D. Sugarman, ed., *Legality, Ideology, and the State.* London: Academic Press.

Taylor, Stuart, Jr. (1981). "On the Evidence, Americans Would Rather Sue Than Settle." *New York Times*, July 5, Section 4, 8.

Taylor, William B. (1985). "Between Global Process and Local Knowledge: An Inquiry into Early Latin American Social History, 1500–1900." In O. Zunz, ed., *Reliving the Past: The Worlds of Social History.* Chapel Hill: University of North Carolina Press.

Thompson, E. P. (1978). "The Poverty of Theory." In *The Poverty of Theory and Other Essays.* New York: Monthly Review Press.

Tocqueville, Alexis de. (1945). *Democracy in America,* 2 vols. H. Reeve, trans.; K. Bower, rev. trans; P. Bradley, ed. New York: Vintage.

Todd, Harry F., Jr. (1978). "Litigious Marginals: Character and Disputing in a Bavarian Village." In L. Nader and H. F. Todd, Jr., eds., *The Disputing Process: Law in Ten Societies.* New York: Columbia University Press.

Tondel, Lyman M., Jr. (1976). "The Work of the American Bar Association Commission on Medical Professional Liability." *Insurance Counsel Journal* 43:545.

Turner, Victor Witter. (1969). *The Ritual Process: Structure and Anti-Structure.* Chicago: Aldine.

Unger, Roberto Mangabeira. (1975). *Knowledge and Politics.* New York: Free Press.

———. (1976). *Law in Modern Society: Toward a Criticism of Social Theory.* New York: Free Press.

Varenne, Hervé. (1977). *Americans Together: Structured Diversity in a Midwestern Town.* New York: Teachers' College Press.

———. (1984). "Collective Representation in American Anthropological Conversations: Individual and Culture." *Current Anthropology* 25:281.

———. (1986). "Drop in Anytime: Community and Authenticity in American Everyday Life." In H. Varenne, ed., *Symbolizing America.* Lincoln: University of Nebraska Press.

——. (1987). "Talk and Real Talk: The Voices of Silence and the Voices of Power in American Family Life." *Current Anthropology* 2:369.

Vidich, Arthur J., and Joseph Bensman. (1958). *Small Town in Mass Society: Class, Power and Religion in a Rural Community.* Princeton: Princeton University Press.

Vollenhoven, C. (1918). *Het adatrecht van Nederlandsch-Indie.* Leiden: E. J. Brill.

Wallace, Anthony F. C. (1978). *Rockdale: The Growth of an American Village in the Early Industrial Revolution.* New York: Knopf.

Warner, W. Lloyd. (1962 [1953]). *American Life: Dream and Reality.* Chicago: University of Chicago Press.

Weber, Max. (1958). *The Protestant Ethic and the Spirit of Capitalism.* Trans. Talcott Parsons. New York: Scribner's.

——. (1967). *Law in Economy and Society,* ed. Max Rheinstein. New York: Simon & Schuster.

Williams, Patricia J. (1987). "Alchemical Notes: Reconstructing Ideals from Deconstructed Rights." *Harvard Civil Rights-Civil Liberties Law Review* 22:401.

Williams, Raymond. (1973). *The Country and the City.* New York: Oxford University Press.

——. (1983). *Keywords: A Vocabulary of Culture and Society,* rev. ed. London: Fontana.

Wilson, James Q. (1970). *Varieties of Police Behavior: The Management of Law and Order in Eight Communities.* New York: Atheneum.

Yamaguchi, Masao. (1977). "Kingship, Theatriciality, and Marginal Reality in Japan." In R. K. Jain, ed., *Text and Context: The Social Anthropology of Tradition.* Philadelphia: Institute for the Study of Human Issues.

Yngvesson, Barbara. (1978). "The Atlantic Fisherman." In L. Nader and H. F. Todd, Jr., eds., *The Disputing Process: Law in Ten Societies.* New York: Columbia University Press.

——. (1985a). "Legal Ideology and Community Justice in the Clerk's Office." *The Legal Studies Forum* 9:71.

——. (1985b). "Re-examining Continuing Relations and the Law." *Wisconsin Law Review* 3:623.

——. (1988). "Making Law at the Doorway: The Clerk, the Court, and the Construction of Community Order in a New England Town." *Law & Society Review* 22:409. [Reprinted in this volume.]

——. (1989). "Inventing Law in Local Settings: Rethinking Popular Legal Culture." *Yale Law Journal* 98:1689.

——. (1993). *Virtuous Citizens, Disruptive Subjects: Order and Complaint in a New England Court.* New York: Routledge.

Yngvesson, Barbara, and Patricia Hennessey. (1975). "Small Claims, Complex Disputes: A Review of the Small Claims Literature." *Law & Society Review* 9:219.

Index